ADVANCED BLACK POWDER HUNTING

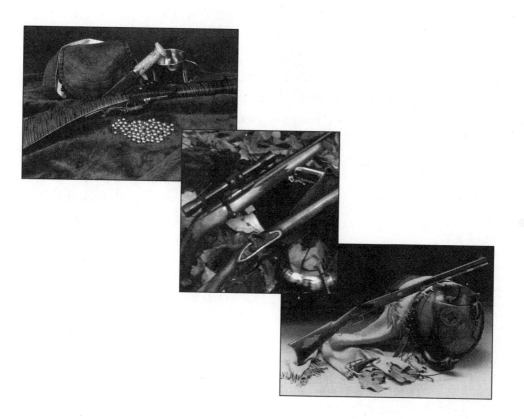

By Toby Bridges

STOEGER PUBLISHING COMPANY

TITLE: Advanced Black Powder Hunting
EDITOR: William S. Jarrett
COVER ART DESIGN: Ray Wells
BOOK DESIGN AND LAYOUT: Lesley A. Notorangelo/DSS
PROJECT MANAGER: Dominick S. Sorrentino
ELECTRONIC IMAGING: Lesley A. Notorangelo/DSS

Published by Stoeger Publishing Company
5 Mansard Court
Wayne, New Jersey 07470

ISBN: 0-88317-209-7
Library of Congress Catalog Card No.: 98-060004
Manufactured in the United States of America

Distributed to the book trade and to the sporting goods trade by Stoeger Industries, 5 Mansard Court, Wayne, New Jersey 07470

In Canada, distributed to the book trade and to the sporting goods trade by Stoeger Canada, Ltd., 1801 Wentworth Street, Unit 16, Whitby, Ontario L1N 8R6.

DEDICATION

Advanced Black Powder Hunting is dedicated to the memory of the late Turner Edward Kirkland, founder of Dixie Gun Works. Without him, the muzzleloading industry may never have found its start. The next time you hear the distant rumble of thunder and see towering cumulus clouds abuilding, it may not be an approaching storm. Ol' Turner has probably just challenged the angels in Heaven to a good ol' fashioned Tennessee muzzleloader shooting match. We will all miss him.

ABOUT THE AUTHOR

Toby Bridges has been shooting and hunting with muzzleloaders since the early 1960s. He has authored more than 1,000 magazine articles, most of which have been on hunting with guns of the frontloading design. He has taken nearly 200 big game animals on his muzzleloading hunts, relying on both traditional and ultra-modern black powder rifles. In 1985, he wrote *Advanced Muzzle Loader's Guide.* This book is Bridges' sixth book on the subject of muzzleloading. It is the first modern-day publication to be filled from cover to cover with the guns...the loads...the projectiles...the accessories...and the techniques needed to get the absolute most from any of today's frontloading guns.

Bridges has been actively involved with the muzzleloading industry for more than 20 years and has contributed to the design of several popular modern in-line percussion rifles. His involvement with these products has won him the title of "Mr. In-Line" among other writers and noted black powder hunters. It's safe to say that no other writer could have compiled the information included in this book. It is destined to become a classic.

INTRODUCTION

Today, the interest in hunting with a muzzle-loader is booming. In Michigan alone, nearly 200,000 black powder hunters head for the deer woods during the special muzzleloader deer season now held annually in that state. Consequently, the sales of muzzleloading guns, accessories and loading components have exploded. In fact, many experts within the shooting industry claim that muzzleloading is currently recognized as one of the fastest growing segments of the shooting and hunting sports.

One thing is for certain: hunters of whitetailed deer and other big game across the country are picking up a muzzleloader for the first time in record numbers. Indeed, since the publication of *Advanced Muzzle Loader's Guide* in 1985, the number of muzzleloading hunters in this country has more than doubled. Somewhere between two and three million hunters now rely on a front-loader for at least some of their big game hunting—and a growing number are using a muzzleloader for some of their small and upland game hunting as well. The reasons are simple; for example, shooting and hunting with a muzzleloader is fun and offers new challenges. But the real driving force behind the increasing popularity of hunting with a muzzleloader is the emergence of hunting opportunities. A study of new deer and other big game hunting opportunities in most states reveals that the majority involve hunting with a muzzleloading gun. Bag limits may have been relaxed for both archery and modern gun hunters in many states, but the structure and length of those seasons in most states remain about the same as they were a decade ago.

Black powder shooters of the 1940s and '50s often had no option but to shoot original guns from the last century and earlier. This group photo (circa mid-1950s) reveals a broad spectrum of custom-crafted rifles. Photo courtesy Homer Dangler.

Simply put, the establishment of new (or expanded) muzzleloading seasons over the last ten years represent the majority of new hunting opportunities available in this country. Keep in mind that many of the earlier muzzleloading deer seasons were established during the late 1960s and early 1980s. The purpose then was to allow the growing number of black powder shooters to experience what it was like to hunt with an old-fashioned rifle of pre-1860s frontloading design. That, coupled with an explosion of the white-tailed deer population in the last 20 to 30 years, explains why new muzzleloading seasons in the 1990s have been established, providing hunters with greater opportunities for harvesting more deer.

NEW MANAGEMENT TOOL

During the 1960s, when some of the first muzzleloader deer seasons were established, whitetail herds were just beginning to prosper, climbing from all-time low population levels. Game managers of the day were concerned about over-harvesting this resource; as a result, hunting regulations became very restrictive. Today's game manager, however, finds himself on the other side of the fence, because we simply are not harvesting enough deer. In some states, the whitetail population has tripled or quadrupled since the 1960s. Take Virginia, for example. During the late 1970s and early 1980s, that state was home to a healthy whitetail herd of about a half-million deer. By the early 1990s, the size of the herd skyrocketed to nearly a million. Throughout Virginia's vast wooded regions whitetails played havoc with farm crops in agricultural areas, not to mention their presence in many a suburban backyard. To help curtail further growth, the Virginia Department of Game and Inland Fisheries established in 1990 its first statewide muzzleloader deer season.

Originally, the Virginia game department required the strict use of traditionally-styled muzzleloaders with open sights and patched round balls. But over the course of the next five years, these regulations were slowly relaxed. Today, muzzleloading hunters in Virginia can head for the deer woods with as modern a muzzleloader as they care to pack, with more and more relying on the new, more efficient in-line percussion rifle, complete with telescopic sights and loaded with hard-hitting saboted bullets. Now, around 100,000 hunters cash in each fall on the bonuses offered by Virginia's two muzzleloader deer seasons, harvesting between 40,000 and 50,000 whitetails each fall.

A NEW BREED OF BLACK POWDER RIFLE EMERGES

Nostalgia is no longer the driving force behind the modern-day shooters' and hunters' decision to embrace muzzleloading. Their reasons vary, from an opportunity to enjoy more time in the deer woods to the availability of ever more efficient front loaders available on the market. Until the mid-1990s, traditionally-styled rifles were number one in popularity. Then, gradually, rifles

The sight of a scope on a muzzleloading hunting rifle is fast becoming more commonplace.

Muzzleloading today has matured into a hunting sport, with the most popular models incorporating modern features similar to the efficient in-line percussion ignition system of the Thompson/Center "Fire Hawk" (top) or the corrosion resistant stainless steel of the "Grey Hawk" (bottom).

hammer, fire from the exploding cap traveled only a fraction of an inch to reach the powder charge.

Most of these "New Wave" frontloaders bear little or no resemblance to past designs. Most appear more like a modern bolt-action centerfire rifle; in fact, some more recent models even have "bolt-action" in-line ignition systems. Other modern features include safeties, modern stock lines, comfortable rubber recoil pads, and receivers that are drilled and tapped for easy installation of scope bases. For the most part, these are serious big game rifles that just happen to load from the front, all designed and built to deliver the kind of performance today's muzzle-loading hunters demand.

WRINKLES FOR AN OLD PERFORMER

Since the early 1800s, muzzleloading shooters and hunters have had two basic choices when selecting a muzzleloader projectile: the patched round ball or the heavier, longer, bore-sized conical bullet. Now, modern in-line riflemakers offer a third choice: the plastic-saboted pistol bullet. Indeed, performance-minded hunters began to steer away from the patched round ball more than a decade before in-line rifles had

with shorter, faster-handling 24- to 28-inch barrel lengths began to outsell those with barrels stretching to 40 inches. These new models also featured quicker rates of rifling twist for better accuracy and hard-hitting, heavy conical bullets, all of which soon won favor in the deer woods.

The modern in-line percussion rifle first began to capture the market during the late 1980s. Here was a modern frontloading design that offered many of the same features found on popular centerfire hunting rifles. The heart of these new models was an efficient, sure-fire percussion ignition system, one that positioned a nipple in the rear center of the breech plug. Once the capped nipple was struck by a plunger-style

Most of today's modern in-line rifles and saboted bullet projectiles are capable of centerfire rifle quality accuracy at 100 yards.

Muzzleloading never did completely die out in many parts of southern Appalachia. Backwoods riflemen and hunters continued to rely on original muzzleloaders until the introduction of modern reproduction guns.

designed to expand and transfer energy at velocities basically equal to those produced by muzzleloading rifles and heavy powder charges. As for accuracy, fast rifling twists of one turn in 20 inches to one in 38 inches produce centerfire rifle accuracy at a hundred yards. Many in-line rifles and saboted bullet loads are now capable of printing inside of $1^{1}/_{2}$ inches at a hundred yards.

SOME OLD FAVORITES REMAIN

No book on the topic of muzzleloading would be complete without covering the traditional side of the sport. For many black powder shooters, the rifle with authentic styling—the kind you throw over the shoulder—offers a chance to relive some of the past, whether at the range or in the field. Often, getting the best accuracy from a traditionally-styled muzzleloader requires more skill and knowledge of loading techniques than when one loads and shoots a modern in-line percussion rifle with saboted bullets. This book provides its readers with many loading techniques and tips for obtaining the best accuracy with traditional patched round ball projectiles fired from a traditional muzzleloading rifle. We also include detailed information on traditionally styled rifles and projectiles, loading and shooting the big .58 caliber Civil War rifled-muskets, the

established their popularity. Those spheres of soft pure lead simply did not deliver enough energy to ensure a clean kill on big game with consistency. On the other hand, heavy, bore-sized conical bullets made of lead weighed in at about twice that of a round ball for the same caliber rifle, thus causing inaccurate rainbow trajectories. Small plastic sleeves known as sabots now allow black powder shooters to load, shoot and hunt with a wide range of new, jacketed pistol bullets. Most .44, .45 and .50 caliber jacketed handgun bullets, especially those of hollow-point design, have been

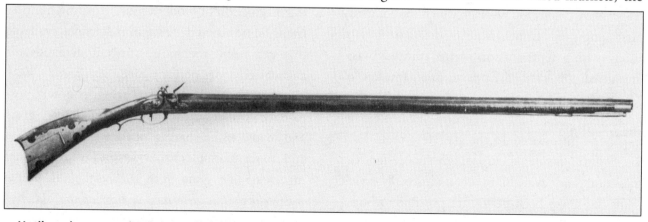

Until modern reproduction muzzleloaders offered shooters a safer, more affordable alternative, fine old originals like this graceful Pennsylvania flintlock were subjected to everyday use and abuse.

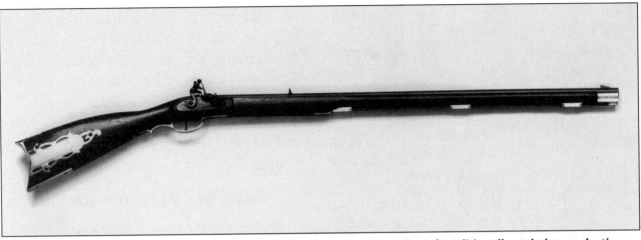

A muzzleloading shooter with an historical curiosity has a great selection of traditionally styled reproduction guns to choose from, such as this Navy Arms flintlock "Kentucky" full-stock rifle.

cleaning and care of all muzzleloading guns, how to accessorize a new frontloader and how to master the muzzleloading shotgun and black powder handgun.

Unfortunately, many of the guns covered in *Advanced Muzzle Loader's Guide* are no longer in production, and a few of the companies featured in that book are no longer in operation. A few standard-setters remain though, and continue to enjoy a certain popularity. Thompson/Center's Hawken rifle, introduced in the early 1970s, remains the best-selling traditionally-styled muzzleloading rifle. Another good example is Dixie Gun Works's Tennessee Mountain Rifle. Navy Arms still offers its faithful copy of the Colt 1851 Navy percussion revolver, which the company first imported from Italy in the late 1950s, along with a reproduction of the colorful brass-mounted .58 caliber Zouave rifled-musket of Civil War fame.

Even though the vast majority of muzzleloading guns introduced in the past few years have been of the in-line percussion ignition design, the selection and availability of traditionally-styled guns has never been better. It's possible to buy a reasonably faithful copy of a 1777 French Charleville flintlock smoothbored musket (circa 1780), a percussion Hawken half-stock rifle, a Model 1803 Harpers Ferry flintlock rifle, a high-quality Whitworth percussion sporting target rifle, or an 1830 Colt Paterson revolver. Other possibilities include faithful copies of Civil War rifled-muskets used by both the North and the South, stylish side-by-side percussion shotguns, an English flintlock sporting rifle, a Swiss percussion off-hand target rifle, a European flintlock fowling piece, or even a 16th Century-style Japanese smoothbored matchlock.

The sport of muzzleloading continues to expand its boundaries, each year encompassing more and more guns from the past, and yet at the same time incorporating advanced technology in the production of modern muzzleloading hunting rifles. Somewhere there's a muzzleloader available that can fulfill the most stringent demands for authenticity or performance. *Advanced Black Powder Hunting* seeks to bring shooters up-to-date information about the latest guns and loads, while sharing tips for better accuracy and performance from a variety of traditional muzzleloading guns from the past. *It is, as the muzzleloaders it describes, a mix of the old and the new, designed for black powder shooters and hunters everywhere.*

TABLE OF CONTENTS

TABLE OF CONTENTS *(CONTINUED)*

A Search For The Ultimate Muzzleloading Hunting Rifle

When handing out advice to novices, experienced black powder shooters too often forget what it's like to get started in the muzzleloading sports. Today's astounding array of guns, accessories and loading components is nothing less than mind-boggling to anyone looking at the sport for the first time. For many, in fact, buying that first muzzleloader can be downright frightening. The best move is to seek the advice of someone with lots of experience in shooting and hunting with muzzleloaders. Learning what works and what doesn't through trial and error can be costly—and frustrating. Most knowledgeable muzzleloading shooters are more than happy to share what they know about the sport, and almost any muzzleloading gun shop can put you in contact with an experienced black powder burner.

During the 1930s and '40s, not many black powder shooters were around. Even as recently as the mid-1960s, fewer than 200,000 muzzleloading shooters and hunters were active in the U.S.

Most were still shooting the old guns from the past, but an infant reproduction muzzleloading industry was slowly beginning to replace centuries' old antiques with safer and more serviceable, up-to-date copies of those guns. Still, trying to locate an experienced black powder shooter for advice was next to impossible. With little more than old publications about loading and shooting frontloading guns to turn to, beginners in the muzzleloading sports were as often as not self-taught. How these hopeless romantics got hooked on the frontloading rifle and began a lifelong pursuit of the ultimate muzzleloader is detailed in the following pages of this book.

How I Got Bitten by the Bug

To begin with, the first whitetail I ever took was downed with a muzzleloader. That special moment in my hunting career took place on the opening morning of my second season chasing whitetails. The year before, I had spent both

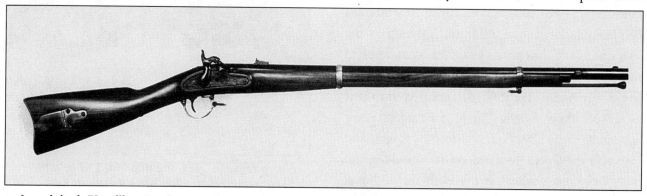

An original .58 caliber Remington Zouave rifle musket put in the finishing shot on the author's first whitetail.

halves of the split six-day deer season in Illinois hunting the same ridgetop. During the hunt, from atop my bulldozed pile stand, I had spotted a half-dozen whitetails, but none had come close enough for me to take a shot with the 30-inch Winchester 12 gauge pump I was carrying.

When a fire in the family home destroyed that prized old pump shotgun the following summer, I began hunting with a borrowed Stevens side-by-side 12-bore loaded with rifled slugs. While sighting in before the hunt, I discovered that the right barrel printed satisfactorily out to about 40 yards, but the left barrel threw large hunks of lead about two feet to the right. Regardless, the next morning found this 14-year-old hunter filled with anticipation and hope as I perched on top of a pile of logs. Little did I realize that my life was about to be changed forever.

To ward off the chill of that early November morning, I had slipped on all the warm clothing I owned, plus an old Army surplus wool blanket around my shoulders. By ten o'clock, nothing had moved within sight of my stand. The sun was bright and temperatures quickly rose into the upper 50s. I slipped out of the blanket, took off the heavy coat, and settled back for another hour or two of hunting before heading back to camp. Moments later, I heard the unmistakable sounds of deer running through the dry leaves that covered the ground. Suddenly, a big doe appeared, followed by two yearling deer. Since all whitetails had been declared legal in Illinois, I swung on the lead doe as she shot past 30 yards away and pulled the right trigger. The shot missed, and before I could fire again she had disappeared into the safety of heavy brush. Then, the second deer appeared magically right in front of me, and instinctively I put the bead on its shoulder and pulled the left trigger. In my excitement, I had forgotten to lead, but fortunately the left barrel

had the lead built in. The whitetail rolled, regained its feet, turned and headed down the side of the ridge.

By the time I could reload the double, the deer was already too far out to try another shot. It had been hit hard, though, and stumbled several times as it went down the ridge. I followed the wounded animal about a quarter of a mile down the valley below until I'd closed the distance to 50 yards or so. Two quick shots both missed their target, but as I set to reload I discovered that I'd left my other rifled slug loads in the jacket back at the stand. I heard someone shout and turned to see another hunter approaching. When I explained my predicament, he offered me the use of his gun so I could put in a finishing shot. What he handed me was his original Civil War era .58 caliber Remington "Zouave" rifled-musket. After we'd eased up to within 50 yards of the standing deer, he insisted I take the shot from there, which I thought was too far away. But to my amazement, the big hollow-based Minie bullet drove home exactly where I'd been holding and dropped the small button buck cleanly. That single shot changed the way I'd hunt whitetails from that day on.

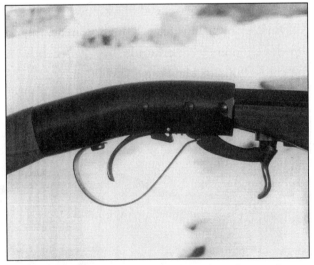

First offered in 1963, the Hopkins & Allen under-hammer muzzleloading rifles were efficient, accurate and economically priced.

That following winter, I read every magazine article on muzzleloading I could lay my hands on, which wasn't too many. Apparently not many writers in 1964 were specializing in black powder shooting. Among the early pioneers was the late Al Goerg, who often wrote about hunting in the Pacific Coast mountains, Hawaii and Alaska with muzzleloading rifles, most of which he had fitted with a scope. One of his favorite rifles for deer-sized game was Hopkins & Allen's .45 caliber underhammer rifle, which sold for about $50 in the early 1960s. In any event, I learned a great deal from his articles about hunting with a muzzleloader.

WELCOME TO MY FIRST MUZZLELOADER

When in the following spring I bought my first frontloader, I discovered the selection was a far cry from what today's shooters have to choose from. There were, in fact, less than a dozen long guns available suitable for hunting deer. The Hopkins & Allen underhammer rifles were popular because of their low price, which allowed a shooter to buy a rifle, a flask full of black powder, 25 round balls and patches, and a tin of No. 11 percussion caps for only $49.95. Other popular muzzleloaders of the day included a modern version of the .58 caliber Zouave imported from Italy by Navy Arms Company, along with a

"sporterized" half-stock version of the same gun, known as the "Buffalo Hunter." One of the first reproduction muzzleloaders to feature what came to be known as "Hawken" styling was the Tingle half-stock percussion hunting rifle.

But the first modern-day production muzzleloader was reputed to be the "Kentucky Rifle" introduced by Dixie Gun Works in 1956 in .40 caliber. By 1963, the caliber of this Belgium-made front loader had been upped to .45, making the rifle more suitable for deer hunting. Perhaps it was the rifle's graceful and slender lines, its long 40-inch rifled barrel, or simply the gleam of its polished brass trigger guard, buttplate and other furniture; but for whatever reason, I chose that .45 caliber Dixie percussion rifle for my first muzzleloader.

The long barrel of that frontloader, I soon learned, performed well with a 70 grain load of DuPont FFFg black powder behind a tightly patched .440" diameter round ball. Three- to four-inch groups at 50 yards were the rule, and I felt confident that I could keep hits inside the kill zone of a whitetail out to 75 or 80 yards. Back then, I knew absolutely nothing about the down-range ballistics of muzzleloading guns; if I had, I'd never have chosen to hunt deer with a .45 caliber rifle loaded with a patched 128 grain soft lead ball. That load pushed the ball from the muzzle of

The Navy Arms "Buffalo Hunter" was one of only a few muzzleloading hunting rifles available during the early 1960s. The big .58 caliber rifle was a sporter version of the Remington Zouave rifle musket (also offered by Navy Arms).

the 40-inch barrel at about 1,900 f.p.s. Even so, the light 128 grain lead sphere developed only 1,100 foot pounds of muzzle energy. By the time the ball reached 100 yards, it was good for slightly more than 300 ft. lbs. of leftover energy. The .45 caliber muzzleloading rifle loaded with a patched round ball was simply a poor choice for whitetails, but what could a 14-year old know about such things?

Still, that first season with my Dixie .45 caliber rifle rewarded me with my first two branch-antlered bucks. The first was a six-pointer taken on my first out-of-state deer hunt in neighboring Missouri. The deer was shot at 35 yards and ran another 75 yards before it fell dead. The round ball had caught the whitetail through both lungs and the top of its heart. The following week, back in Illinois, I made a 90-yard shot on an eight-point buck. From the way the deer reacted, I knew I had hit it solidly. Foamy blood indicated a lung shot, and after a long tedious tracking job I jumped the buck and managed to get a second ball into him. Still, he ran another 400 yards before going down. Later, during a stint with the U.S. Marine Corps, I was fortunate enough to take a couple of blacktail bucks with my long-barreled .45 caliber Dixie rifle. I also had an opportunity to hunt feral goats on some of the coastal islands, which Al Goerg had once hunted regularly with his underhammer .45 caliber rifles.

In 1971, Thompson/Center Arms' half-stocked "Hawken" rifle caught my eye. This short-barreled muzzleloader (28-inch) seemed more ideally suited to hunting from an elevated tree stand. Its fully adjustable rear sight was a definite improvement over the non-adjustable "fixed" rear sight of the Dixie longrifle. For years, the Dixie .45 caliber had shot about three inches high at 50 yards. I didn't realize at the time that I could have remedied the problem by replacing the front sight with

The author installed a long eye relief handgun scope on his favorite old Thompson/Center Hawken to improve its long range accuracy.

a higher blade, or filing the notch in the rear sight slightly deeper. I always compensated for the higher impact by aiming a little lower with shots out to about 60 yards, then dead on at 75 to 100 yards. The adjustable rear sight of the new Thompson/Center muzzleloader made sight adjustments a breeze.

My first Thompson/Center Hawken was also a .45 caliber rifle. I found the rifle shot well with the patched round ball, but the faster rate of rifling twist (one-turn-in 48 inches) seemed to perform best with Thompson/Center's Maxi-Ball. With 80 grains of FFFg black powder behind one of the 240 grain .45 caliber conical bullets, this rifle and load produced enough energy to drop even the largest whitetail buck.

Soon I began experimenting with the .50 caliber rifle, beginning a love affair for the half-inch bore that lasts to this day. One of my favorites was a .50 caliber Thompson/Center Hawken, which I came to regard as my first "serious" big game muzzleloading rifle. During several seasons, I took more than a dozen whitetails with the rifle, shooting both the patched round ball and Thompson/Center's Maxi-Ball. I quickly discovered that the big Maxi-Ball bullet, which had done so much for the smaller bored .45, really turned the .50 caliber Hawken into a powerhouse. But the load that performed best for me consisted of a 90 grain charge of FFg black powder behind one of the whopping 370 grain Maxi-Ball projectiles. This combination pushed the big slug from the muzzle at a little over 1,450 f.p.s., generating a muzzle energy of nearly 1,800 ft. lbs. At 100 yards, the hefty Maxi-Ball could smack a whitetail with almost 1,000 ft. lbs. of remaining energy, or about three times what the 128 grain round ball fired from my old .45 caliber Dixie rifle could produce at that distance.

Throughout the 1970s, I shot and hunted with a wide range of .50 and .54 caliber muzzleloading rifles. I had started writing for a number of shooting and hunting magazines, often finding myself doing a "test report" on new models for publication. Muzzleloading had suddenly become fashionable, causing U.S. and foreign gun manufacturers alike to introduce new models to satisfy the growing demand. Interest in the guns of the Civil War era continued to grow, and more and more black powder shooters were participating in rendezvous reenactments of the Revolutionary War and fur trade eras. All these developments caused manufacturers to begin offering guns with more authentic styling and better quality. Unfortunately, a few get-rich-quick operations also opened up, offering cheap, shoddy front loaders that were often functional at best and quite dangerous to shoot.

Once shooters were introduced to quality muzzleloaders, however, they quickly weeded out these junk guns. New companies like Connecticut Valley Arms showed how serviceable muzzleloaders could be offered at reasonable prices without jeopardizing safety. But low cost was not the only reason shooters were turning to muzzleloading. The sport had taken a new turn, and shooters didn't seem to mind paying a little more. In 1977, Dixie Gun Works was forced to discontinue production of its original "Kentucky Rifle," replacing it with a copy of a southern-styled longrifle known as the "Tennessee Mountain Rifle." This .50 caliber full-stock muzzleloader was built for Dixie by the B.C. Miroku Gun Works (Japan), makers of the Charles Daly shotguns. The gun is still in production in the original .50 caliber bore size, along with a smallbore .32 caliber model for the small game hunter.

Another survivor of the 70s is the Ithaca/Navy Hawken rifle, which was first introduced by the old Ithaca Gun Company. Unfortunately, the company had some serious financial problems and was forced to shut down operations. Navy Arms purchased the tooling for the rifle and began producing it as the "Ithaca/Navy Hawken." The

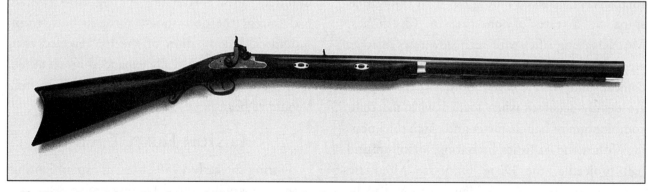

The Navy Arms/Ithaca Hawken, which was among the first true reproductions of the famous half-stock sporting rifle ever offered, is still available.

When the Knight MK-85 in-line percussion rifle was introduced in 1985, it changed how black powder hunters would look at muzzleloading again.

31½-inch barreled percussion rifle is still available in .50 and .54 caliber.

Both the Dixie Tennessee Mountain Rifle and the Ithaca/Navy Hawken are true round ball rifles. The long 41-inch barrel of the .50 caliber Dixie rifle features six-groove rifling that spirals with a one-turn-in 56 inches rate of twist. The Ithaca/Navy Hawken bore is cut with rifling that spins at a rate of one-turn-in 65 inches. Muzzleloading rifles with such slow rates of twist are traditionally poor performers with longer conical bullets. However, both of these guns are deadly accurate when loaded with the right combination of ball diameter and patch thickness.

Within the ballistics limitations of the round ball projectile, the Dixie Tennessee Mountain Rifle and the Ithaca/Navy Hawken proved to be excellent whitetail rifles. I relied on these and a few other similar rifles, but I always came back to my old Thompson/Center Hawken and hard-hitting Maxi-Ball when heading out on serious big game hunts. The rifle and load have rewarded me with a number of memorable trophies, including a superb 12-point Illinois whitetail buck which literally dropped in its tracks at almost a hundred yards. Fortunately the big hunk of lead had caught the deer square through both front shoulders. Examination of the hit revealed that the Maxi-Ball hadn't really expanded much at all. If the hit had struck back four or five inches, I could've been faced with a long tracking job.

CUSTOM HUNTING RIG

During the early 1980s I began experimenting with every known muzzleloading projectile design available. My goal was to find a hard-hitting

Not only do modern saboted bullets and handy Pyrodex Pellets make muzzleloading easier than ever, they make today's modern in-line rifles more accurate and effective.

conical bullet that performed as accurately as the Thompson/Center Maxi-Ball, but which promised better expansion and transfer of energy on big game. One lengthy practice session after another at the shooting bench convinced me that the stylish, curved brass buttplate of my old Hawken satisfied the whims of traditionally-minded shooters more than it provided shooting comfort for shooters with its hefty powder charges and heavy hunting bullets. Switching to Thompson/Center's Renegade model in .50 caliber, with its flat shotgun-style buttplate, did alleviate some of the shoulder pain generated by heavy hunting loads. But its low comb still caused some discomfort, so I decided to build my own muzzleloading hunting rig.

Reinhart Fajen (Warsaw, Missouri) offers a variety of replacement stocks for several of the more popular muzzleloading rifles, including the Thompson/Center Hawken. Most of the stocks feature traditional lines while retaining the pronounced crescent-shaped buttplate. One particular stock, however, had all the features I was looking for: A comfortable flat buttplate, high Monte Carlo shaped comb, and a comfortable pistol grip. I soon transferred all of the component parts from my Thompson/Center Hawken onto a beautifully striped "curly" maple stock. Fajen's superb inletting of the wood made the transition easy. The job required minor fitting of parts, some light contour shaping, sanding and finishing with a hand-rubbed, boiled linseed oil finish. The completed rifle was as good-looking as it was practical.

The flat buttplate and higher comb tamed down the recoil from shooting 90 to 110 grains

The author poses with the first buck—a Missouri eight- pointer—he ever took with a modern in-line rifle, a Knight MK-85, during the 1986 season.

of FFg black powder and equivalent loads of Pyrodex "RS" behind conical bullets of 300 to more than 400 grains. Just as I'd completed work on the rifle, a new "Maxi-Bullet" from a then new California firm, Buffalo Bullet Company, arrived. Precision swaged from pure, cold lead, the new Maxi-Bullets were neatly knurled and featured a hollow point for much-needed expansion. They were available in several calibers, but the .50 caliber Maxi-Bullet was my only interest. They came in two versions: One featured a lightly cupped hollow base and weighed 385 grains; the other had a flat solid base and tipped the scales at 410 grains. Both shot well out of my customized Thompson/Center Hawken, but the lighter, hollow-based design had an edge in accuracy. With the factory open sights still mounted on the Hawken barrel, I could group

The Marlin MLS-50 in-line percussion muzzleloader is the first frontloading firearm produced by this old-line maker of cartridge firearms.

This big Minnesota ten-pointer was no match for the author's scope-sighted .50 caliber stainless steel Knight MK-85 rifle. The buck was dropped at about 150 yards with a modern saboted handgun bullet.

shots inside of five inches at a hundred yards.

Preparing for a pronghorn hunt in Wyoming, I replaced the rear sight with a scope base and installed a 4x long eye relief handgun scope. By reducing some of the human error of sighting and shooting with open sights, I discovered how accurately my old Thompson/Center barrel could shoot. The size of the groups fired at a hundred yards were practically cut in half.

Allowing for a full two feet of drop, I took a beautiful 15-inch horned buck at 200 yards. Buffalo Bullet's hollow-pointed conical had expanded nicely and dropped the pronghorn on the spot. Later on, the rifle and bullet accounted for a record book class whitetail at 120 yards. Here at last, I felt, was the muzzleloading hunting rig I could live with forever—or so I thought.

In 1996, Remington took in-line ignition muzzleloader development to another level with the introduction of its Model 700 bolt action rifle in a new muzzleloading configuration.

MODERN IN-LINE PERCUSSION RIFLES

Late in 1985, I was asked by a gun designer named William A. "Tony" Knight to field test an innovative in-line percussion ignition system rifle he hoped to manufacture and market. It was an early version of the now famous Knight MK-85. Its one-turn-in 48 inches rate of twist was the same as the Thompson/Center barrel on my custom hunting rifle. Accuracy with Buffalo Bullet's conical bullets was every bit as good with Knight's rifle as the one I had built. However, Knight's rifle was built with features that made it even more practical as a hunting rifle. One was its unique double safety system. In addition to a side-mounted thumb-operated trigger safety, the Knight rifle featured a secondary safety located at the rear of the hammer. When threaded forward, this knurled collar safety prevented the hammer from striking a capped nipple. Other great features of the Knight rifle included a removable breech plug for easy cleaning of the muzzleloader, a receiver drilled and tapped for easy installation of scope bases, and a modern stock design with a rubber recoil pad.

Compared to the nearly ten-pound weight of my custom rifle, Knight's new rifle was, at less than seven pounds, a real lightweight. During a wild boar hunt in the rugged mountains of Tennessee, I quickly grew to appreciate its light weight and outstanding balance. Even with hefty 100 grain charges of Pyrodex "RS" behind a 385 grain Maxi-Bullet, this muzzleloader was still a delight to shoot, thanks to the high comb of its modern stock and the extra cushioning of its rubber recoil pad. Together, those features combined to help me drop a 250-pound wild boar at 75 yards.

Early in 1986, Tony Knight switched to a faster one-turn-in 32 inches rate of twist. A small company in Arkansas had introduced a new sabot projectile system, one that allowed shooters to load, shoot and hunt with modern jacketed pistol bullets out of a .45, .50 or .54 caliber muzzleloading hunting rifle. This combination proved deadly accurate and ultimately changed the way many big game hunters looked at black powder hunting from then on.

Tony Knight's new rifle-making operation soon became known as Modern Muzzleloading,

The Ruger M77/50 bolt-action in-line muzzleloader basically shares the same receiver and bolt as the Ruger M77/22 bolt-action rimfire.

Inc. At first, there was tremendous opposition to a muzzleloader that didn't look like one. But attitudes changed as the sport of muzzleloading matured. Traditionalists hated the new in-line rifle, but hunters who had decided to cash in on the bonus afforded by the new muzzleloading deer (and other big game) seasons liked what they saw. Here, they now realized, was a serious hunting rifle that just happened to load from the front.

A few years later, Modern Muzzleloading went to a still faster one-turn-in 28 inches rate of rifling twist, which proved to be even more accurate using a wider range of bullet and sabot combinations. I still shoot a .50 caliber stainless steel Knight MK-85 rifle produced at that time. To date, more than 7,500 saboted bullets have been fired through it. Armed with 100 grains of Pyrodex "Select" and a saboted .45 caliber Speer 260 grain jacketed, hollow-point pistol bullet, this rifle consistently shoots well inside of two inches at a hundred yards, with many groups shrinking closer to 1½ inches. That kind of performance has made the new in-line rifle popular and caused gunmakers like Thompson/Center Arms, Connecticut Valley Arms, Traditions, Lyman, Dixie Gun Works, Navy Arm and Marlin to begin marketing their own in-line percussion rifles.

MUZZLELOADING ENTERS A NEW ERA

In 1996, Remington Arms Company shook up the shooting world when it introduced its revered bolt-action Model 700 Centerfire rifle in a new muzzleloading configuration, while retaining the stock design, trigger, receiver and even the bolt of its Model 700 cartridge models. Modifications included a removable breech plug and nipple threaded into the rear of the barrel, plus replacement of the standard firing pin with a larger

diameter and flat-faced cylindrical pin for positive ignition of a No. 11 percussion cap. The new Remington Model 700 ML (blued) and Model 700 MLS (stainless) feature the fast one-turn-in 28 inches rate of twist that has become a standard for modern in-line rifles. This rifle shoots extremely well with a wide range of saboted .44 and .45 jacketed bullets. Its crisp, clean trigger is among the finest available on a muzzleloader today, and the lock time is so quick you'll never feel—or hear—the hammer fall. Ignition is spontaneous. Another feature certain to make this muzzleloader attractive to those whitetail hunters who head out no matter how bad the weather is the special plastic "weather shroud" that can be locked securely into the face of the bolt. When the bolt is in the forward "closed" position, the shroud completely encloses the capped nipple, protecting it from rain, snow or any other wet hunting condition. It's this promise of reliability in damp weather that has really put the new Remington muzzleloader in the forefront. The gun has also helped set the stage for the next round of muzzleloader development.

Modern Muzzleloading also offers a "bolt-action" in-line ignition muzzleloader known as the D.I.S.C. Rifle (Disc Ignition System Concept). Small plastic ignition discs allow the shooter to switch from standard No. 11 percussion cap ignition to hotter No. 209 shotshell primer ignition in mere seconds. Also unique is the D.I.S.C. rifle's bolt, which cocks the action as the bolt handle is lifted upward. This design feature also causes the bolt to cam rearward slightly, exposing a priming port at the face of the bolt for the priming disc. The plastic discs accept either a special No. 11 nipple insert or they can be primed with a No. 209 shotshell primer. When priming the rifle, one of the discs is simply dropped into the opening at the face of the bolt and the bolt handle is pushed back downward. This cams the bolt forward to enclose the plastic disc for a precise, moisture-proof fit with the flash hole of the breech plug. Ignition with either No. 11 caps or No. 209 shotshell primers is spontaneous. Fired with two 50 grain Pyrodex pellets (100 grain charge) using the No. 11 percussion cap ignition disc, a .50 caliber D.I.S.C. rifle can average about 1,640 f.p.s. at the muzzle with a saboted Barnes 250 grain all-copper Expander-MZ bullet. The same load fired with one of the shotshell primer disc inserts increases the velocity to slightly less than 1,670 f.p.s.

Not all advances in muzzleloader performance have been made with the guns themselves. During the mid-1970s Pyrodex became the first successful black powder substitute. Introduction of the plastic sabot allowed hunters to load and shoot a modern bullet design superior to a simple piece of lead. Bullets are now designed specifically for shooting with a sabot out of a muzzleloading big game rifle, such as the all-copper Barnes Expander-MZ. This bullet has been designed to expand fully at velocities of less than 1,000 f.p.s., or about what a .50 caliber hunting load will produce once the bullet reaches 150 yards or so. Still, this bullet holds together when driven into a deer or elk at close range.

It still seems strange to combine the words "bolt-action" and "muzzleloader" when describing the same gun. When I look at muzzleloading today, I suddenly realize how little I knew about the sport some 30 years ago when I acquired that .45 caliber Dixie "Kentucky Rifle." The sport now has many different facets; fortunately, we're served by an industry that has responded to the needs of all black powder shooters, whether they're in the market for a Brown Bess musket of Revolutionary War days or a deadly accurate, scope-sighted in-line percussion hunting rifle. *There's something out there for all of us.*

A NEW BREED OF MUZZLELOADING HUNTING RIFLE

Many experts in the shooting industry consider muzzleloading the fastest growing of all the shooting and hunting sports. Whether they're correct or not, no one can deny that it's become one of the fastest changing sports. Today's most popular muzzleloaders are a far cry from the frontloaders we knew during the 1970s. Nostalgia plays a much lesser role now in causing shooters and hunters to turn to muzzleloaders. For one thing, they're motivated by the special muzzleloader-only big game hunting seasons now held across the country. The new breed of muzzleloading hunter could care less about historically correct lines and styling. Instead, he's making new demands on the performance of that rifle, constantly trying to make it perform more like a modern centerfire big game rifle. Fortunately, some significant changes and improvements in muzzleloader design and performance have been made. Muzzleloading has gone modern, giving the newer rifles the capability of delivering centerfire quality accuracy at a hundred yards and more.

The one rifle that has done more than any other to change the way today's big game hunter looks at muzzleloading is Tony Knight's MK-85. At first glance, it bears little, if any, resemblance to the heavy and awkward frontloading rifles with traditional side-hammer styling. In fact, this muzzleloader displays all of the classic lines and handling characteristics of a top-quality bolt-

William "Tony" Knight hand-crafted this first prototype of the Knight in-line percussion rifle during the winter of 1983.

Built in early 1985, this Knight MK-85 prototype was the first to feature the now famous double safety system.

One of the first 25 Knight MK-85 rifles, all of which were built in November 1985.

Currently in production is Knight's MK-85 stainless steel "Predator" model.

action centerfire rifle. The idea for the MK-85 first arose during the late 1970s and early 1980s, when several of Tony Knight's friends, eager to enjoy the newly sanctioned muzzleloader elk season, took up the sport. Most had never loaded and fired a muzzleloader before, and as a result often returned from hunting trips with horror stories about how their rifles failed to perform in bad weather. Others complained about how cumbersome the ten-pound rifles were when carried all day at high altitudes, and how unsafe they were in rough terrain, with only a half-cock notch preventing the hammer from striking a capped nipple.

These shortcomings caused Knight to shift his attention to the design and production of a new breed of muzzleloading hunting rifle. Work on the first prototype began during the winter of 1983. Along with two other early prototypes, this rifle featured a unique in-line percussion ignition system, one that positioned the nipple directly in the rear center of the breech plug. Knight's muzzleloader action also featured a plunger-style hammer that was fitted inside a machined receiver. When the trigger was pulled, the hammer slammed forward, striking the capped nipple and

sending fire from the exploding cap only a fraction of an inch. Without any turns or angles in the flash channel, the flame entering the barrel was much hotter than a traditional cap-lock ignition system could ever produce. The efficiency of this ignition system all but eliminated several major causes of misfires with percussion hunting rifles.

Knight's prototypes were built with fully tapered round barrels so as to reduce weight; even with a 26-inch, .50 caliber barrel, the rifles weighed barely seven pounds. Other "hunter friendly" features included a thumb-operated safety and a receiver drilled and tapped for easy installation of a scope. Knight's rifles also featured a removable breech plug and a design which allowed them to be completely broken down, including removal of the breech plug, in a minute or two.

In 1984, Knight added a second safety. The primary safety could be slipped into the "on" position before the hammer was pulled back into the "cocked" position. Earlier prototypes had featured a small handle on the side of the hammer for cocking; but this new prototype was cocked simply by grasping the rear of the plunger hammer and pulling it rearward until it engaged the sear of the trigger. The extension of the hammer from the rear of the receiver made it possible to add a secondary safety in the form of a threaded collar. With the hammer cocked, the collar can turn forward a half-inch or so. In the forward position, the collar bottoms out against the rear of the receiver, so that the nose of the hammer cannot reach the capped nipple. To fire the rifle, the secondary safety must first be turned to the rear, allowing the hammer to fall forward far enough to strike the cap.

By early 1985, Knight's final prototype displayed the lines and features to be carried over to his first production rifle. The gun boasted a stylish modern stock complete with rubber recoil pad and sling swivel studs. Weighing 6 1/2 pounds, this rifle with its 24-inch barrel was a delight to carry. Later that year, it was introduced to the muzzleloading fraternity as the "Knight MK-85." Since then, several refinements have been added to the original design, but the basic concept has not changed. Some recent models now utilize either rifle or shotgun primers rather than No. 11 percussion caps for hotter ignition, but most changes from one model to the next have been purely cosmetic.

All this does not mean that Tony Knight "invented" the ignition system. Original in-line percussion guns existed shortly after the invention of the percussion cap itself, and several in-line flintlock guns are known to have been built in Germany around 1730. A few muzzleloading benchrest target shooters have been shooting in-line percussion rifles since the early 1970s. One of these, an early in-line sporting rifle, known as the "Eusopus Pacer," appeared on the market during the early 1970s, but it failed to gain popularity, mostly because shooters were more interested in muzzleloading purely for nostalgic reasons. During the early 1980s,

Michigan Arms produced the modern in-line "Wolverine" hunting rifle that utilized hot shotgun primers for ignition. Unfortunately, it was only a "round ball" version with a heavy octagon barrel and slow-twist rifling, which was not what hunters wanted.

Tony Knight's earliest prototypes were built with barrels made by Numrich Arms, featuring an extremely slow one-turn-in 66 inches rate of rifling twist. Knight had earlier been a custom centerfire riflesmith, so it didn't take long for him to discover that a little more spin was needed to stabilize the elongated conical bullets. He then switched to Bauska barrels with a twist of one-turn-in 48 inches. In 1986, Knight went to a still faster one-turn-in 32 inches rate of twist, which performed even better with conical and saboted handgun bullets. About this same time, Del Ramsey, another enterprising black powder fan from Harrison, Arkansas, discovered that modern jacketed handgun bullets could be fired with great accuracy from the larger bore of a muzzleloading hunting rifle. Ramsey had tried for years to come up with an improved hunting projectile for his muzzleloaders. It finally dawned on him that the large selection of jacketed .44 and .45 caliber pistol bullets available to handloaders had been designed to perform at velocities equal to those derived from a .50 or .54 caliber muzzleloading hunting rifle. Ramsey quickly devised a mold for producing his now widely used plastic sabots. This combination—of saboted handgun bullets and the Knight MK-85 rifle—were to change muzzleloading forever.

Most of Knight's guns built around 1990 were fitted with McMillan barrels, but quite a few were also imported from Lothar Walther in Germany. Since 1990, however, all Knight rifles have been built with barrels made by the Green Mountain Rifle Barrel Company. It's now estimated that

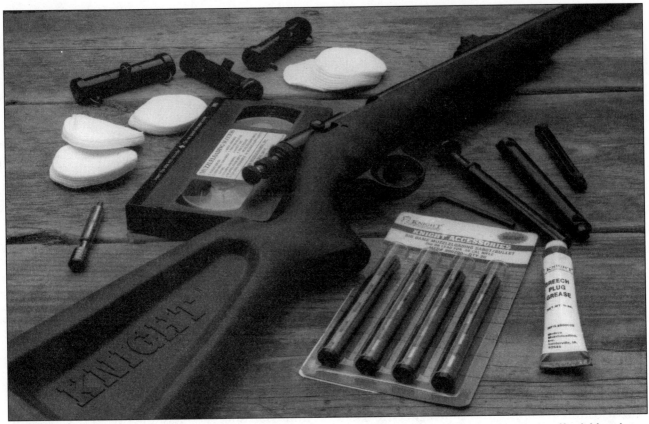

The Knight Wolverine delivers the accuracy, reliability and safety of the revered MK-85, but at a more affordable price.

nearly 300,000 in-line muzzleloading rifles made by Modern Muzzleloading head for the deer woods each fall. Thus, in the course of a single decade, this updated muzzleloading hunting rifle grew from a virtual unknown to one of the most recognized muzzleloaders on the market. The lightest model in the current line tips the scales at only 6 pounds, with the heaviest version weighing in at about 7 pounds. Compared with the 9 and 10 pound rifles that hunters were forced to haul around, this lighter weight became one of Modern Muzzleloading's biggest selling points.

One factor that kept the Knight rifle from winning even quicker acceptance among black powder hunters was the original price tag ($349.95). Back then, the best-selling muzzle-loader in America was the Thompson/Center Hawken, whose percussion version carried a suggested retail price of $270.00, while the basic

Thompson/Center Renegade sold for only $225.00. This disparity caused Modern Muzzleloading to introduce in 1992 its now discontinued "BK-92 Black Knight" with all the bells and whistles of the MK-85 but at a price closer to that of top quality traditional side-hammer rifles. The following year, the company introduced an early version of the "Knight LK-93 Wolverine," which retailed for $289.95. In 1993, that model's stock was replaced with a synthetic version, causing the price to drop another $20.00. While this gun lacked many of the features found on the MK-85, it maintained the same efficient in-line percussion ignition system, patented double safeties, and easy take-down design. Most of all, it delivered the same accuracy and down range performance that had made the Knight rifle the most revered muzzleloading hunting rifle on the market.

The Knight MK-85 "Knight Hawk" takes on an avant garde appearance with it's ultra-modern composite thumbhole stock.

Two more recent entries from Modern Muzzleloading are the MK-95 Magnum Elite and the MK-86 Multiple Barrel System. The former is built with one of the hottest in-line ignition systems available. Instead of a No. 11 percussion cap, this innovative "bolt-action" muzzleloader utilizes an extremely hot primer for ignition. Built without a nipple, this "percussion" muzzleloader features a chamber into which a small plastic capsule (with the primer at the rear) is inserted. A tiny hole—about the size of one found in a nipple—runs from the chamber into the barrel. This allows fire from the primer to enter the barrel, eliminating blow-back as the powder charge ignites and burns. The Multiple Barrel System allows shooters to switch from a .50 to .54 caliber rifle barrel to a 12 gauge shotgun barrel in just minutes, using only a hex-head wrench to loosen two lock screws. The barrel can now be pulled forward out of the receiver and replaced with either of the two other options. The MK-86's versatility as an in-line muzzleloader offers shooters and hunters a quick choice of .50 or .54 caliber bores with the flexibility of a muzzleloading shotgun barrel, whether hunting wild turkey or upland game.

For serious black powder handgunners, Modern Muzzleloading offers an in-line percussion muzzleloading pistol, dubbed the "Hawkeye." This .50 caliber frontloader resem-bles a muzzleloading version of the Remington XP-100 single-shot bolt-action centerfire pistol. The 12-inch barreled handgun comes with laminated stock, double safeties, removable breech plug and an accurate Green Mountain barrel capable of delivering .44 Magnum ballistics with a saboted handgun bullet and 60 grain charges of FFFg or Pyrodex "P" grade powder.

Today, every major manufacturer of muzzleloading guns offers a broad selection of modern in-line percussion frontloaders. Thompson/Center Arms, Connecticut Valley Arms, Traditions and others have been joined by the likes of Austin & Halleck, Kahnke Gun Works, and Markesbery Muzzle Loaders, not to mention such well established armsmakers as Remington and Marlin. The improved reliability and performance of these new guns continue to appeal to deer and other big game hunters who were previously unimpressed with muzzleloading. Today's powders, bullets and efficient modern in-line percussion rifles, bolt-action or otherwise, enable the black powder hunter to head out knowing that when the smoke clears there will be meat laying on the ground.

The following reports represent an in-depth look at the latest in modern in-line guns. As these seven reports clearly show, muzzleloading is now a hunter-driven sport involving rifles capable of amazing accuracy and devastating knockdown power.

PRODUCT REVIEW #1: KNIGHT D.I.S.C. RIFLE

SPECIFICATIONS

CALIBER: *.50 only*

BARREL LENGTH: *22"*

RATE OF TWIST: *1-turn-in-28"*

STOCK: *Composite Monte Carlo - black or camouflage*

WEIGHT: *6 lbs., 14 oz.*

FEATURES: *Blued or stainless Green Mountain*

barrel, adjustable Timney trigger, removable stainless steel breech plug, receiver drilled and tapped for scope bases, Knight double safety system, fully adjustable rear sight, rubber recoil pad, and instructional video.

MANUFACTURED BY: *Modern Muzzleloading, Inc., 234 Airport Road, Centerville, IA 52544*

Perhaps the best word to use in describing the new Knight D.I.S.C. rifle (Disc Ignition System Concept) is *controversial.* This .50 caliber rifle is now pushing saboted bullets at velocities previously unattainable in a muzzleloader. Faster velocities, improved ignition and an ultra-modern bolt-action in-line ignition system have led some black powder hunters to ask: "When does a muzzleloader stop being a muzzleloader?"

Modern Muzzleloading has taken the new "bolt-action" muzzleloader trend to yet another level of development with the D.I.S.C rifle, whose innovative system allows the shooter to switch from percussion cap ignition to the much hotter

optional No. 209 shotshell primer ignition in a matter of seconds. It utilizes special plastic ignition discs and can be primed by lifting the handle of the bolt upward. The bolt cams rearward to expose a priming port at the face of the bolt. Once a disc has dropped into the opening, the bolt handle is pushed down. The bolt cams forward, compressing the plastic disc between the fact of the bolt and the rear of the breech plug. Fire from either the standard No. 11 percussion cap or No. 209 primer travels through a small flash hole in the breech plug to the powder charge, which is located only one-quarter inch from the source of ignition.

When the bolt handle is lifted upward, the bolt cams slightly to the rear, exposing the priming port at face of bolt.

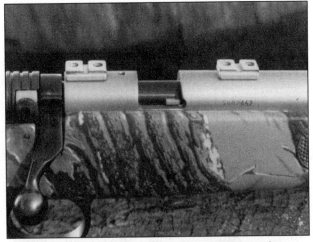

With the bolt handle in the down position, the bolt cams forward to form a compressed fit with the plastic disc.

Modern Muzzleloading developed the D.I.S.C. Rifle at the same time the Hodgdon Powder Company introduced the new Pyrodex Pellet charges. These compressed powder charges were designed to be loaded into and fired from almost any modern in-line percussion muzzleloading rifle, but the Knight D.I.S.C. rifle was the first new-age muzzleloader designed especially for shooting these pellets. The face of the removable breech plug was hollowed out, allowing the compressed pellets to drop into the plug, thereby placing the powder charge closer to the source of fire for better, more spontaneous ignition.

The plastic discs were designed to accept either the percussion cap insert or a No. 209 primer. Either can be pressed into the plastic disc with nothing more than thumb pressure. The percussion cap insert features a cone for the No. 11 cap; once the insert has been seated in the disc, it can be easily capped. To remove a cap that may not have split upon firing, the insert is usually pushed out of the disc with a small pin punch or finishing nail. Shotshell primers can be easily pushed into the disc with finger pressure as well, but it takes a punch pin or nail to de-prime them. With the No. 11 cap insert, each disc can be re-used dozens of times. However, the added fire and heat tend to loosen the snug fit after two or three primers have been fired. These discs are relatively inexpensive, though, and can be purchased by the dozens and carried in a small zip-lock bag. Using the No. 209 primers for ignition adds more fire for ignition. While this by itself doesn't result in grater velocity using standard hunting powder charges, it can produce a more complete burn when shooting the "magnum" charges now marketed by Modern Muzzleloading. With 100 grains of Pyrodex "Select" in the loose grain form and a saboted 260 grain Speer .45 caliber jacketed hollow point, this 22-inch barreled .50 caliber muzzleloader produces an average muzzle velocity of about 1,630 f.p.s. when fired with the No. 11 disc. A similar load fired from the same rifle using the No. 209 shotshell primer disc increases velocity to about 1,650 f.p.s. Apparently, the hotter fire from the primer promotes better initial burn of the powder charge along with slightly higher pressures. When the rifle is loaded with two 50 grain Pyrodex Pellets behind a saboted Speer .45 bullet, velocity jumps to 1,680 f.p.s. with the primer disc being used for ignition.

Modern Muzzleloading's shooting tests with this rifle involved firing three 50 grain pellets

These unique plastic discs are the heart of the D.I.S.C. Rifle bolt-action ignition system. They can be fitted with a No. 11 percussion cap insert (left) or a hot No. 209 shotshell primer (right).

The D.I.S.C. Rifle proved quite accurate with a wide range of saboted bullets, generally printing 100-yard groups of 1½ inches.

behind a variety of saboted bullets. As a result, the D.I.S.C. pushes a saboted 250 grain all-copper Knight "Red Hot" bullet from the muzzle at just over 2,000 f.p.s., while a 300 grain all-copper "Red Hot" bullet emerges at 1,900 f.p.s. Best accuracy occurred when the rifle was loaded with two 50 grain pellets and fired with a No. 209 primer disc. Groups fired with the saboted 260 grain .45 caliber Speer bullet generally averaged around 1½ inches across at 100 yards, while the 250 and 300 grain Knight all-copper "Red Hot" bullets fared about the same. When pushed out of the 22-inch barrel by three 50 grain pellets, groups opened up to 3 or 4 inches at 100 yards, whether fired with standard pressure sabots or the Knight high pressure sabots. The most accurate "high velocity" load fired from the rifle was shot with 100 grains of Pyrodex "P" behind a saboted 260 grain Speer .45 bullet. This load is about the equivalent of shooting 120 to 130 grains of "Select," pushing the Speer bullet from the muzzle at about 1,850 f.p.s. Loaded with a standard velocity sabot, groups averaged just under 2 inches, but when loaded with Knight

high pressure sabots, groups shrunk closer to 1½ inches.

The barrel and action of the D.I.S.C. rifle are quickly removed from the stock assembly by loosening one 5/32" allen screw. The adjustable Timney trigger is also removed by loosening one allen head screw from the left side of the receiver. The bolt is then slipped easily from the receiver. The breech plug is removed using a special take-down tool provided with the rifle. It takes only a minute or two to break down the D.I.S.C. rifle to this point, allowing the bore and inside of the receiver to be cleaned much like a modern centerfire rifle.

When small amounts of fouling reach inside the bolt of a muzzleloader like the D.I.S.C., the internal surfaces must be cleaned. Knight's rifle features a special bolt take-down ring that compresses the bolt spring, allowing the bolt to break down in a minute or less. With the striker and bolt spring removed from the bolt housing, fouling can be quickly wiped from internal surfaces. This quick take-down design also allows a hunter to remove the breech plug and push out both bullet and powder charge. An unfired rifle is a lot easier to clean than one filled with burnt fouling residue.

To sum up, the Knight D.I.S.C. Rifle is a remarkable frontloader, but its futuristic disc ignition concept may take a few years to catch on. Moreover, the plastic discs may be hard to find. Also, several states have already enacted or reviewed regulation changes that effectively make this modern rifle and magnum pellet powder charges illegal for use during the special muzzleloader seasons. Where allowed during the general gun season in those states requiring the use of a shotgun with slugs—or a muzzleloader as an option—the Knight D.I.S.C rifle could add another 50 yards to your effective range.

PRODUCT REVIEW #2: THE REMINGTON ARMS COMPANY: MODEL 700 ML/MLS BOLT ACTION MUZZLELOADING RIFLE

SPECIFICATIONS

CALIBER: *.50 or .54*

BARREL LENGTH: *24"*

RATE OF TWIST: *1-turn-in-28"*

STOCK: *Black or Camo Composite*

WEIGHT: *7 3/4 lbs.*

FEATURES: *Blued (ML) or stainless (MLS) barrel and receiver; fully adjustable rear sight; solid aluminum ramrod, sling swivel studs, removable breech plug, receiver drilled and tapped for scope bases; standard Model 700 trigger; easy take-down bolt design*

MANUFACTURED BY: *Remington Arms Company, Corporate Headquarters, 870 Remington Drive, Madison, North Carolina 27025-0700*

In 1996, Remington Arms Company shook up the shooting world with its introduction of the company's revered Model 700 bolt action centerfire rifle in a brand new muzzleloading version. Not content to jump onto the rapidly growing in-line percussion bandwagon, Remington's new "bolt action" in-line ignition design took muzzleloader development to a new level. This concept was far from being a new idea, however. During the late 1970s and early 1980s, several custom muzzleloading riflemakers utilized a Mauser bolt action to build similar designs that actually pre-date the popular non-bolt action in-line rifles. Earlier, before the Knight MK-85 started the in-line rifle craze, there was a "bolt action" in-line rifle on the market known as the Marathon "First Shot," which offered shooters an opportunity to switch from a smallbore percussion .32 caliber barrel to a .22 rimfire barrel.

What makes the Remington Model 700 ML (blued model) and MLS (stainless model) so special is that they're built with all of the great features of the company's respected Model 700 centerfire, plus features demanded by black powder hunters in a modern in-line ignition rifle. The Model 700, which is available in .50 and .54 caliber, retains the stock design, trigger, receiver and even the bolt of the original Model 700 cartridge rifle. Modifications include a removable breech plug and nipple threaded into the rear of

Remington Model 700 ML (blued with black composite stock).

Remington Model 700 MLS (stainless steel with black composite stock)

the barrel, replacement of the standard bolt firing pin with a larger diameter and flat-faced striker for positive ignition of a No. 11 percussion cap, and the addition of a solid aluminum ramrod. Wisely, Remington went with the one-turn-in-28 inches rate of rifling twist. A growing number of companies now accept this twist as superior with a wider range of conical and saboted bullets. The .50 caliber rifle tested for this book performed well with most of the saboted bullets fired through it, along with several of the heavy bore-sized "maxi-styled" conical designs.

Not surprisingly, one of the best shooting

The receiver and bolt of the Model 700ML/MLS are basically the same action found on the company's line of centerfire bolt action rifles.

projectiles was the new 289 grain Remington Premier Copper Solid bullets. This all-copper .45 caliber bullet loaded into the .50 caliber muzzleloader using Remington's own sabot design, is a lot like other one-piece designs on the market. The base of this sabot, however, has a unique taper which expands into the rifling for a good gas seal. It also grips the rifling grooves for outstanding accuracy. In testing the stainless steel .50 caliber rifle, it shot extremely well using the all-copper Remington bullet. To tap the accuracy potential of this modern percussion hunting rifle, a Pentax 3-9X Lightseeker scope was mounted on the receiver (drilled and tapped) using a set of Weaver bases and rings. With a 100 grain charge of Pyrodex "Select," the Model 700 MLS repeatedly printed the all-copper Remington bullet inside of 1½ inches at 100 yards, with some groups registering close to an inch. This load pushes the 289 grain bullet along at about 1,600 f.p.s., generating close to 1,600 ft. lbs. of muzzle energy. With two 50 grain Pyrodex pellets, groups opened slightly from 1½ to 2 inches, while the compressed pellets upped velocity to almost 1,650 f.p.s. Loaded with either loose-grained Pyrodex "Select" or the new compressed pellets and a 289 grain Premier Copper Solid bullet, the Remington Model MLS rifle and load make an excellent choice for large game from whitetails to elk.

The Model 700MLS proved highly accurate with a variety of saboted bullets. This tight 100-yard group was fired with the new 289 grain Remington Premier Copper Solid Bullets.

Like most .50 caliber in-line rifles with a fast-twist barrel, the Remington Model 700 MLS showed a real preference for saboted .45 caliber bullets over saboted .44 bullets. This is due largely to a slightly thinner plastic sabot, which makes up the difference between the larger bore and smaller bullet diameter. A .429" diameter .44 bullet requires a heavier sabot than a .451" diameter .45 caliber bullet; moreover, the heavier sabot tends to stay with the bullet slightly longer after exiting the muzzle. The quicker the sabot peels away from the bullet, the better the accuracy. The combination of a .45 caliber Speer 260 grain jacketed hollow point, Hornady 250 grain and 300 grain .45 XTP jacketed hollow points, plus the .45 caliber Sierra Sports Master jacketed hollow point bullets and sabot, all produced highly acceptable hunting accuracy. The jacketed pistol bullets are also a lot cheaper to shoot than the new, all-copper bullets.

Another feature that makes this muzzleloader attractive to whitetail hunters is the special plastic "weather shroud" locked into the face of the bolt. With this in place, the capped nipple is completely enclosed with the bolt closed, thus protecting the cap from rain, snow or any other wet hunting conditions. Remington's bolt-action Model 700 ML/MLS is also easy to break down and clean at the end of a long day at the shooting range or in the deer woods. Each rifle is shipped with a combination nipple and breech plug wrench, allowing these to be removed and the rifle cleaned from the breech end, much like a modern center-fire rifle. The directions that accompany the rifle explain the easy take-down procedure for cleaning the bolt using a vise and a coin to relieve spring tension. The bolt housing can then be unthreaded from the cocking piece, striker and bolt spring; or, the face of the bolt can be placed against a wood surface, with pressure then applied against the bolt in order to force the striker back into the bolt. The cocking piece, striker and spring are now unthreaded easily from the bolt housing.

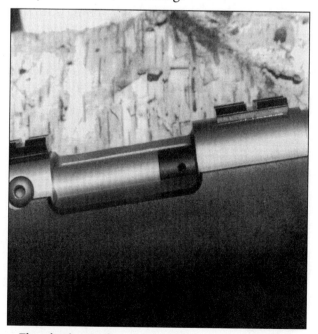

The plastic weather shroud, shown here at the face of the bolt on the Remington Model 700 ML/MLS, makes this rifle virtually weatherproof.

PRODUCT REVIEW #3: CONNECTICUT VALLEY ARMS: ACCU-BOLT AND FIRE-BOLT RIFLES

SPECIFICATIONS

CALIBER: *Fire-Bolt .50 or .54 (.50 only with Accu-Bolt)*

BARREL LENGTH: *24"*

RATE OF TWIST: *1-turn-in-32" (1-turn-in-26" in Accu-Bolt Pro and custom Badger barrel)*

STOCK: *Composite Monte-Carlo in black or camouflage; or Bell & Carlson black composite thumbhole*

WEIGHT: *Fire-Bolt 7 lbs. (7 1/2 lbs. in Accu-Bolt)*

FEATURES: *Fire-Bolt available in blued or stainless steel (Accu-Bolt in blued only); fiber-optic adjustable rear and front sight on Fire-Bolt/Accu-Bolt standard models; synthetic ramrod; easy bolt take-down; removable breech plug; receiver drilled and tapped; rubber recoil pad; sling swivel studs; mechanical trigger safety*

MANUFACTURED IN SPAIN AND IMPORTED BY:
Connecticut Valley Arms, 5988 Peachtree Corners East, Norcross, Georgia 30071

Connecticut Valley Arms was among the first companies to recognize the demand for a modern in-line percussion hunting rifle. Shortly after the Knight MK-85 hit the market, this importer quickly introduced its own, less expensive in-line percussion rifle, known as the "Apollo." And with the fast growing interest in "bolt-action" muzzle-loading rifles, CVA has once again answered with several of its own. Top of the line model in this series is the Accu-Bolt Pro, which is built around a modern bolt-action receiver. What sets the Accu-Bolt Pro apart from the others in the series is a custom-cut Badger barrel, featuring .005" deep grooves that spin with a one-turn-in-26 inches rate of rifling twist. All other variations in this series are built with an extruded, hammer-forged barrel promoted by CVA as "The Most Accurate Production Barrel in The World." These barrels are rifled with a one-turn-in-32 inches rate of twist. The Accu-Bolt models also come with a special Accu-System bullet sizer made from a section of the barrel installed on the rifle. This ensures bore-sized lead conicals will be a perfect match for the bore of each rifle. All Accu-Bolt and Fire-Bolt barrels measure 24 inches in length and are counter-bored at the muzzle, thus creating a false muzzle for easier starting of either bore-sized lead conical or saboted bullets.

Connecticut Valley Arms has also developed a special lubaloy-coated bullet for its rifles. These bullets are slightly larger than land-to-land

The bolt of the CVA Accu-Bolt is a simple, easily maintained design that cocks as the handle is lifted and strikes the cap with an exceptionally fast lock time.

The Accu-Bolt barrel has been designed to shoot a sized copper plated soft lead bullet (left). It shoots best with a number of saboted bullets such as the .45 caliber Hornady jacketed hollow point (top of box).

measurement of the bore; when loaded directly into the rifle without first being pushed through the sizer, they load extremely tight. But once they are pushed through the sizer with the steel rod provided, the bullets literally ride right squarely on top of the lands and seat easily down the bore. The 300 grain copper clad Accu-System bullets for the .50 caliber Accu-Bolt review rifle performed relatively well in our tests. With a 100 grain charge of FFg black powder, this rifle consistently printed 3- to 4-inch groups at 100 yards. Not bad hunting accuracy for a bore-sized lead conical.

The fast one-turn-in-26 inches rate of twist found in the Badger barrel of the Accu-Bolt Pro review rifle makes the muzzleloader an excellent choice for shooting the longer all-copper bullets, such as the saboted Barnes Expander-MZ and the Remington Premier Copper solid bullets, which, being longer, require a faster twist for good stabilization. With two 50 grain Pyrodex Pellets behind the saboted 289 grain Remington bullet,

CVA's Accu-Bolt produced groups of around $1\frac{1}{2}$ inches. This bullet is only 11 grains lighter than the bore-sized 300 grain Accu-System bullet, yet it prints groups half that size. The unique design of its deep, hollow-point cavity promises exceptional expansion, while the copper solid base continues to push the expanded bullet through it's target, whether a 200-pound whitetail or a 600-pound elk.

The .45 caliber Hornady XTP 250 and 300 grain jacketed hollow point bullets, loaded with a black sabot (made by Muzzleload Magnum Products), shot well inside of 2 inches (most groups, in fact, were around $1\frac{3}{4}$ inches across). With loads of 100 grains of Pyrodex "Select" the 250 grain bullet left the muzzle of this particular rifle at about 1,640 f.p.s., generating 1,550 ft. lbs. of muzzle energy. This makes an excellent whitetail load, whereas a 300 grain XTP loaded with 110 grains of "Select," cranking out more than 1,700 ft. lbs. of energy, is ideal for elk.

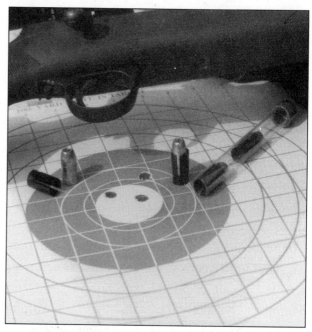

Topped with a 3-9x Pentax Lightseeker scope, the CVA Accu-Bolt consistently printed sub 2-inch groups at 100 yards with saboted bullets.

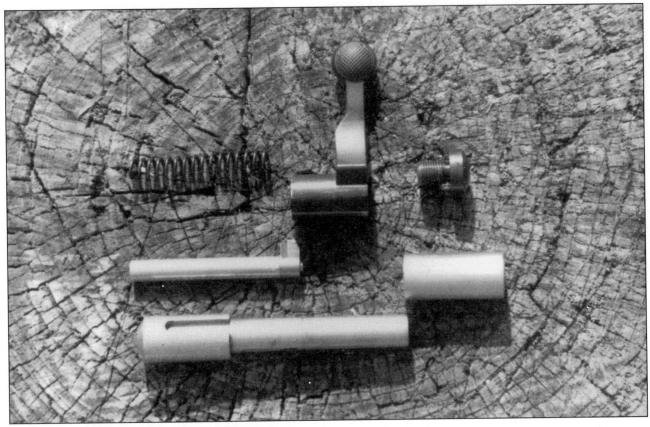

The CVA bolt breaks down easily for cleaning.

The modern synthetic stock design and rubber recoil pad of the Accu-Bolt make this 7$^1/_2$-pound rifle a delight to shoot. The receiver comes drilled and tapped for easy installation of scope bases (we used a 3-9x Pentax Lightseeker on the modern bolt-action muzzleloader). The raised semi-Monte Carlo comb of the stock allows positive sighting through a scope without having to lift your head, producing tighter down range groups and more comfortable shooting.

When several black powder shooters were asked to evaluate the Accu-Bolt, they agreed Connecticut Valley Arms should install a different trigger. The trigger on the test rifle, while crisp, required about 5 pounds of pull to drop the hammer. The design of this trigger positions the safety to the rear of the trigger, where it's handy when ready to shoot. The mechanism, however, is located inside a beefy housing, with no means of adjusting the pull lighter. Imagine what kind of groups this rifle would fire with a 2$^1/_2$-pound trigger pull!

Cleaning and disassembling are relatively easy tasks, requiring only a 1/8" wrench to loosen and remove the cap at the rear of the bolt. All Fire-Bolt models and the standard Accu-Bolt model come with fully adjustable fiber-optic front and rear sights for positive sighting in low light conditions. The Accu-bolt Pro with a custom Badger barrel comes without sights. Other standard features include a tough synthetic ramrod and an over-sized trigger guard with plenty of room for a gloved trigger finger during cold weather hunts. Some variations include a camouflaged or ultra-modern Bell & Carlson composite thumbhole stock.

PRODUCT REVIEW #4: TRADITIONS, INC.: LIGHTNING BOLT-ACTION IN-LINE MUZZLELOADER

SPECIFICATIONS

CALIBER: *.50 or .54*

BARREL LENGTH: *24"*

RATE OF TWIST: *1-turn-in-32" (.50 caliber); 1-turn-in-48" (.54 caliber)*

STOCK: *Available in walnut finished hardwood, black composite, camo composite, brown laminate*

WEIGHT: *7 lbs. (composite stock)*

FEATURES: *Blued or stainless steel barrel and action; adjustable trigger, rubber recoil pad; sling swivel studs, adjustable rear sight; thumb operated safety, removable breech plug, receiver (drilled and tapped)*

MANUFACTURED IN SPAIN AND IMPORTED BY: *Traditions, Inc., 1375 Boston Post Road, P.O. Box 776, Old Saybrook, CT 06475*

In recent years, Traditions, Inc. has been changing its name to "Traditions Performance Muzzleloading," probably because of the excellent modern in-line percussion rifles it now offers. With the introduction of the company's new Lightning bolt-action in-line ignition rifle, Traditions Performance Muzzleloading has taken a giant step forward. Remove the ramrod and ramrod thimble from this rifle and it has all the appearance and lines of a very stylish bolt-action centerfire. As much as this frontloader may look like a bolt-action cartridge rifle, it's a pure hunting muzzleloader through and through.

The Lightning offers a wide range of stock choices and metal finishes. The standard model comes with a blued barrel and receiver and a walnut-stained hardwood stock. A stainless steel version built with a tough black synthetic stock is also available. And for the ultimate in bad weather protection, Traditions offers its All-Weather model made with a Teflon-coated stainless steel barrel and tough synthetic stock. All three barreled actions are available with a camouflaged synthetic stock in a choice of popular camo patterns. And for those seeking a top-of-the-line model, there's a laminated, stainless steel version as well.

Every Lightning model is available in either .50 or .54 caliber with a 24-inch hammer-forged barrel. The former has a one-turn-in-32 inches

Traditions Lightning (blued with walnut stained hardwood stock)

Traditions Lightning (stainless steel with black synthetic stock)

rate of rifling twist, while the larger bore .54 caliber gun comes with a one-turn-in-48 inches rate of rifling twist. Apparently, Traditions concluded that when shooting saboted bullets, there is absolutely no advantage in shooting a .54 caliber. The .50 caliber will do everything the .54 can—usually with more accuracy. With a faster rate of twist in the .50 caliber models, these guns seem destined for plastic saboted bullets, while the slower rate of twist of the .54 rifles indicates they were made with the round ball and "maxi" shooter in mind.

The one-turn-in-32 inches rate of twist found in the .50 caliber rifles does an excellent job with a wide range of saboted pistol bullets. In fact, the .50 caliber rifle fired for our tests actually turned in much better groups with some bullets than its competitors' rifles costing as much as 50 percent more. When loading and shooting saboted .44 and .45 caliber jacketed lead handgun bullets, the Lightning performed extremely well with bullets in the 200 to 300 grain range. Traditions packages the 240 grain Hornady XTP with a green sabot for .50 caliber fast-twist barreled muzzleloaders. This bullet and sabot, loaded in front of 80 to 100 grain charges of Pyrodex "Select," grouped inside of two inches at 100 yards repeatedly.

The most accurate loads fired with the Lightning were comprised of two 50 grain Pyrodex Pellets, a black Knight "Hyper-Shock"

sabot and a .45 caliber Speer 260 grain jacketed hollow-point. This load left the muzzle of the .50 caliber Lightning at just under 1,700 f.p.s., with nearly 1,600 ft. lbs. of muzzle energy. Down range at 100 yards, the Traditions rifle printed the modern jacketed hollow point inside of 1½ inches (several groups actually measured less than an inch across). Either of these two bullets would make an excellent choice for hunting whitetails and other big game. For elk and larger game, however, muzzleloading hunters tend to move up to a heavier saboted bullet. The new all-copper bullets, such as the Barnes

The Traditions Lightning bolt ranks among the easier bolts to break down for cleaning.

The Lightning's removable breech plug and nipple allows the bore to be cleaned quickly and easily from the breech end.

Expander-MZ and Remington Premier Copper Solid Bullets can deliver a knockout punch against any big game animal weighing 500 pounds or more.

The 300 grain Barnes Expander-MZ and 289 grain Remington copper Solid bullets, being so long, require a faster rate of twist for proper stabilization and accuracy. The .50 caliber Lightning, with its one-turn-in-32 inches rate of twist, simply isn't fast enough to do the job. Most 100-yard groups fired with this bullet opened to six inches across or more, with many impact holes on the target paper mirroring outlines of the bullets to indicate severe keyhole-ing. That doesn't mean the rifle's rate of twist won't shoot a heavier bullet for larger game, though. The 300 grain Speer .45 caliber jacketed flat-nose soft-point bullet is a full one-third shorter than either the Barnes or Remington all-copper bullets; with 100 grains of Pyrodex—either loose grained "Select" or two of the 50 grain compressed pellets—this bullet consistently shot 1½ to 2 inch groups with enough authority to down

even the largest of North American game.

The Lightning uses standard No. 11 percussion caps for spontaneous ignition with either black powder, Pyrodex "RS/Select" or Pyrodex Pellets. To disassemble the bolt for cleaning, a single 2mm allen-head screw must first be loosened on the cocking piece of the bolt. The front part of the hammer or striker is then turned counter-clockwise until the shank of the striker has been removed from the cocking piece. The striker and bolt spring can now be separated from the rest of the bolt without any tension on the spring whatsoever. It takes mere seconds to break down the bolt for cleaning.

The Lightning also features a fully removable nipple and breech plug, along with all the tools needed to do the job. Other features include an adjustable trigger, sling swivel studs, an adjustable rear sight, and a receiver that's drilled and tapped for scope installation (such as a Pentax 3-9x Lightseeker scope).

Using the shorter saboted handgun bullets, the Traditions rifle proved to be a real tack driver. This 100-yard three-shot group measuring an inch across was fired with a saboted 260 grain Speer .45 jacketed hollow point.

SPECIFICATIONS

CALIBER: *.32, .50, .54, .58 rifle, 12 gauge shotgun (interchangeable)*

BARREL LENGTH: *26"*

RATE OF TWIST: *1-turn-in-38"*

STOCK: *Walnut or Black/Camo Composite*

WEIGHT: *7 1/2 lbs. (avg.)*

FEATURES: *Blued or stainless steel, adjustable trigger,* *removable stainless steel breech plug, interchangeable barrels, receiver drilled and tapped, folding adjustable rear sight, rubber recoil pad, sling swivel studs, thumb operated safety, synthetic ramrod*

MANUFACTURED BY: *Thompson/Center Arms Co., Inc., P.O. Box 5002, Farmington Road, Rochester, New Hampshire 03866*

The word that best describes the new System 1 in-line percussion muzzleloader from Thompson/Center Arms is *versatile*. This muzzleloading system is an ideal choice for any black powder hunter who seeks an economical approach to hunting large or small upland game or waterfowl. The system's unique interchangeable barrel allows shooters or hunters to switch from a large bore rifle barrel to a small one or to a frontloading shotgun barrel in just minutes.

Thompson/Center Arms offers the System 1 with a choice of .32, .50, .54, or .58 caliber rifle barrel, or a 12 gauge barrel. All barrels are 24" long and can be purchased separately. This enable black powder hunters to put together a multiple barrel hunting rig that is ideally suited for hunting nearly all North American game, big and small. To switch System 1 barrels, the barrel and action must first be removed from the stock. The two screws holding the trigger guard in place also secure the bottom of the receiver to the stock, using a standard bit screwdriver. With the receiver and barrel lifted from the stock, a 5/32nd allen head screw (located at the front of the recoil or barrel lug) is loosened and removed. This screw passes through a lug on the removable barrel and then into a permanent lug located on the bottom of the receiver.

Forming a precise fit of barrel to receiver is necessary to ensure accuracy and positive return to the point of impact each time a rifle barrel is installed. On all barrels, a breech plug protrudes

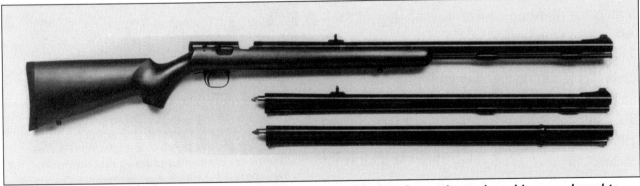

The versatile Thompson/Center System 1 enables hunters to switch from a larger bore big game barrel to a small caliber small game barrel, or even a shotgun barrel for turkey and upland game.

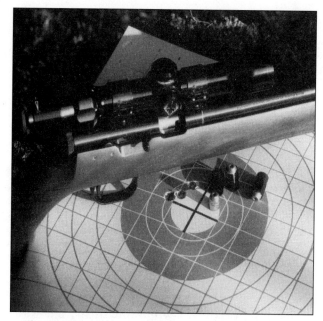

The Thompson/Center System 1 with a .50 caliber barrel and Bushnell 1.75-5x Trophy scope produced this 1 ½-inch group using .45 caliber 260 grain Speer jacketed holow point and plastic sabot.

from the rear of the barrel approximately one inch. The outside surface of this breech plug and the inside surface of the receiver are precision machined to ensure a snug, tight fit. To install a barrel, the smooth shoulders of the breech plug are first slipped into the face of the receiver. A 5/32nd allen screw enters through the barrel lug and threads into the lug on the bottom of the receiver. When this screw is cinched down tight, the barrel becomes an integral part of the receiver.

The Thompson/Center System 1 muzzleloader was tested with both .50 caliber rifle and 12 gauge shotgun barrels, a versatile combination for any muzzleloading hunter looking to cash in on the muzzleloading big game season as well as the spring turkey hunting season (the addition of a .32 caliber small bore barrel also allows sharpshooters to snipe at a few bushytails and cottontails). The System 1's receiver is drilled and tapped for easy installation of scope bases. A Bushnell 1.75-5x Trophy one-inch tubed scope proved out well on both rifle and shotgun barrels. This scope

offers a full 3½" of eye relief, keeping the rim of the rear objective away from the forehead even when the relatively light 7½ pound muzzleloader is fired with heavy turkey loads from its shotgun barrel. At lower magnifications, the scope offers a good field of view for locating an oncoming gobbler; and when turned up to 5 power it generates enough magnification to tap the accuracy potential of the rifle barrel.

All system 1 barrels are machined with Thompson/Center's QLA muzzle system, which is basically a recessed (or false) muzzle that provides easier starting of almost all types of projectiles. The 12 gauge shotgun barrel is built with an interchangeable screw-in choke system. The barrel is shipped with a full choke tube (Thompson/Center offers optional improved-cylinder and modified choke tubes, making this smoothbored tube well suited for loading and shooting a wide range of lead, steel or Bismuth shot). Thompson/Center has elected to stay with the one-turn-in-38 inches rate of rifling twist, which is slower than most other in-line rifles. As we expected, this slower rate of twist seemed to prefer the shorter and more stabilized saboted bullets.

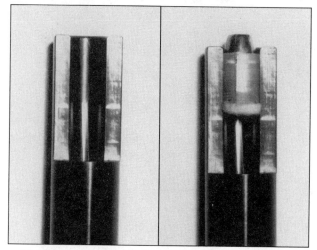

The QLA muzzle allows easier loading of projectiles, especially tight-fitting saboted bullets. Shown are an unrifled portion at muzzle (left) and the Break-O-Way saboted bullet in the QLA muzzle (right).

The .45 caliber Speer 260 grain jacketed hollow-point bullet performed nicely out of the .50 caliber System 1 barrel. Matched with a black sabot, this bullet consistently printed 1½ to 2 inch groups at 100 yards when fired ahead of 90 or 100 grain charges of Pyrodex "Select." With two 50 grain Pyrodex Pellets, this bullet excelled, often printing three-shot groups closer to an inch across. Optimum accuracy was realized when the bore was wiped between shots and the barrel allowed to cool for a few minutes before reloading.

Accuracy with the Barnes all-copper bullets wasn't nearly as effective. The 250 grain Expander-MZ (a .45 caliber bullet with black sabot) grouped inside 2½ inches at a hundred yards, but the longer 300 grain bullet spread all over the target paper. The all-copper construction of these bullets must be longer to achieve the same weight of all lead or jacketed lead bullets. The 300 grain Expander-MZ for the .50 caliber is easily a third longer than, say, a 300 grain .45 caliber Speer or Hornady bullet. The one-turn-in-38

The rifle barrels of the System 1 come equipped with an adjustable folding rear sight.

inches rate of twist in the Thompson/Center barrel simply lacks enough speed to stabilize this long bullet in flight. Many of the holes found in the target paper were elongated, indicating that the long slugs were beginning to tumble. Almost every shorter 220 to 275 grain jacketed bullet and sabot fired from the barrel produced acceptable accuracy, however.

Patterns with the shotgun barrel were excellent, especially with the full choke tube (the owner's manual recommends loading with one or two Natural Lube-treated felt wads over the powder charge and another over the shot charge). The System 1 shotgun barrel produced much better patterns when one of the felt wads was loaded directly over the powder charge, followed by a plastic shot cup and shot charge, with the entire load topped by a single styrofoam over-shot wad. The full choke tube consistently printed around 90 percent of its 1¼-1½ ounce shot charges inside a 30-inch circle at 30 yards. The best patterns were usually achieved when the smoothbore barrel was loaded with nearly equal volumes of powder, either FFg black powder or Pyrodex "RS/Select," and shot.

Thompson/Center Arms offers its System 1 with a great line-up of standard features, including an adjustable trigger, sling swivel studs, synthetic ramrod, adjustable folding rear sight, and recessed QLA muzzles. The shotgun barrel comes with an interchangeable choke system and a receiver drilled for scope bases. The removable breech plug and easy take down of the in-line action make this one of the easier muzzleloaders to clean. The company ships each System 1 muzzleloader with the tools required for disassembly (except for the screwdriver needed to remove the trigger guard/action screws).

PRODUCT REVIEW #6: NAVY ARMS "COUNTRY BOY"

SPECIFICATIONS

CALIBER: *.50*

BARREL LENGTH: *24"*

RATE OF TWIST: *1-turn-in-32"*

STOCK: *Black Composite*

WEIGHT: *8 lbs. 1 oz.*

FEATURES: *Blued or chromed barrel and receiver, removable nipple and breech plug, take-down tool* storage compartment in stock, rubber butt pad, double safety system, adjustable trigger, receiver drilled and tapped, adjustable rear sight, synthetic ramrod, sling swivel studs

MADE IN CHINA AND IMPORTED BY: *Gibbs Rifle Company, Route 2, Box 214, Hoffman Road, Cannon Hill Industrial Park, Martinsburg, WV 25401*

Val Forgett, who founded Navy Arms Company with the help of the first reproduction percussion revolver in 1958, also unknowingly built one of the first modern-day in-line percussion muzzleloaders. In 1960, he took an M1A1 Thompson machine gun, welded a breech plug in the barrel, then welded the barrel to the receiver. The breech plug had been threaded to accept a musket nipple. The .45 caliber barrel was loaded from the muzzle with black powder and a projectile, which was pushed down the bore with a ramrod. To fire, the Thompson action was pulled back and a winged musket cap placed on the nipple. When the trigger was pulled, the hammer/bolt/breech block of the action slammed forward, igniting the cap. This remains the same basic type of action found on

many of today's in-line percussion hunting rifles. Navy Arms went on to become one of the leading importers of quality reproductions from the past. Only recently did the company put its own name on a modern in-line hunting rifle. Even then the rifle was imported from China (under the Navy Arms International banner) and not as a division of Navy Arms. The new venture is now a part of Gibbs Rifle Company (Martinsburg, West Virginia) headed by Val Forgett, III, the founder's son.

Navy Arms' "Country Boy" in-line percussion rifle has been designed and built to fill a special niche as the lowest-priced full feature rifle of its kind on the market. Similar to the "Buckhunter" in-line percussion rifles imported from Spain by Traditions, this rifle features a barreled receiver

The inexpensive Navy Arms "Country Boy" offers hunters good shooting with an efficient in-line percussion hunting rifle.

A handy compartment in the butt of the Navy Arms in-line rifle offers convenient storage for take-down tools.

with a plunger-style hammer that strikes a capped nipple positioned in the rear center of the breech plug. This in-line design was made popular by the Knight MK-85 model during the late 1980s, and the majority of in-line rifles introduced since then have been built with a similar action; that is, they deliver fire from the percussion cap directly into the powder charge for sure-fire ignition. At the same time, the action is simple enough for easy tear down for a fast and thorough cleaning.

Like many other, higher-priced models, Navy Arms' rifle has a removable nipple and breech plug. Another feature of the Country Boy in-line rifle is a compartment located in the butt of the composite stock for storing and carrying a special nipple/breech plug wrench. A removable plug in the rubber butt pad is easily unthreaded, whereupon the combo wrench slides in and out of the recess.

For those who are tired of getting slammed by the recoil of heavy hunting charges fired from a light 6 or 7 pound rifle, the Country Boy weighs in at slightly more than 8 pounds. It's still light enough to pack all day, but that extra pound or

two really helps to absorb recoil generated rearward by 100 or 110 grain powder charges. Unlike barrels found on some cheap imports, Navy Arms' barrels are made from true rifle barrel steel; the Chinese manufacturer button rifles the bore with 8 lands and groves, creating a one-turn-in-32 inch spiral. Groove depth is .005".

More than 25 years ago, Navy Arms began lining the bore with chrome on some of its traditionally-styled rifles imported from Italy. This made the bore slicker and easier to load with tight-fitting projectiles; it also made the steel less susceptible to the corrosive effects of black powder or Pyrodex fouling. The Country Boy, not surprisingly, also features a chrome-lined bore, which makes loading a tight sabot and bullet combination easier than one finds in rifles without a chromed bore. While this coating helps to fight the effects of fouling, it doesn't mean the rifle can be fired, then put away without being properly cleaned. The plating simply buys the black powder hunter time during a rainy day hunt, or when there's no time for cleaning until the following day.

The "Country Boy" has standard features not found on higher-priced models, witness this chrome-lined bore.

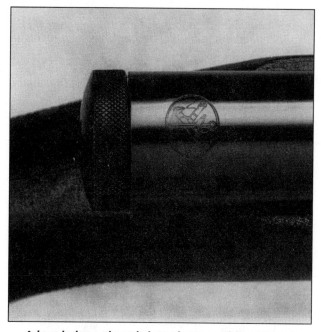

A knurled cap threads into the rear of the "Country Boy" receiver to retain the plunger-style hammer and hammer spring.

The Country Boy rifle comes standard with a 24-inch barrel and in .50 caliber only. It's available with a blued barrel and receiver or with all-weather chromed metal parts. The latter is a matte finish chrome plating with less shine than some all-stainless steel models. Both blued and chromed models come with a tough black plastic composite stock that is indestructible. Other features include a metal trigger guard, steel ramrod thimble, sling swivel studs, adjustable rear hunting sight, synthetic ramrod, and an adjustable trigger. The receiver comes drilled and tapped, allowing easy installation of a scope. The rifle requires two Mauser Model 98 front bases, such as the Weaver No. 46.

The Country Boy action operates by pulling back on the bolt handle until it cocks and the hammer stays to the rear. The rifle is built with two safeties, the primary one being a standard thumb-operated arrangement along the right side of the receiver. The secondary safety—a deep, upward angling notch in the receiver—engages this safety, whereupon the bolt handle is pulled past the machined cut and lifted upward. The bolt or hammer spring keeps the handle securely in the notch until it's pulled back and out of the safety notch. The rifle cannot fire while the handle is locked into this notch.

With its one-turn-in-32 inches rate of twist, this rifle shot effectively with a good variety of saboted handgun bullets. The Country Boy favors .45 caliber bullets of around 260 to 300 grain weight range. Both the 300 grain Hornady XTP and Speer 260 grain jacketed hollow-point bullets printed inside of 2 inches at 100 yards with consistency when pushed out of the chrome-lined bore by a pair of 50 grain Pyrodex Pellets. The 40 grain lighter Speer bullets clocked in at a slightly higher 1,665 f.p.s., compared to 1,610 f.p.s. for the heavier 300 grain Hornady. However, the heavier bullet is good for more than 1700 ft. lbs. of energy at the muzzle, while the 260 Speer produces around 1,550 ft. lbs. at the muzzle with the 100 grain Pyrodex Pellet load.

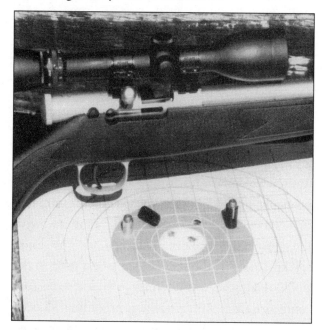

The "Country Boy" proves that good accuracy and performance don't have to cost a lot. The rifle consistently shot 1 ½-inch groups at 100 yards.

SPECIFICATIONS

CALIBER: *.50 only*

BARREL LENGTH: *26"*

RATE OF TWIST: *1-turn-in-28"*

STOCK: *Model 420 LR: Monte Carlo and Classic (Curly Maple) • Model 320 LR: Blued and Stainless Steel (Black Synthetic)*

WEIGHT: *7 lbs., 14 oz.*

FEATURES: *Model 420 LR, blued only; Model 320 LR, blued or stainless steel; adjustable Timney trigger; thumb operated safety; receiver drilled and tapped; adjustable rear hunting sight; high tensile strength aluminum ramrod; rubber recoil pad; sling swivel studs; removable breech plug*

MANUFACTURED BY: *Austin & Halleck, Inc., 1099 Welt, Weston, MO 64098*

Behind every successful venture there lies a good mix of people. At Austin & Halleck it is definitely the quality of the people involved who have made the company's new bolt-action in-line muzzleloading rifle an instant success. The rifle began with gunmaker Ted Hatfield's idea and Niles Burkett, whose manufacturing facilities make it all happen. This pair teamed up with Neil Oldridge (a former president of Remington) to form a trio that has made the Austin & Halleck name synonymous with quality and top hunting performance.

The Austin & Halleck Model 420 rifles bring to muzzleloading a new level of class, one that had been missing from the fast-growing modern bolt-action in-line rifle market. Most of the competition featured plain-Jane hunting guns built to take the abuse of hard hunting; but if you wanted a similar gun with a touch of class, you'd probably have to take it to a custom gunmaker and have it totally reworked. Not so with the Austin & Halleck Model 420. The lines, workmanship and quality of the wood used in the stock rivals the work found in modern custom centerfire rifles with price tags exceeding $2,500. For one-fourth that price, a discerning muzzleloading hunter could own a top-of-the-line Austin & Halleck muzzleloader of the same quality.

The Model 420 comes in two versions: the 420 LR Monte Carlo and the 420 LR Classic, the only difference being variations in the stock. Both guns come with a beautiful, tiger-striped curly maple stock, with the 420 LR Monte Carlo sporting a high-combed butt. The Classic version has the lines of a high-quality sporter (similar to the stock found on the old Super Grade Model 70 Winchester rifles). The Monte Carlo comes with a high gloss finish, much like that found on

The sleek bolt-action of the Austin & Halleck rifle looks much like the receiver and bolt of a Weatherby centerfire rifle.

Even with the plastic weather guard in place at the front of the bolt, the Austin & Halleck bolt-action leaves plenty of room for capping the nipple.

Weatherby Mark V rifles, while the Classic stock sports a low-luster satin finish. Both versions feature 20-lines-per-inch cut checkering at the wrist and along the forearm.

The beauty of the new Austin & Halleck rifle is more than wood and finish, though. Designer Ted Hatfield set out to make this one of the most user-friendly modern rifles currently available. First, he did away with the screw-like bolt detent, or keeper, found on many rifles of similar design. The Austin & Halleck action incorporates a unique spring-loaded bolt stop pin that protrudes up through the bottom of the receiver. To remove the bolt for cleaning, this bolt is easily opened and pulled to the rear about 3 inches. Then, by applying slight downward (clockwise) pressure on the bolt handle, the bolt stop pin engages a milled ramp, which depresses the bolt-stop pin. The bolt can then be pulled rearward and out of the action.

Once removed, the bolt is easily disassembled for cleaning, first by loosening a small allen screw on the bolt shroud. The face of the striker or hammer can then be turned counter-clockwise to unthread the striker from the bolt shroud. The bolt breaks down into four basic parts: bolt housing, shroud, striker and bolt spring. This design allows the bolt to be disassembled in about 15 seconds, giving shooters no excuse whatsoever for failure to clean the fouling from the internal surfaces of the bolt assembly. These rifles also feature a fully removable stainless steel nipple and breech plug, along with a combination nipple and breech plug wrench. It takes only a minute or two to disassemble the bolt, remove the barreled action from the stock, and remove the nipple and breech plug from the rear of the barrel. The barrel and receiver can now be easily cleaned through from the breech end.

The 26 inch .50 caliber barrel is produced by a unique extrusion process that forces the barrel blank though a special die to form the .006" deep rifling grooves. This process produces one of the best internal surface finishes found in any of today's muzzleloader barrels. Eight lands and grooves of equal width spiral with a one-turn-in-28 inches rate of rifling twist, making the Austin

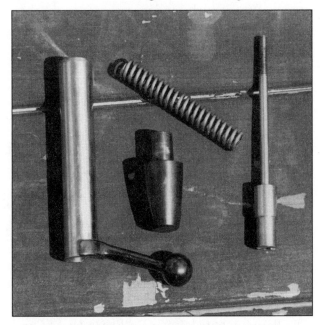

In just seconds, the Austin & Halleck bolt breaks down into four parts to make cleaning a breeze.

The high Monte Carlo comb and generous cheek-piece of the Model 420 LR Monte Carlo make this Austin & Halleck model one of the most comfortable modern muzzleloaders to shoot. Note the beautiful curly maple stock.

& Halleck muzzleloader a true saboted bullet rifle. The Monte Carlo model we tested was fitted with a set of high quality Leupold bases and rings, and topped with a Burris 6-24X Signature Series scope. While such optics are far more than needed for a muzzleloader, the higher magnification revealed the true capabilities of the Austin & Halleck rifle.

Not surprisingly, one of the best shooting sabot and bullet combinations turned out to be the .45 caliber Speer 260 grain jacketed hollow point, loaded with a black sabot (produced by Muzzleload Magnum Products). With two 50 grain Pyrodex Pellets, the Monte Carlo often clustered shots into a one-hole group at 100 yards. The heavier 300 grain Speer .45 jacketed flat-nose soft point with 50 grain Pyrodex Pellets didn't fair quite as well, however, producing 1½ inch groups at 100 yards. That is still exceptional accuracy. The Barnes saboted 300 grain Expander-MZ and 100 grain Pyrodex Pellet charge turned in about

the same results. Most three-shot 100 yard groups averaged just over 1½ inches. The new saboted 289 grain Remington Premier Copper Solid bullet ahead of two 50 grain Pyrodex Pellets produced less than 1½ inch groups, an outstanding combo for elk and more than needed for even the largest whitetail buck.

Austin & Halleck installs a crisp, fully adjustable Timney trigger, a stylish sporter rubber recoil pad, and a ramrod guide mounted where a ramrod guide should be: up close to the muzzle. Even the barrel, which is offered in blued only, has been given a unique contour, starting out full octagon at the receiver, then changing over to a tapered round configuration from the tip of the forearm on out to the muzzle.

All of these great features found on the Austin & Halleck Model 420 LR actions and barrels are available on the lower-priced 320 LR series models. These rifles are offered in a choice of blued or stainless steel, stocked with a tough black synthetic stock.

Ted Hatfield checks out a 1½-inch 100-yard group with his Model 420 LR.

CONCLUSION: A LOOK INTO THE FUTURE

A great selection of hi-tech, in-line percussion rifles, especially the latest bolt-action designs, is taking muzzleloading into the 21st Century with tremendous momentum. Just when you think you own the hottest, safest, most user-friendly muzzle-loading system available, someone introduces still a better mouse trap. One new system, which is now available as a custom-built muzzleloader only, has been dubbed the "21st Century Muzzleloader," a brainchild of Henry Ball, who owns and operates Bill's Custom Guns in Greensboro, North Carolina. Following an unfortunate accident involving a traditionally styled percussion rifle, Ball decided there had to be a better system. He sat down and designed, then built a better and safer system.

The two rifles we tested were built on modern centerfire rifle actions. A .45 caliber version was built with a medium-length Howa action, while a .50 caliber rifle featured a short action Interarms Mark X receiver. Ball's patented ignition system utilizes a special module that utilizes a hot No. 209 shotshell primer for ignition. It, in turn, is chambered into a special breech plug, much like a cartridge case is chambered into a centerfire rifle. A small-diameter orifice at the face of the breech plug allows the fire from the primer to enter the barrel, while at the same time preventing excessive blowback once the powder charge has ignited. In addition to installing this system on bolt-action designs, this creative custom maker has also utilized the big Martini and Remmington rolling block single-shot actions to build muzzleloaders with this ignition system.

The ignition modules can be primed and de-primed right at the shooting bench. A No. 209 primer can be started with nothing more than finger pressure. Full seating is then completed by the camming force of the action as the bolt is closed behind the module. To remove the spent primer, one simply places a portable decapping pin into the front of the module and taps the rear of the pin against the bench. The primer pops right out and the module is ready for another primer. The stainless steel modules can be re-used a hundred times or more.

The modules Henry Ball machined for the smaller Interarms Mark X action are basically the same size as the rear of a .223 cartridge. The Howa action, on the other hand, uses a module with a slightly larger diameter and with the same rear dimensions as a .308 Winchester cartridge case. The action, chamber and module are so precise that absolutely no fouling escapes. Even after 20 or 30 shots, the outside surfaces of the module remains free of fouling. This ignition system also forces every bit of fire into the barrel; in fact, when a primed module was test-fired through an empty barrel in total darkness, fire shot out of the muzzle for nearly two feet.

Henry Ball built this modernistic muzzleloader with a Howa centerfire bolt action receiver and bolt (shown with ignition module ready to be chambered).

Built with a mini-mark X action, this Henry Ball rifle repeatedly printed 1 1/4- to 1 1/2-inch groups with Pyrodex Pellet and saboted bullet loads.

Ball's .45 caliber Howa action muzzleloader was built for shooting jacketed .45 caliber bullets, but without a sabot. With charges consisting of 140 grains of Pyrodex "P" grade, the rifle can push a 300 grain Hornady .452" XTP jacketed hollow point out of the muzzle of the 24-inch barrel at about 2,000 f.p.s. With hotter 100 to 140 grain charges of Pyrodex "Select" or finer "P" grade, the gun consistently prints 1 to 1½ inch groups at 100 yards. The .452" bullets fit the one-turn-in-14 inches rifling snugly, yet they remain relatively easy to ramrod down the bore.

The .50 caliber Mark X action rifle was built with a more conventional "sabot" barrel, with a one-turn-in-24 rate of rifling twist. Loaded with three 50 grain Pyrodex Pellets, this rifle printed 300 grain

Hornady .45 caliber XTP and Knight Hi-Per Shock sabots well inside of two inches at 100 yards, with many groups right at 1½ inches. With two 50 grain Pyrodex Pellets behind this bullet and sabot, group size averaged slightly over an inch across. Muzzle velocity with the three pellet load was right at 2,000 f.p.s., while two pellets pushed the 300 grain bullet out of the muzzle at around 1,600 f.p.s.

Both of the rifles tested were extremely easy to tear down for a thorough cleaning at the end of the day. The breech plugs and barrels alike were fully removable. A minute or two is all it takes to remove the barreled action from the stock assembly, loosen a lock screw, and snap the barrel free from the action. The breech plug can then be easily removed from the barrel using a

Muzzleloading hunter Mike McDaniels took this mulie buck at 180 yards shooting a custom "sabotless" .45 caliber rifle using a 300 Hornady .45 XTP and a load of Winchester 571 smokeless powder.

special wrench designed by Henry Ball. Amazingly, once the barrel has been cleaned, the breech plug reinstalled, and the barrel locked back in place in the receiver, the point of impact at 100 yards remains unchanged. Now, that's precision!

As a serious centerfire benchrest shooter and competitor, Henry Ball's custom bolt action centerfire rifles are built for other top shooters. When he sat down to design his innovative muzzleloading system, his goal was to produce cleaner-burning smokeless powder loads. Until now, shooting smokeless powder out of any muzzleloader was strictly taboo, mostly because open ignition systems and barrels weren't built to withstand smokeless powder pressures. The 21st Century Muzzleloader has been designed

and built to do just that, thanks to an ignition system that is totally enclosed, a rifle that's built with a strong modern centerfire bolt action, and a gun fitted with a centerfire rifle grade barrel.

This futuristic frontloader has been safely fired with as much as 37 grains of Alliant 2400 smokeless powder behind a non-saboted 300 grain bullet out of a .45 caliber barrel, and 35 grains behind a saboted bullet out of a .50 caliber barrel. Most groups fired with the 300 grain Hornady XTP bullets at 100 yards measured about $1\frac{1}{2}$ inches. The .50 caliber barrel turned in exceptional accuracy with 34 grains of Alliant 2400 and a .45 caliber 260 Speer jacketed hollow point loaded with an orange Knight Hi-Pressure

A "sabotless" .45 muzzleloader produced this excellent group with a load of 37 grains of Alliant 2400 and a non-saboted Hornady .45 caliber 300 grain XTP jacketed hollow point.

sabot, creating 100-yard groups measuring less than one inch across. With the powder charge, a 260 grain bullet leaves the muzzle at more than 2,250 f.p.s. The drop from 100 yards to 150 is just 2¹/₂ inches. The .45 caliber rifle loaded with 37 grains of 2400 behind a non-saboted .45 Hornady 300 grain XTP produces a muzzle velocity of over 2,300 f.p.s.—without leaving any corrosive fouling behind. *But beware: DO NOT ATTEMPT TO SHOOT THESE LOADS OUT OF ANY OTHER MUZZLELOADER.*

AN INTRODUCTION TO THE TRADITIONAL MUZZLELOADER

The next time you're browsing through the catalog section of an annual shooting publication, spend a few moments to study the wide range of traditionally styled muzzleloaders currently available. Some muzzleloading fans can probably remember when there were only a dozen or so guns to choose from, most of which lacked any real style or any valid link to an original gun from the past. Today there is something for every shooter, whether he or she fancies an authentically styled early American longrifle, hefty Hawken half-stock rifle, flintlock fowler, side-by-side percussion shotgun, high quality Swiss target rifle, big-bored Civil War rifled-musket, lightweight hunting rifle, flintlock Revolutionary War snoothbored musket, handy single-shot target pistol, percussion double rifle, or a duplicate of an original percussion revolver from the past. Somewhere, there's a model on the market to satisfy your needs.

The success of today's muzzleloading firearms industry is attributed largely to the forethought of two individuals: Turner Kirkland of Dixie Gun Works and Val Forgett of Navy Arms. Both men grew up shooting original muzzleloading guns during the 1930s and 1940s, each realizing that the supply of serviceable originals would eventually dwindle, while prices for collector quality guns would skyrocket. Each set out to create a modern day solution to the age-old dilemma of supply and demand.

Until Turner's death in 1997, he and Val Forgett remained the best of friends. Both were actively involved with collecting fine originals from the past, each specializing in a slightly different field but sharing a common love for all old guns. They were also highly competitive, with each man striving to actually produce the first "reproduction" black powder gun. The following success stories may not determine who was

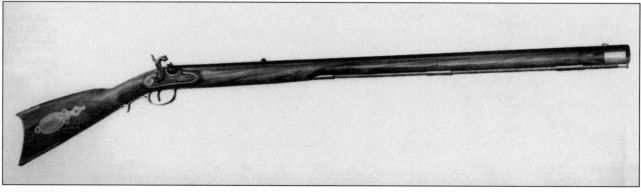

During the late 1960s, black powder shooters in this country had only a handful of models to choose from. This Kentucky rifle served a small, but growing family of muzzleloading fans.

actually first, but perhaps they will offer readers a better understanding of how this industry got its start.

TURNER KIRKLAND

The beginnings of the Dixie Gun Works can be traced back to an entry in Turner Kirkland's Boy Scout diary, dated October 9, 1931. The entry read: "Today I saw an old gun at school." It was an old rusted Colt 1849 Pocket Model five-shot .31 caliber percussion revolver, and it cost the young Kirkland seventy-five cents. He loved that old gun so much he practically slept with it. Even so, his entrepreneurial instincts soon took over. He drilled out the rusted screws that held the revolver together and sold the salvaged brass trigger guard and backstrap for $3, realizing a profit of $2.25. Little did he know then that those early dealings in antique gun parts would eventually become his life's work, not to mention the genesis of a whole company.

During the early 1930s, the country was in the grip of the Great Depression. Money was scarce, especially for spending on old guns. Still, Kirkland's father occasionally found the extra cash to buy an old Kentucky rifle, a Civil War musket or a percussion revolver, many of them in excellent shooting condition. by the mid-1930s, the sport of shooting old muzzleloading guns in the backyard had become almost a daily routine at the Kirkland household. Later, during World War II, Turner was stationed overseas where he had an opportunity to discover a wide range of antique guns. After the war, he returned to west Tennessee with a greater love of old muzzleloading guns. While traveling in the South as a jewelry salesman, he often traded old guns and gun parts with gun collectors he ran into along the way. By 1948, Kirkland had accumulated a relatively large collection, whereupon he placed his first ad in Muzzle Blasts magazine, the official publication of the National Muzzle Loading Rifle Association. Every gun listed sold quickly, encouraging Kirkland to expand his offerings.

Inquiries overseas uncovered small inventories of old, inexpensive original muzzleloading gun parts that had been in storage for a hundred years or more. Kirkland quickly added these parts to his collection of original American gun parts, and by 1954 he had founded Dixie Gun Works. Not only were muzzleloading fans eager to restore old guns, they wanted to shoot them as well. But the supply

Turner Kirkland's hand-made prototype of the Dixie Squirrel Rifle (top) is shown with the first modern-day production muzzleloader (bottom).

of shootable original guns had already started to dwindle, causing a steady rise in the prices demanded for top quality muzzleloaders.

Because Belgium had been a major source for many of the original parts found in the first 12-page Dixie Gun Works catalog, Kirkland established strong contacts with the F. Dumoulin & Company, a large armsmaking operation in Liege, Belgium. By late 1955, he had contracted the manufacturer to assemble the first modern-made "production" muzzleloader, the Dixie "Squirrel Rifle," which retailed for $79.50. Its design was a composite of features taken from dozens of originals in his collection. Kirkland, being cost-conscious, realized he had to keep the rifle relatively free of fancy patchboxes and inlays, but still he chose brass over steel for the furniture to make his product more aesthetically appealing. To determine the size of the bore, he averaged the bore sizes of the original guns in his collection. The new rifle was offered in .40 caliber only, with a choice of flint or percussion ignition.

The Dixie Squirrel Rifle may not have been a true reproduction of any particular gun from the past, but it did represent the "first" true modern manufactured muzzleloader on the market. In 1963, the caliber was changed to .45, making it a more effective muzzleloader for hunting game as large as the whitetail deer. That same year, a fancier version of the rifle, known as the Dixie Pennsylvania Rifle, was added to the line.

VAL FORGETT

While a young man, Val Forgett developed a fascination for old guns of all types. Even before establishing the Service Armament Company in 1957, he had already won a reputation as a "wheeler dealer" when it came to buying and selling old guns. And even before getting into the

A young Val Forgett introduced the first true reproduction black powder gun in 1958, when he began marketing Italian copies of the Model 1851 Colt Navy.

business, Forgett had long been a muzzleloading shooter with a special interest in the guns of the Civil War. He became an active member of the North-South Skirmish Association, which specialized in target competition using military arms from the Civil War era, including reenactments of historical engagements on the battlefield. During those war years in the early 1860s, millions of the big .58 caliber rifled muskets were produced. Even as late as the mid-1950s, originals in excellent condition could be bought for less money than a modern day manufacturer would need to reproduce these guns. What attracted Forgett, though, were various percussion revolvers dating from that period, especially the revered Colt and Remington military issue sidearms.

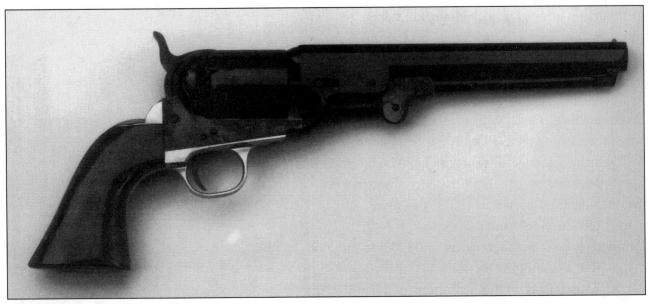

Val Forgett introduced the first true reprodcution black powder gun in 1958, when he began marketing Italian copies of the Model 1851 Colt Navy.

Forgett hated the thought of subjecting fine specimens of original Civil War revolvers to the rigors of day-to-day service. They were truly irreplaceable. Likewise, originals in mint condition were in high demand by those collectors and shooters who could afford the escalating prices. The real need, Forgett now realized, was a modern copy of a Civil War military issue percussion revolver—that is, a black powder handgun that faithfully reproduced the original in every detail, matching or even surpassing it in quality, and still be affordable. And so, during the fall of 1957, he visited the old armsmaking centers of Europe; specifically, Birmingham, England; St. Etienne,

France; Liege, Belgium; Ferlach, Austria; and Gardone, Italy. He settled on the region around Gardone, Italy, as the best environment for a limited production of replica or reproduction black powder firearms.

The most widely used percussion revolver of the Civil War was the .36 caliber Colt Model 1851 Navy. Between 1850 and 1873, Colt manufactured 215,348 of these revolvers, a significant number in those days. It became the first gun manufactured with the use of investment cast parts, a process that was also used to make the first replica revolvers bearing the name of a new armsmaker: the Navy Arms Company.

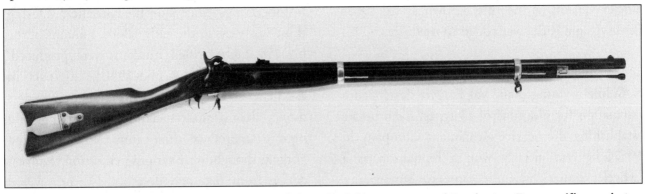

Navy Arms' first long gun was a modern copy of the colorful brass-mounted Remington Zouave rifle-musket.

Forgett's first replica Colt 1851 Navy model revolvers hit the U.S. market in 1958. To help distinguish the modern-made copies from the original handguns made by Colt, he made slight changes, such as the arc of the grip and backstrap. Even so, few knowledgeable shooters could discern a well-used Navy Arms replica from a well-kept original Colt. Eventually, the steel-framed Colt copy became known as the "Yank." A few years later, Forgett introduced the first of the reproduction long guns made in Italy, an authentic copy of the .58 caliber Remington "Zouave" rifled musket from the Civil War era. Often referred to as the most colorful of all the rifled muskets dating from that period, this large bore muzzleloader featured a yellow brass butt plate, trigger guard, barrel bands and nose cap. Like the modern copy of the 1851 Colt Navy, the Navy Arms Zouave was an immediate success, becoming an affordable alternative to the original rifled musket.

Just as Turner Kirkland was the first to offer black powder shooters a modern manufactured muzzleloading rifle, so Val Forgett was the first to offer faithful copies of original frontloading guns. Together, these two men established a new industry that has since produced more muzzleloading guns than all the makers of the past combined could ever produce. Consider these facts: today's black powder gun manufacturers have produced more Colt percussion revolvers than were ever produced by Colt, more Kentucky rifles than were ever made by all of the early longrifle makers combined, more Remington Zouaves than Remington ever dreamed of, and more sporting muzzleloading hunting rifles than

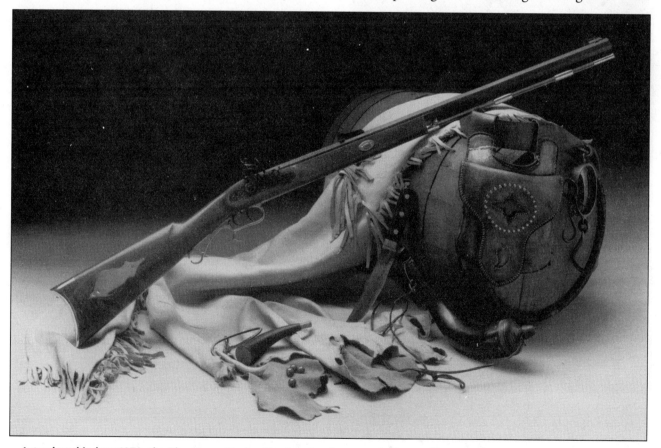

Introduced in late 1970, the Thompson/Center Hawken has become the best-selling sporting muzzleloader of all times.

were ever produced by all of the riflemakers of the 1700s and 1800s.

More than a dozen different manufacturers and importers now provide traditional black powder shooters with an outstanding selection of models. Original guns in shooting condition costing $50 to $100 during the 1950s now demand prices starting at $1,000, depending on the scarcity of the model in question. Not many gun buyers are prepared to pay $20,000 for an original Colt Walker revolver, but for only a few hundred dollars anyone can own and shoot an excellent copy, which for the most part is made of higher quality materials than can be found in any of the old guns.

Dixie Gun Works and Navy Arms, along with Connecticut Valley Arms, Traditions, Lyman and a number of others, continue to expand the

Thompson/Center led the way in the use of many modern manufacturing techniques, such as investment casting of brass and steel parts. Here a mold is poured in the company's own foundry.

variety of traditionally styled modern-made black powder guns. Another company that has learned to "roll with the flow" since the early 1970s is Thompson/Center Arms, which has survived an ever-changing muzzleloading market by continuing to meet the demands of today's black powder shooters. Thompson/Center introduced its first muzzleloader—the now famous "Hawken" rifle—in December of 1970. Designed by Warren Center, this half-stock muzzleloader was more the product of contemporary styling than that of the true original Hawken. Few, if any, original Hawken rifles left the St. Louis shop of Samuel and Jacob Hawken with a brass buttplate and trigger guard. The originals were generally big, heavy steel or iron-mounted guns that weighed as much as 12 pounds. Warren Center's version featured brass furniture and was slimmed down considerably, weighing in at about 8½ pounds. It had a fast-handling, short 28-inch octagon barrel, handsome walnut half-stock, and the reliability one looks for in a serious muzzleloading hunting rifle.

To say that Thompson/Center's version of the Hawken rifle was an instant success is putting it lightly. Since 1971, it has easily been the number-one selling sporting muzzleloader of all time. The only frontloading long guns produced in greater quantities were doubtless the millions of contract Civil War rifled muskets. In any event, it's probably safe to say that the number of Thompson/ Center Hawken rifles and other variations of the basic design that have been shipped from the Rochester, New Hampshire, plant exceeds a million guns.

The following test reports offer a much closer look at six of today's more popular and unusual traditionally styled frontloaders, including a few that have been around for several decades. The guns covered here, of course, represent only a fraction of what's available in today's market.

SPECIFICATIONS

CALIBER: *.45, .50, .54, flint or percussion (Silver Elite .50 percussion only)*

BARREL LENGTH: *28" Octagon*

RATE OF TWIST: *1-turn-in-48"*

STOCK: *Satin finished American black walnut (Silver Elite premium walnut)*

WEIGHT: *8 1/2 lbs.*

FEATURES: *Double-set triggers; modern coil spring powered lock; fully adjustable rear sight; brass butt-plate, trigger guard, cap box, thimbles and nosecap; blued barrel on standard modern; stainless steel barrel, lock, triggers and hardware on Silver Elite model*

MANUFACTURED BY: *Thompson/Center Arms Co., Inc., P.O. Box 5002, Farmington Road, Rochester, New Hampshire 03866*

The only muzzleloader made in greater numbers than the Thompson/Center Arms Hawken was the U.S. Model 1861 rifled musket from the Civil War era. Even then, it took the U.S. Armory at Springfield, Massachusetts, and some 32 contractors to build the nearly one million .58 caliber muskets produced from 1861 to 1866. The U.S. Model 1861 was the most widely used arm during the war, while the Hawken is easily today's number-one used muzzleloading sporting rifle. Many a veteran black powder hunter who has gone afield with a frontloader since the early 1970s considers the Thompson/Center Hawken the first serious modern-made muzzleloading hunting rifle. Prior to its introduction in late 1970, nearly all reproduction rifles available featured rifling that spun with a markedly slow rate of twist, and which were designed for shooting the patched round ball.

Most were also built with long 32- to 40-inch barrels, which often proved unsatisfactory in the deer woods.

When Warren Center sat down to draw up plans for the Hawken, he did so with one goal in mind: to design a hunters' rifle. His decision to use a 28-inch barrel was often criticized by black powder experts of the time. The barrel, they warned, was too short to burn heavy hunting powder changes effectively. The trend today is for even shorter 22- to 24-inch barrels without significant loss of velocity. Center also designed a hard-hitting conical bullet that proved much more effective on big game than the patched round ball. Realizing that many shooters preferred the patched round ball for target shooting, plinking and even some hunting, Center settled on a slower rate of rifling twist, enough to produce

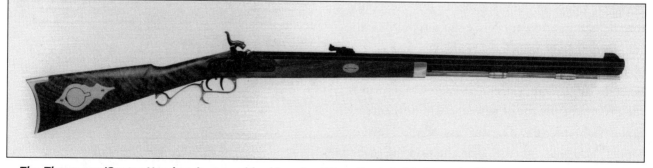

The Thompson/Center Hawken is a good looking, traditionally styled half-stock rifle.

Thompson/Center's 1-turn-in-48 inches rate of twist in the Hawken barrel was designed to shoot both the round ball and the longer maxi-ball. The twist usually performs best with a patched ball.

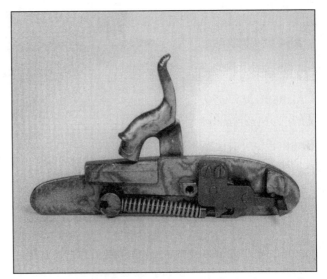

Externally, the Thompson/Center lock displays traditional looks; internally, the mechanism incorporates modern coil springs that are more reliable than old-style flat V-springs.

good accuracy with a patched ball but fast enough to stabilize the heavy conical bullet. Since then, the Thompson/Center Hawken has been rifled with a one-turn-in-48 inches rate of rifling twist.

The Thompson/Center Hawken was also one of the first reproduction muzzleloaders to feature double-set triggers as standard equipment and to utilize modern coil springs in the lock. The company took this short, fast-handling barrel and crisp double-set triggers and created a reliable, traditionally-styled side-hammer lock together with a stylish walnut half-stock. The rifle was then dressed up with a flashy brass butt plate, trigger guard, cap box, nose cap, wedge plates and ramrod thimbles. Thus did the Thompson/Center Hawken establish new standards for the young muzzleloading industry. Since the early 1970s, the standard Thompson/Center Hawken has not changed much. The only noticeable change has been the adjustable rear sight, which was improved for easier adjustment of windage and now offers a better sight picture. The success of the Hawken model also led to the introduction of other Thompson/Center muzzleloading rifles, including

the very popular Renegade and New Englander models. The Hawken is available now in flint or percussion ignition, and in three calibers (.45, .50 and .54).

Among several different variations of the Hawken rifle produced by Thompson/Center is the Silver Elite. It displays the same lines and features that have made the Hawken so popular; the barrel, lock, triggers, butt plate, trigger guard and all other pieces of furniture, however, are

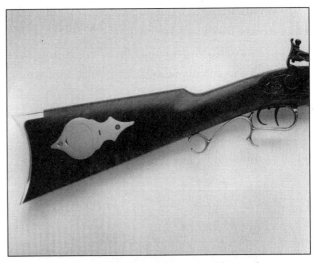

The standard Hawken model comes with a walnut stock and brass butt plate, patch box and trigger guard.

With open sights and the patched round ball, the Silver Elite is an excellent 50- to 75-yard deer rifle.

made of satin-finished stainless steel. The only Hawken feature not included on the Silver Elite is the cap box. Thompson/Center also stocks this new rifle with a premium grade of walnut.

The Silver Elite's 28-inch octagonal stainless steel barrel is offered in .50 caliber percussion ignition only. Its muzzle features Thompson/Center's recessed QLA system, which makes it easier to start almost any projectile this rifle will shoot, whether a patched round ball or any number of conical bullets. In testing the Silver Elite, we found it was most accurate with a .495" round ball patched with lubed .015" Ox-Yoke Originals "Wonder Patches" and 70 grains of FFg black powder. The ball and patch combination did load a little tight into the button rifled bore (appx. .005" deep grooves), but it consistently produced one-inch groups at 25 yards and two-inch groups at 50 yards, which isn't bad for a rifle equipped with open sights. A stainless steel auxiliary loading/cleaning rod made by Tennessee Valley Manufacturing (Corinth, Mississippi) made loading a little easier. When a smaller diameter .490" ball was loaded with .025" patching, it

started and made its way down the bore with no problem, but groups did open slightly. Even with as much as 90 grains of FFg or Pyrodex "Select", though, the ball and patch combination still produced acceptable hunting accuracy, with groups measuring three inches at 50 yards.

One of the more accurate conicals fired out of the Silver Elite was Thompson/Center's 350 grain Maxi-Hunter. With 90 grains of FFg, this big hunk of lead consistently printed inside of three inches at 50 yards, while most 100-yard groups fired with the same load measured around five inches across. All shooting was done with open sights, and at a hundred yards the front bead nearly covered the center of the bulls-eye. Both the 385 grain Hornady Great Plains and Buffalo Bullet Company hollow-point conicals shot just as well. The one-turn-in-48 inches rate of twist of this barrel, however, failed to digest saboted bullets very well. A half-dozen different sabot and bullet combinations were fired through the barrel, with the best group still measuring more than five inches across from 50 yards out.

The Thompson/Center Hawken features a hooked breech barrel for easy take-down and cleaning.

PRODUCT REVIEW #2: DIXIE GUN WORKS: TENNESSEE MOUNTAIN RIFLE

SPECIFICATIONS

CALIBER: *.32, .50*

BARREL LENGTH: *41 1/2" Octagon*

RATE OF TWIST: *1-turn-in-56"*

STOCK: *Satin finished Japanese cherry*

WEIGHT: *8 1/2 lbs. (.32 cal.), 9 1/2 lbs. (.50 cal.)*

FEATURES: *Brown finished barrel and steel hardware,* *double-phase double-set triggers; interchangeable flint and percussion ignition system (with conversion unit); traditional non-adjustable rear sight; .50 caliber available in right or left hand*

MANUFACTURED BY: *B.C. Miroku Gun Works, Japan*

IMPORTED BY: *Dixie Gun Works, Inc., Gunpowder Lane, Union City, Tennessee 38261*

Some historians feel that if the South had been better funded, enough to at least equal the North in arms production, the Civil War results might have been quite different. Indeed, the Confederate soldier has often been considered a better shot than his Yankee counterpart. The vast majority of the southern troops came from rural communities, where they honed their shooting abilities as youngsters by hunting squirrels for the family dinner table. They became such great shots with their long, slender rifles that many later carried these same guns into battle. Those who survived early confrontations with Union forces quickly replaced their "sporting" rifles with .58 caliber Springfield or Enfield guns recovered from the battlefield.

In stark contrast to the elaborate and highly decorated Pennsylvania and Kentucky rifles used in the north, most of the long guns produced in backwoods gun shops throughout southern Appalachia were quite plain and crude in their construction. Most were built with hand-forged iron or steel trigger guards and butt plates, with the hammer and file marks still clearly visible. These were hard-working rifles built without frills; in fact, quite a few southern mountain rifles were built without butt plates or trigger guards.

A few graceful, long-barreled muzzleloaders were produced, but these were the exception, not the rule. A "fancy" southern mountain rifle —often referred to as a Tennessee mountain rifle—was built with a good grade of curly maple, walnut or cherry. Some were built with a crescent steel butt plate, often a side plate and nose cap, and sometimes with a long, slender patchbox,

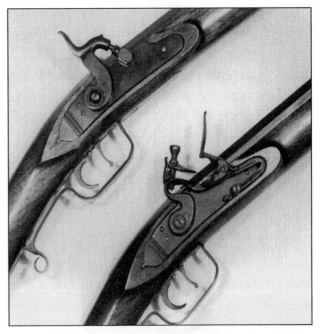

This classic American long rifle reproduction is available in either flintlock or percussion ignition. Shooters can also purchase a conversion kit so that the same rifle can be converted back and forth to either ignition system.

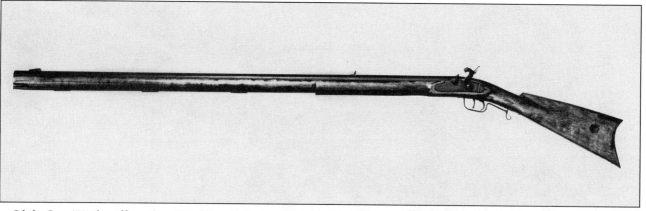

Dixie Gun Works offers the .50 caliber Tennessee Mountain Rifle in a left-hand version.

commonly known as a "banana-shaped" patch-box. Occasionally a brass-mounted original would show up, but most southern gunmakers preferred hand-forged steel for their furniture or hardware. Back in 1978, Dixie Gun Works introduced an outstanding reproduction of a higher-than-average grade of southern longrifle, called the Dixie Tennessee Mountain Rifle. It replaced the Dixie Kentucky Rifle, which happened to be the first modern-made muzzleloader ever offered to blackpowder shooters in this country. When the cost of this Belgian-made muzzleloader escalated, the company contracted with the B.C. Miroku Gun Works of Japan to build a more affordable replacement for the discontinued Kentucky Rifle.

Dixie's modern copy of a Tennessee mountain rifle is built with one of the longest barrels (41½ inches) available on a current production frontloader, and it is offered in .32 or .50 caliber. The .50 caliber comes with a hefty 15/16" diameter octagonal barrel and weighs in at close to 9½ pounds. The .32 caliber "squirrel rifle" is built with a smaller 13/16" diameter barrel and weighs 8½ pounds. Either caliber is available in a choice of flint or percussion ignition (a conversion kit can be purchased for those who switch from one ignition system to the other). For about one-fourth the cost of a new rifle, a percussion rifle owner can now shoot with a flint ignition

and vice versa. The .50 caliber models are also offered in both right and left hand (the smallbore version comes in right hand only).

Those who enjoy the graceful lines of the full-stocked long rifles built in this country during the late 1700s and early 1800s appreciate the lines of Dixie's Tennessee Mountain Rifle. Its features include a nicely shaped one-piece cherry stock with classic southern mountain rifle contours, a substantial drop to the comb, a comfortable raised cheekpiece, proportionately shaped wrist and a full-length fore-stock that extends all the way to the muzzle of this long-barreled rifle. These guns are also built with a steel butt plate, side plate, toe plate and three steel ramrod thimbles. Instead of a patch box, the butt is drilled with a grease hole for carrying patch lubricant (a feature common to many originals lacking a patchbox). The square-bowed trigger guard on the Tennessee Mountain Rifle has the look of a hammer-forged steel original, but without its many dings and file scars.

Both the .50 and .32 caliber versions of this reproduction are definitely round ball rifles. The .50 caliber model features a true .500" land-to-land measurement, with a groove depth of .008", while the .32 caliber rifle runs slightly shallower at just under .006". Land-to-land measurement of the smallbore was just over .319". The grooves in both the .50 and .32 caliber models spin with a

With light powder charges and small diameter soft lead round balls, the .32 caliber Dixie Tennessee Mountain Rifle proved exceptionally accurate at 25 yards.

one-turn-in-56 inches rate of twist. Dixie Gun Works recommends loading and shooting a 70 grain charge of FFg black powder behind a .015" patched .490" round ball in the larger bore model. For the smallbore .32 caliber their recommended load is 25 grains of FFFg black powder and a .015" patched round ball (a switch to .010" may make loading a little easier without affecting accuracy).

The one-turn-in-56 inches rate of twist is actually a little slow for the .32 caliber bore. If that same ratio was used for the .50 caliber, its barrel would have a one-turn-in-85$\frac{1}{2}$ inches! With such slow rifling, it would take 100 grain-plus charges to achieve accuracy with a patched .490" ball. Likewise, the slow twist of the .32 caliber rifle needs to be stoked up slightly for best accuracy. In fact, the percussion smallbore version

tested for this report shot best when loaded with a 30 grain volume equivalent of Pyrodex "P". At 25 yards, the rifle printed tight clusters less than an inch below point of aim. Although this load is fine for target shooting or plinking, it's too hot for hunting small game. A 30 grain charge of Pyrodex "P" pushes a 45 grain .310" ball out of the muzzle of the long barrel at nearly 1,800 f.p.s., generating around 350 ft. lbs. of muzzle energy, or about the same as a .22 Magnum rimfire. On game as small as a squirrel or rabbit, this could cause considerable destruction. To get velocities and energy levels down to that of a .22 long rifle round, the Dixie long rifle would have to be loaded with 20 grain (and lighter) charges. Together with the slow rate of twist, accuracy would suffer, producing slightly open groups even at 25 or 30 yards.

PRODUCT REVIEW #3: PACIFIC RIFLE COMPANY: "ZEPHYR UNDERHAMMER RIFLE"

SPECIFICATIONS

CALIBER: *.62*

BARREL LENGTH: *30" Octagon*

RATE OF TWIST: *1-turn-in-144"*

STOCK: *Hand-rubbed linseed oil/beeswax finished walnut butt and fore stock*

WEIGHT: *7 3/4 lbs.*

FEATURES: *Browned barrel, blued receiver and bottom-mounted hammer, crescent steel buttplate, traditional nonadjustable rear sight*

MANUFACTURED BY: *Pacific Rifle Company, 1040-D Industrial Parkway, Newberg, OR 97132*

Of all the original muzzleloader designs, one that stands out as being uniquely American is the underhammer percussion ignition system. All others had their beginnings in Europe or Great Britain, including the now popular in-line percussion ignition system. Back in the 1830s and 1840s, sportsmen turned to the underhammer percussion rifles for more "sure-fire" ignition, and soon several American riflemakers were busy building a wide range of excellent underhammer hunting and target rifles.

Two or three decades before the Civil War, riflemen in this country set out to improve the accuracy of the muzzleloading rifle. Many considered the patched round ball an inferior projectile, for both long range target shooting and for hunting larger game. The development of longer and heavier conical bullets, along with faster rifling twist for better accuracy with the elongated bullets, extended the effective range of the muzzleloading rifle. But for best accuracy, shooters realized that ignition

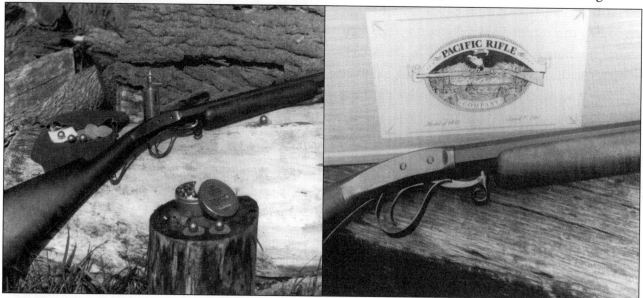

The Zephyr underhammer rifle from Pacific Rifle Company is reminiscent of an authentic American muzzleloading design dating from the mid-1800s.

This section of a .62 caliber Zephyr barrel shows the Forsyth rifling, with its narrow lands and wide, shallow grooves.

had to be faster and more spontaneous. Thus was the underhammer rifle born.

In its design, the nipple was threaded directly into the bottom side of the barrel. A hammer mounted on the bottom swung in an upward arc, striking the capped nipple. The fire from the exploding cap traveled only a fraction of an inch before reaching the powder charge in the barrel. With no corners or bends in the flash channel to keep the hot flame from producing fast, hesitation-free ignition, accuracy was greatly improved. Using this underhammer percussion ignition, William Billinghurst, Norman Brockway and other American riflemakers built some of the most accurate muzzleloading target rifles ever made, with some guns grouping ten shots inside two inches at 200 yards.

Pacific Rifle Company (Newberg, Oregon) now manufactures a well-made copy of an early American underhammer percussion rifle, which they've dubbed the "Zephyr Model of 1837."

Rather than offering this rifle with the same fast rifling twist found in most original underhammer rifles, the Zephyr is rifled with an extremely slow one-turn-in-144 inches, making it ideal for shooting the patched round ball. Instead of building the rifle with the more popular .45, .50 or .54 caliber bores, Pacific Rifle Company offers this underhammer frontloader in .62 caliber. Actually, the Zephyr is the result of joining two entirely different muzzleloading concepts from both sides of the Atlantic. The bottom-mounted hammer and nipple are genuinely American, while the extremely slow rate of rifling twist and huge bore size closely imitate the English concept conceived by James Forsythe during the mid-19th Century. The result is a unique muzzleloading rifle indeed.

Because it offers the muzzleloading hunter the most knockdown power possible with a

The 325 grain .600" round ball (left) fired out of the Zephyr is compared to the 178 grain .490" ball (center) for the .50 caliber and a 45 grain .310" ball (right) for the .32 caliber rifles.

patched round ball, Pacific Rifle Company recommends shooting a full 175 grains of FFg black powder behind a patched 325 grain .600" round ball. At the muzzle of the 30" octagonal barrel, this load produces 1,700 f.p.s. and more than 2,000 ft. lbs. of muzzle energy. Down range at 100 yards the big ball slows to around 1,100 f.p.s., but it still smacks the target with more than 900 ft. lbs. of energy. For those shooters who still feel the need for more knockdown power, the company recommends using as much as 200 grains of FFg black powder, pushing the muzzle velocity to 1,800 f.p.s. and muzzle energy to around 2,400 ft. lbs. Surprisingly the recoil generated by such loads from a 7 3/4 pound underhammer rifle isn't all that objectionable. It's the equivalent of shooting magnum slug loads out of a modern 20 gauge shotgun, due in large part to the fact that the Zephyr is practically a true 20-bore rifle. The very slow twist of the rifling and the relatively loose-fitting patched ball, moreover, offer little resistance as the projectile is being pushed down the bore by the powder charge. Still, you'll know for certain when the trigger is pulled on this big bore frontloader. The recoil will push the shooter back father than the recoil of a .50 caliber rifle loaded with 100 grains of powder and a heavy lead conical bullet. The large bore of the Zephyr consumes powder and lead as if there were no tomorrow.

As noted, the design of the underhammer ignition systems makes it as sure-fire as any modern in-line ignition systems. To ensure positive ignition even further, Pacific Rifle installs a large musket nipple on its Zephyr, producing three or four times as much fire as a standard No. 11 percussion cap. Because the nipple faces downward when the Zephyr is being carried, the manufacturer installs a nipple

Underhammer rifles are known for their sure-fire ignition. Pacific Rifle Company makes the Zephyr even more sure-fire by installing a nipple for larger and hotter musket caps.

with a noticeable taper to the cone. To force the musket cap all the way down onto the taper of the nipple, Pacific Rifle recommends using a thin slat of wood and a healthy shove. This serves a dual purpose. First, the tight fit ensures the cap won't fall off while hunting; and second, the hammer needn't employ any force to bottom the cap out on the nipple before it fires—a common cause of delayed ignition or misfires with any percussion ignition system.

The pride shown among craftsmen who build the Zephyr is quite evident in the excellent

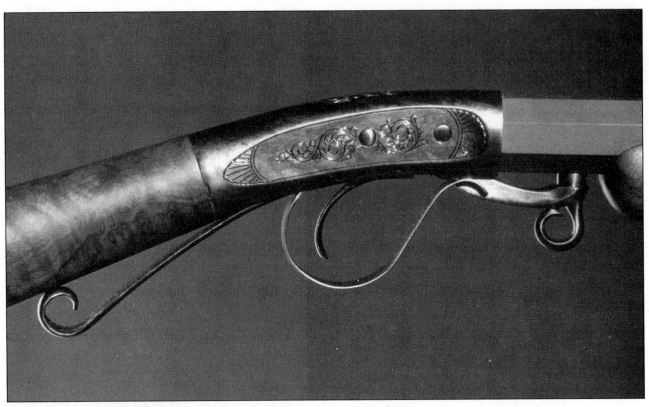

A dressed up version of the Zephyr sports nice engraving and a beautifully color case-hardened receiver.

workmanship found in this rifle. All underhammer rifles share some common features and traits, but in no way should today's shooter compare this rifle to the low-cost Hopkins & Allen underhammer rifles offered intermittently since the mid-1960s. Pacific Rifle Company offers so many options that it could be considered a custom gun. The standard model comes with a blued receiver, browned barrel, crescent steel buttplate, hand-rubbed boiled linseed oil and a beeswax-finished walnut butt and fore stock, plus standard open sights sighted at the factory for 175 grains of FFg. Recommended options include several different styles of rear sight, special stock contours, engraving and metal finish—and for those who prefer shooting 200 grains of FFg, venting at the muzzle to reduce recoil and muzzle jump.

Those who enjoy hunting with the patched round ball and who look for all the punch a muzzleloading rifle can deliver will gravitate toward this rifle. Serious black powder shooters and hunters who admire what the Pacific Rifle Company refers to as "the thinking man's rifle" advocate a faster twist version in .45 or .50 caliber, one that shot well with conical or saboted bullets. In other words, they want a fast twist underhammer rifle for superior accuracy with elongated bullets. Sounds familiar, doesn't it?

PRODUCT REVIEW #4: PEDERSOLI TRYON CREEDMORE TARGET RIFLE

SPECIFICATIONS

CALIBER: *.451*

BARREL LENGTH: *32" Octagon*

RATE OF TWIST: *1-turn-in-21"*

STOCK: *Low luster finish European walnut*

WEIGHT: *9-10 lbs.*

FEATURES: *Matte brown finish on barrel and steel hardware; authentic aperture rear and globe front sights; hooked breech; target quality adjustable*

double-set triggers; cap box; sling swivels

MANUFACTURED BY: *Davide Pedersoli & Company, 25063 Gardone V.T., Brescia, Italy 25063*

IMPORTED BY: *Flintlocks, Etc., P.O. Box 181, Richmond, MA 01254*

AND: *Navy Arms Company, 689 Bergen Blvd., Ridgefield, NJ 07657*

Once upon a time—before baseball, basketball and football—shooting was the great American pastime. Every Sunday afternoon, shooters from every walk of life would gather at a local range or nearby meadow and compete in serious target competition. Often, the prize was little more than the satisfaction of having won, while in some instances the top shooter went home with a cash prize, a new rifle, or perhaps even a cow or pig.

Following the Civil War, and well after the introduction of breechloading firearms, a few

riflemakers kept building muzzleloading rifles until the end of the 19th Century. Handy repeating rifles, such as the Henry and Winchester or the hard-hitting big bore single-shot rifles, became hunter's rifles. Those who could not afford a modern breechloader still hunted with a muzzleloader. The muzzleloading target rifle, however, had just reached its pinnacle of development, so serious target shooters continued to rely on frontloaders until the end of the century.

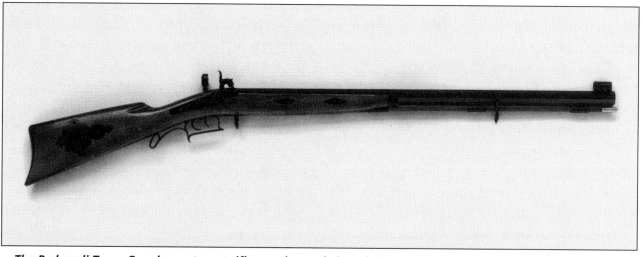

The Pedersoli Tryon Creedmore target rifle may be made in Italy, but the design is all American, dating from the mid- to late 1800s.

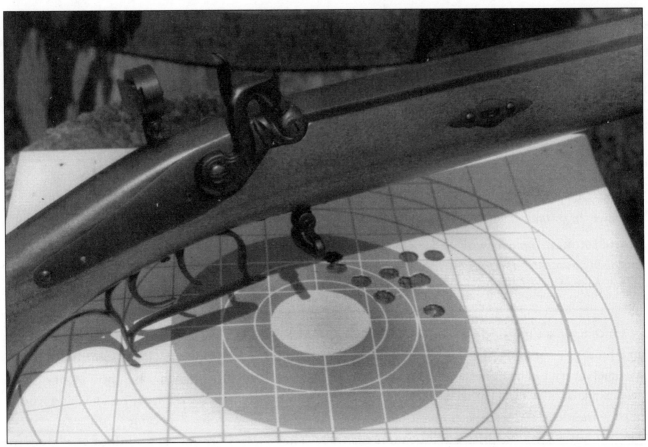

Ten shots fired at 100 yards with the Pedersoli target rifle and a big 500 grain conical bullet all printed inside of 3 ½ inches.

From this period emerged some of the finest, most accurate muzzleloading rifles ever built.

The Tryon "Creedmore" target rifle built by Davide Pedersoli & Company of Brescia, Italy, is an excellent reproduction of a rifle style that enjoyed considerable popularity among target competitors in the late 1800s. Basically a copy of an American design, this Pedersoli Tryon Creedmore bullet rifle enjoys its greatest popularity in Europe, where muzzleloading remains a target shooting sport. This particular rifle is now capturing top honors in several matches held during the World Muzzleloading Championships, an international target shooting competition that takes place every two years.

The hefty one-inch diameter .45 caliber barrel of the Tryon Creedmore measures 32 inches in length and is rifled with five lands and grooves for an exceptionally fast one-turn-in-21 inches rate of rifling twist (groove depth is .006"). Rifling of this type, often referred to as "Whitworth-style" rifling, was developed to perform top accuracy with a long, heavy conical bullet. Original Whitworth rifles from the 1800s and 1860s featured an hexagonal bore that fouled easily; but they did establish the superiority of a lengthy bullet and a fast twist bore for long range shooting. The bore of the Tryon Creedmore target rifle measures exactly .451" from land-to-land and shoots accurately with commercially available conicals, such as the hollow-pointed bullets from Buffalo Bullet or Hornady. In our tests, these bullets performed well when fired ahead of 60 or 70 grain charges of FFg black powder or Pyrodex "Select." The rifle comes with a sizing die that swages slightly oversized bullets to exactly .450,"

The Tryon Creedmore rifle has been designed and built to shoot lengthy pure lead bullets, such as this specially-sized 500 grain slug.

loading easily with little resistance on the ramrod. Both Buffalo Bullet and Hornady .45 caliber bullets feature .001" to .002" oversized bearing surfaces, which offered only slight resistance in our tests when forced through the muzzle of the Tryon Creedmore. After being pushed through the sizing die, however, these bullets practically fell down the bore. Groups shot with the 285 grain Hornady Great Plains Bullet and the 285 grain Buffalo Bullet and 70 grains of FFg black powder averaged 3½ inches at 100 yards when fired from the Pedersoli target rifle. But that was without first being sized; the same load using bullets that had been pushed through the sizer tightened to less than three inches on average.

This rifle tends to shoot best when fired with an extra long bullet. Pedersoli offers a .451" bullet mould for casting a long 500 grain conical bullet especially for this and other "Whitworth-style" bores. The bullet itself measures more than 1½" in length, which is nearly three times longer

than its diameter. The rifle's fast twist bore is essential in stabilizing the big hunk of lead. The perfectly round holes punched in the target paper at 100 yards indicate the rifling was doing a good job of that; one 10-shot group fired with a 70 grain charge of FFg black powder behind a 500 grain conical measured only 2½ inches center-to-center.

Being a target rifle, the Tryon Creedmore comes with a diopter, or "peep" sight, mounted on the tang. Elevation adjustments are made by loosening a lock screw and threading the aperture up or down. The front sight is a globe-type that comes with a variety of post and circular inserts. With the rear sight lowered all the way, a group fired with 70 grains of FFg behind the heavy bullet impacted about 1½ inches above point of aim at 100 yards. A lighter 60 grain charge placed the bullet about an inch low at 100 yards. While no groups in our tests were

This "peep" sight, which is an authentic copy of the original, comes standard on the Pedersoli Tryon target rifle.

The Tryon rifle features a back-action lock, which means the hammer lies forward of the mainspring.

fired with 65 grains of FFg, that load would probably print the big bullet just about dead on.

The rifle's fast rate of rifling twist indicates that it should shoot equally well with saboted bullets. Several .38/.357 bullets were fired from the Tryon Creedmore with more than acceptable results. Loaded with a blue sabot and 50 grains of Pyrodex "P", Hornady's 158 grain XTP flat-point bullets produced several 2-inch groups at 100 yards. When loaded with a tan sabot and a 180 grain 10mm (.40 caliber) XTP hollow point and 50 grains of Pyrodex "P", this rifle produced several sub 2-inch groups at 100 yards.

Pedersoli's stylish, high quality reproduction rifle features a "back action" lock, which means its hammer rides ahead of the mainspring, sear and other internal workings of the mechanism. While many original guns featuring locks of this design were generally considered inferior to guns with a front-action lock, this back action muzzleloader measures up to any current reproduction muzzleloader with traditional styling. Other features found on the Tryon Creedmore include adjustable target-grade double-set triggers, European walnut stock, sling swivels, stylish steel hardware, and a hooked breech barrel. There's also a field model in .45, .50 and .54 caliber that comes with an adjustable open rear sight and blade front sight. The .45 and .50 caliber standard Tryon models come with one-turn-in-48 inches rate of twist, while the .54 has a slower one-turn-in-66 inches rifling.

PRODUCT REVIEW #5: NAVY ARMS COMPANY: MODEL 1851 COLT NAVY

SPECIFICATIONS

CALIBER: *.36*

BARREL LENGTH: *7 1/2" tapered octagon*

RATE OF TWIST: *1-turn-in-32"*

STOCK: *One-Piece European walnut*

WEIGHT: *2 3/4 lbs.*

FEATURES: *Polished brass backstrap and trigger guard;* *blued barrel and cylinder; color case-hardened frame; loading lever and hammer; brass bead front sight and hammer notch rear sight*

MANUFACTURED IN: *Italy*

IMPORTED BY: *Navy Arms Company, 689 Bergen Blvd., Ridgefield, NJ 07657*

When Val Forgett of Navy Arms Company first hit the U.S. market in 1958 with his modern Italian-made copies of Civil War era percussion revolvers, everyone in the industry was amazed at how well these guns duplicated the originals. In fact, the new guns were such close copies of the old they were shunned by collectors who reasoned that it could become too difficult to distinguish one from the other. In fact, several firearms magazines catering to antique arms collectors refused to accept ads for the guns.

Navy Arms' first venture into the reproduction industry was a rendition of the Colt Model 1851 Navy, often simply referred to as the Colt Navy. Navy Arms has since introduced a variety of other excellent reproductions, including modern day copies of the Colt Model 1860 Army, the Confederate Griswold & Gunnison, the huge Colt Walker, the Remington Model 1858 New Model Army, the Rogers and Spencer .44 revolvers, and even the first model Colt ever produced: the Colt Patterson. But it was the Colt Model 1851 Navy reproduction that gave this major importer its start.

After Colt introduced the Model 1851, it continued production of the .36 caliber "Navy" model until 1873, when the new single-action Army Colt cartridge handguns ended all production of Colt percussion models. Many arms experts and collectors feel that the Colt Navy represented the best of the company's percussion revolver line. During its production, this revolver was made in a number of variations, and the one chosen by Navy Arms for reproduction became what collectors refer to as the "Third Model." The originals of this variation bore serial numbers ranging from 4,200 to 85,000 (only the "Fourth

The Navy Arms reproduction of the Colt Model 1851 Navy was the first true modern reproduction black powder gun introduced in this country. (Holster by Oklahoma Leather)

Model" was produced in greater numbers). The feature that most distinguishes the "Third" from the "Fourth" model is the trigger guard. The first and second variations featured a square-backed trigger guard; the third variation had a small rounded trigger guard; and the fourth variation featured a slightly larger, rounded trigger guard. The modern version of the Navy Arms Model 1851 Navy is built with the same rounded trigger guard found on the original "Third Model."

Another authentic feature includes a rounded six-shot cylinder engraved with a naval battle scene, hence the "Navy" model designation. True to the original, the Navy Arms copy is built with a 7 1/2-inch tapered octagon barrel attached to the frame by a steel wedge that passes through the barrel assembly and a slot in the cylinder pin. This feature facilitates breaking down Colt percussion revolvers for cleaning. In seconds, the wedge is tapped from the slot and the barrel removed from the frame.

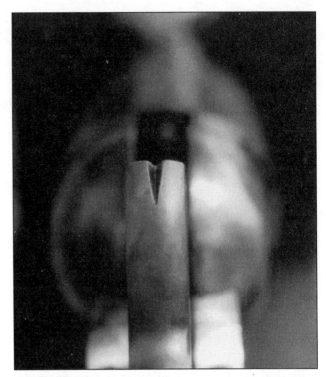

The rear sight of the Navy Arms percussion revolver –a simple V-notch in the nose of the hammer–is the same type found on the original Colt Model 1851.

This six-inch, six-shot grop fired at 25 yards is actually good for a percussion service revolver like the reproduction 1851 Navy.

When loading and shooting the test revolver, we found the cylinder chambers could be loaded with as much as 29 grains of Gearhart-Owens FFFg black powder and still have room for seating a .376" soft lead ball. The inside of the chambers measured .368" from wall to wall. A loading lever forces the ball into the smaller chamber, peeling soft lead from the circumference of the projectile. The result is a tight, swaged fit, ensuring that the balls in adjacent chambers can not be jarred loose (or forward) by the recoil. It is common practice to place a lubed felt wad between the ball and powder charge or to seal the mouth of the chamber with a heavy grease-type lube. This provides the lubricants needed to keep the powder fouling soft, allowing the cylinder to rotate freely. The grease also prevents the fire from one chamber to work around a seated ball in another and create what is known as a chain fire. When loaded with a 29 grain charge of FFFg black

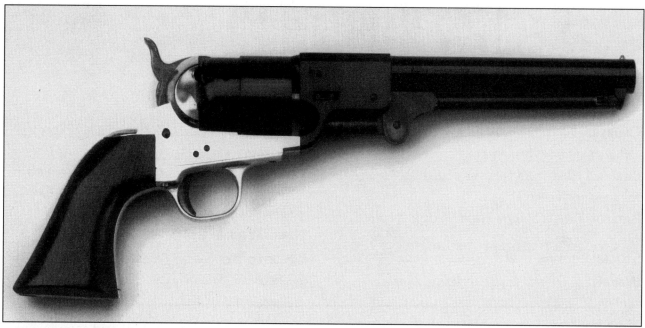

Navy Arms offers a great selection of reproduction revolvers, including this Confederate brass-framed copy of the Colt Navy.

powder, there isn't enough room to place a felt wad between the ball and powder charge. A small dab of Hodgdon "Spit Ball" lube over each chamber kept our test revolver functioning perfectly without simultaneous firing.

Best accuracy with the Navy Arms .36 caliber percussion sixgun was achieved with much light loads. In fact, only 18 grains of Pyrodex "P" (volume equivalent to FFFg) produced the best accuracy. A problem for shooters who attempt to load and shoot reduced loads from a percussion revolver often arises because the seated projectile sits so far from the rear of the barrel. Anytime a projectile can build up velocity before reaching the rifling, accuracy will usually suffer. To prevent this free flight, a filler, such as cornmeal, can be used to take up chamber space between the powder charge and projectile.

Loaded with an 18 grain FFFg volume equivalent charge of Pyrodex "P", along with an Ox-Yoke .36 caliber Wonder Wad and a cast .376" diameter lead ball, each chamber of the Navy Arms Colt Navy printed inside 10 inches at 25 yards. Such accuracy may not seem very impressive compared to that produced by today's modern cartridge revolvers; but keep in mind the technology that was available when percussion revolvers first came on the scene. Moreover, the sighting systems used on both modern reproductions and the originals they copy are nothing more than small rounded beads at the muzzle and a simple V-notch in the nose of the hammer.

Overall, this Navy Arms reproduction handgun is top quality. Its action is smooth and positive, and its cylinder locks up tightly. Fit and finish are as one would expect in a product that has been around for some 40 years—nearly twice as long as the original Colt Model 1851 Navy was in production!

PRODUCT REVIEW #6: LYMAN PRODUCTS: DEERSTALKER RIFLE AND CARBINE

SPECIFICATIONS

CALIBER: *.50 or .54, flint or percussion (rifle); .50, percussion only (carbine)*

BARREL LENGTH: *24" octagon (rifle); 21" octagon to round (carbine)*

RATE OF TWIST: *1-turn-in-48" (rifle); 1-turn-in-24" (carbine)*

STOCK: *Satin-finished European walnut*

WEIGHT: *7 1/2 lbs. (rifle); 6 3/4 lbs. (carbine)*

FEATURES: *Blued barrel; folding adjustable rear sight; white bead front sight; single trigger; matte finished trigger guard and nose cap; case-colored lock plate and hammer; synthetic ramrod; rubber butt pad; sling swivel studs*

MANUFACTURED BY: *Investarms (Italy)*

IMPORTED BY: *Lyman Products Corporation, 475 Smith Street, Middletown, CT 06457*

Lyman Products, headquartered in Middletown, Connecticut, is better known for its excellent gun sights and reloading equipment. But since the early 1970s, this century's old company has also been a major supplier of high-quality black powder guns, including one of the few authentic copies of the Hawken half-stock reproduction model known as the Lyman Great Plains Rifle. The company now offers something of a hybrid muzzleloader for today's black powder hunter, which it calls the Deerstalker. While these frontloaders are built with traditional side-hammer locks and other features, they also incorporate a few features that make them true hunting rifles.

Both the Deerstalker rifle and carbine are built with a European walnut stock fitted with

The Lyman Deerstalker, shown here with a receiver sight, is a hunting muzzleloader built with a combination of traditional and modern features.

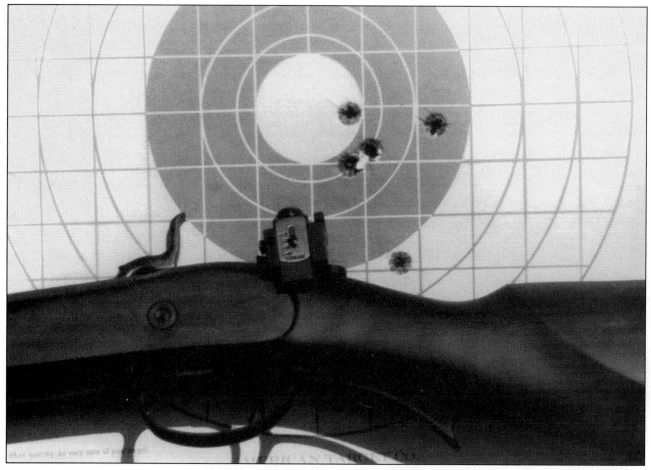

Lyman's 57SML receiver sight is easily mounted on the tang of the Deerstalker. Shooting tests revealed that with a 1-turn-in-48 inches rate of twist, this rifle produced best accuracy with a patched round ball.

a rubber butt pad to soften the recoil from potent hunting powder charges. They are also fitted with steel trigger guard, nose cap and wedge plates, all sporting a matte blued finish to reduce glare. The barrel is blued and the lock has been nicely color case-hardened. The Deerstalker rifle model has a short 24-inch octagon barrel and an overall length of only 41$\frac{1}{2}$ inches. The carbine version has a shorter 21-inch barrel, with an overall length of 38$\frac{1}{2}$ inches, making it one of the shortest muzzleloading big game rifles on the market.

Investarms of Italy, which manufactures the Deerstalker for Lyman, utilizes reliable modern coil springs for the mainspring and sear spring,

but externally the lock has all the appearances of traditional styling. The Deerstalker rifle is offered in .50 or .54 caliber and a choice of flint or percussion ignition (the shorter .50 caliber carbine model comes in percussion ignition only). The Lyman rifle features a one-turn-in-48 inches rate of rifling twist, while the shorte carbine has a much faster one-turn-in-24 inches rate of twist. The slower twist of the rifle barrel produces a muzzleloader that will perform fairly well with either a patched round ball or a "Maxi" style conical bullet. The theory that a one-turn-in-48 inch rate of twist will shoot both types of projectiles with the same degree of accuracy simply doesn't hold water. A barrel rifled with that rate

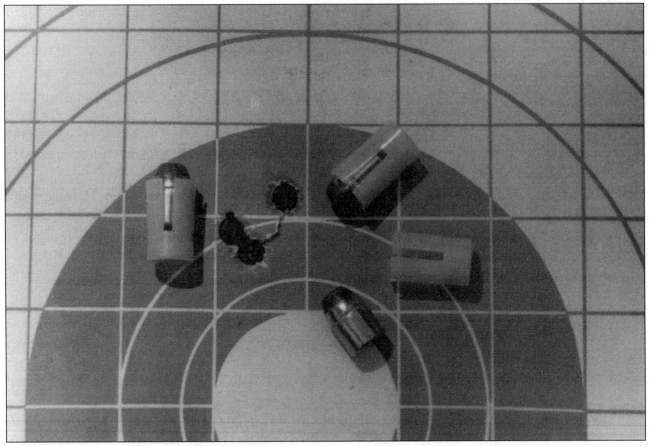

The Deerstalker's 1-turn-in-24 inches rate of twist shot well with saboted Speer 260 grain jacketed hollow point bullets. The best 50-yard group fired was this 1 1/4 inch three-shot cluster.

of twist will usually shoot accurately with one projectile or the other, but not both.

All test shooting for this report was done with standard open sights along with a Lyman 57SML receiver sight attached to the tang of the hooked breech system. As expected, the patched round ball produced the best accuracy in the Deerstalker rifle. The manufacturer lists 90 grains of FFg or 70 grains of FFFg as maximum loads for shooting a patched .490" ball. Patched with .015"lubed Uncle Mike's patches, Speer .490" swaged round balls printed consistently inside of 2½ inches at 50 yards using the standard folding rear sight. With the 57SML receiver sight installed, average groups tightened to slightly under 2 inches at 50 yards, while at 75 yards most

three-shot groups measured around 2½ to 3 inches across. The tightest round ball loads were shot with 50 grains of FFFg. Several three-shot 50 yard groups fired with the receiver sight in place printed less than 1½ inches.

A variety of bore-sized lead conical bullets were fired through the Deerstalker rifle with its one-turn-in-48 inches rate of twist barrel. We used the maximum recommended powder charge of only 80 grains of FFg. Again, the best groups were shot when using the receiver sight. The 385 grain Hornady Great Plains and Buffalo Bullet Company conicals of the same weight shot relatively well, printing 4-inch groups at 75 yards. One of the best shooting bullets was Lyman's own 420 grain Shocker,

The slower twist of the Deerstalker rifle was intended to shoot both the round ball and maxi-style projectiles with equal accuracy.

which placed closer to three inches across at 75 yards. Often it took 90 to 110 grain powder charges to ensure the best accuracy with a heavy conical bullet.

As for the carbine, its faster one-turn-in-24 inches rate of twist is actually better suited for shooting a conical bullet, but this model excels when loaded with saboted bullets. Deerstalker's instruction manual, however, does not cover shooting saboted bullets, clearly stating that black powder is the only propellant recommended by the manufacturer, which we assume excludes Pyrodex. However, Pyrodex has been formulated to duplicate the pressures and ballistics of black powder; in fact, the Deerstalker carbine in our tests liked Pyrodex loads. A 90 grain charge of Pyrodex "Select"

performed well behind a variety of saboted bullets, including the .45 caliber 260 grain Speer jacketed hollow-point, the new Remington 289 grain Premier Copper Solids, and the saboted .45 caliber Hornady 300 grain XTP jacketed hollow-point. As a rule, most grouped inside $2^{1}/_{2}$ inches at 50 yards (using the receiver sight). At 75 yards, most groups still measured within 3 inches. Lyman's own saboted .45 caliber Shocker pure lead hollow point bullets also shot well with 90 grains of Pyrodex "Select," punching groups at 50 and 75 yards on par with the jacketed and all-copper bullets fired through the carbine's short 21-inch barrel.

Had the Deerstalker been fitted with an

The Lyman Cougar is a modern in-line rifle with a fast twist barrel.

adjustable trigger, slightly better groups may have resulted with both barrels. The single non-adjustable trigger that is standard issue breaks at slightly over six pounds of pull. Those who prefer a positive trigger—one that requires more effort to pull the tip of the sear out of the full cock notch—will opt for this arrangement. But those who look for one-hole groups at 50 yards will probably want something that's adjustable to $2^1/_2$ to 3 pounds of pull.

THE ART OF THE
CUSTOMIZED MUZZLE-LOADER

Early settlements along the coastal areas of New England were dependent on gunsmiths to service and maintain the clumsy, often crude smoothbored matchlock muskets that were first brought to this country from England and Continental Europe. As early as 1640, these firearms technicians more often than not hand-crafted each part, spring or screw needed to keep those muzzleloaders firing. It wasn't until the arrival of German immigrants in the remote wilderness areas of southeastern Pennsylvania around 1710 that the American frontier welcomed its first true riflesmiths. Not only were these settlers confronted with a remote wilderness, they were met by wild

cats, wolves and bears, not to mention native inhabitants who had grown increasingly hostile toward the European invaders. These conditions made the proper functioning of the crude muskets all the more important to the settlers.

Those first self-sufficient riflesmiths cut and cured their own stock woods, hammer-forged their own barrel blanks, rifled the bores on crude hand-operated wooden rifling machines, cast their own brass butt plates and trigger guards, and filed every mechanical component of the lock and trigger mechanism. Indeed, these backwoods gunmakers were the cornerstone on which America's gunmaking industry was built.

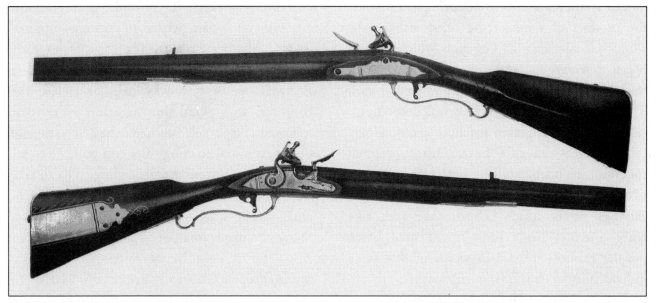

Fine, hand-crafted custom muzzleloading rifles like this early American flintlock (made by riflesmith Homer Dangler) represent hundreds of hours of painstaking work. Such high quality, one-of-a-kind workmanship can cost several thousand dollars.

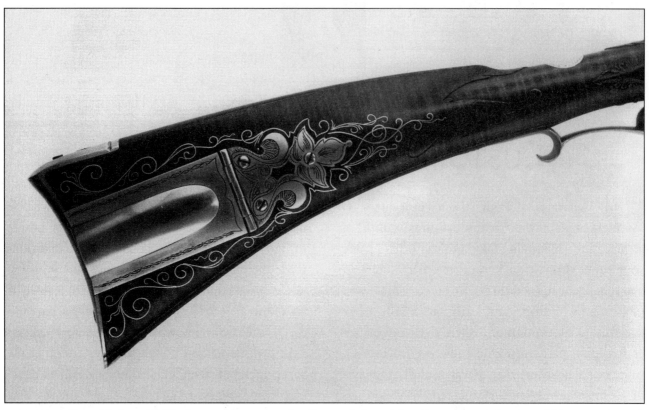

Custom riflesmith Jerry Kirklin is noted for recreating fine early longrifles. Note the preciseness of his engraving and inlay work.

By the time the flintlock Pennsylvania rifle had entered the "Golden Age" of the American longrifle (approx. 1760 to 1800), it had become the product of some of the finest artisans the world has ever known. The guns which evolved began to feature longer barrels and smaller bores, thus making better use of scarce powder and lead. The early rifles also began to reveal decorations, such as a fancy engraved patchbox painstakingly inlayed into the rifle butt. Other personal touches included stylish brass or German silver inlays, engravings and delicate relief carvings, all of which helped make each rifle truly one-of-a-kind. Today's dedicated black powder burners are still in search of that same individuality in their own muzzleloaders.

Today's custom muzzleloading riflemakers are, for the most part, not equipped to craft a rifle from raw materials the way the early Pennsylvania riflesmith did. Still, thanks to an unbelievable selection of component parts for custom riflemakers, it's possible to buy almost any individual part needed to create an original design, whether an authentic copy of an early German jaeger, a transitional longrifle, a Pennsylvania or Kentucky rifle, or any of the flintlock and percussion ignition rifles that followed. The result has been the re-creation of the finest muzzleloading rifles ever built. Even so, a top quality custom muzzleloading rifle can take 100 hours or more to make from scratch; and good quality parts for building a fancy Pennsylvania or Kentucky rifle can cost $500 or more. Many contemporary custom muzzleloaders demand prices of $1000 to $5000, depending on the complexity of design, quality of components used, workmanship and reputation of the builder.

JACK GARNER, ARTIST AT WORK

Perhaps the most prolific of all custom muzzleloading riflemakers is Jack Garner, of Corinth, Mississippi. This modern day riflesmith specializes in building Tennessee mountain rifles, utilizing high-speed power equipment whenever he can to speed up the process. The point is, Jack Garner can start with a blank piece of wood and by the end of the day produce one of these southern mountain rifles fully assembled, sanded and ready for finishing. To observe him cutting the basic lines of a stock design on his saw is to watch an artist at work. Next, he cuts the barrel channel with a power router, then drills the ramrod hole with a special long shank power drill. After that, he installs the butt plate, hand-fitting it with a rasp and a few hard blows with a rawhide mallet. In less than 90 minutes, Garner is ready to add the individual parts that will give each muzzleloader its own distinct personality.

The use of high-speed power equipment enables Garner to complete a rifle in less time than his competitors while still creating a custom muzzleloader superior to most mass-produced reproduction frontloaders. He does this with the same top quality Green Mountain barrels favored by top muzzleloading competition shooters, plus

Jack Garner begins building a rifle by selecting the proper stock blank from the ample supply he keeps on hand.

This high-speed power shaper allows Jack Garner to turn out a true custom rifle faster than most other custom makers.

Garner uses a bandsaw to cut the basic lines for each rifle style he offers.

Garner uses a hand-held power router to make the initial cut before installing double-set triggers on a longrifle.

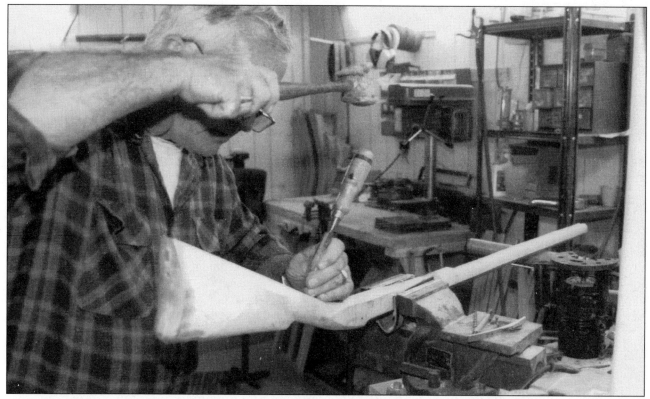

Precise wood-to-metal fit is assured by removing the last of the wood with a hammer and chisel.

locks and triggers that are superior to those found on run-of-the-mill production guns. Garner's craftsmanship also allows a shooter to own a rifle built to a specific trigger pull, caliber, and often with a specified barrel length.

Garner's basic "Poor Boy" Tennessee mountain rifle may be something of a "Plain Jane" in the world of custom muzzleloading rifles, but it is built true to the originals once used throughout Appalachia. Instead of a butt plate, he uses a two-inch section of horn at the heel of the stock and a simple steel toe plate. The standard maple stock is enhanced with a hand-rubbed oil finish. The gun also features a square-bowed steel southern mountain rifle trigger guard and plain steel ramrod thimbles. The barrel is offered in choice of 36- or 42-inch lengths in .32, .36, .40, .45, .50 or .54 caliber. Barrel diameters range from 13/16" to 1" across the bolts.

Double-set triggers are standard. Built to each shooter's choice of trigger pull and barrel length, this custom muzzleloader will set you back an amazingly low cost of $600 in flint or percussion ignition. Fancier versions and more options can increase the final cost to $1000 or so.

Garner also offers a plain copy of the early German jaeger rifle in flintlock or percussion ignition, featuring a wide butt and butt plate that make it extremely comfortable when shooting a large caliber with heavy hunting charges. Garner's basic jaeger is offered in .32, .36, .40, .45, .50, .54 and .58 caliber (optional larger bore .62 and .77 caliber barrels are also available). In a standard caliber and a barrel length up to 36 inches, this custom jaeger will run around $700. Garner can also build stylish copies of a Lancaster "Pennsylvania" rifle and an early "Virginia" longrifle. His Pennsylvania

For about twice the cost of a mass-produced reproduction Hawken rifle, a black powder shooter who desires a recreation of an original can shoot and hunt with a custom Leman rifle such as this one built by Jack Garner.

rifle has all brass furniture, while the Virginia rifle is entirely steel-mounted.. Both guns are available with a flintlock ignition system, or a later percussion conversion ignition system. Both models come with an "A" grade maple stock, double-set triggers, Siler locks, and calibers .32 through .54 with a choice of 36" or 42" length barrel.

Garner also makes a well-built copy of the Leman rifle, an early favorite of western adventurers. It's available in barrel lengths of 30 to 36 inches and in calibers .32 through .58 (flint or percussion ignition). The rifle features standard grade wood, double-set triggers and a choice of either steel or brass hardware. Still another Garner reproduction is a smallbore 20 gauge English flintlock smoothbore fowler. This scattergun is offered with a long 41"

tapered barrel and single shotgun-style trigger. With standard wood and with either steel or brass butt plate, trigger guard and thimbles, this custom long gun costs about the same as the Leman copy ($600-$650).

One reason why many black powder burners pay large amounts to a custom riflemaker for the muzzleloader of their dreams is a strong desire to own something that stands out from the crowd of look-alike reproduction guns. Most of Jack Garner's customers exercise the option of using top quality wood. Choosing "premium" wood adds another $25 to the cost, while a move to "premium plus" can raise the cost by $50 (a "super premium" stock moves it up to a full $100). Selecting something other than the standard maple stock in favor of walnut or cherry increases the price another

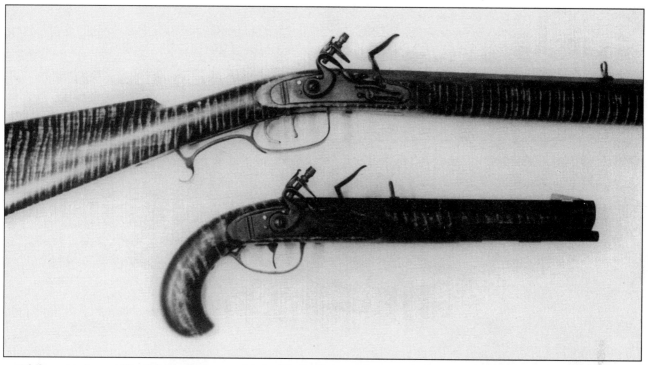

While not a fancy rifle, this southern mountain rifle (built by Jack Garner) is an affordable option for owning a stylish custom muzzleloading rifle (the accompanying flintlock pistol was also built by Garner).

$50. Likewise, the addition of a patchbox, sideplate and inlays tacks on another $150 to $200. A "custom" cut barrel featuring specialized rifling, tapering, or any other additional metal work adds another $100 to $200. Engravings on metal parts and carving on the stock will run anywhere from $250 to more than $750. Thus, one of Jack Garner's standard rifles can, with these options, push the final cost to $2000 or more. The end product, though, is a muzzleloader that can be shot and displayed for the rest of the owner's life.

Garner's top-of-the-line offering is his "Grand Rifle," a fully tricked out Virginia (or Lancaster) rifle built with many options, including a sliding wood patch box cover, super premium curly maple stock wood, a generous amount of engraving, and intricately executed relief carving. The Grand Rifle offers a choice of caliber from .32 to .58, brass or German silver hardware, trigger pull, barrel lengths of

36" to 42", and choice of flint or percussion ignition (right or left hand). With a price tag of approximately $1250, Jack Garner's "Grand Rifle" is a real bargain. At such reasonable prices, it's understandable why he often finds himself behind with orders. To ensure delivery within six months, he has hired other gunmakers to help run his Tennessee Valley Manufacturing Company. Much of the minor inletting and finish work is delegated to other gunsmiths, but Garner still does most of the stock work.

To those who contemplate ordering a custom muzzleloader, Garner highly recommends that customers let the gunmaker know exactly what they want before placing an order. His pet peeve is the shooter who calls once a week to change something, whether a standard feature or an option. Often he has received an order for a relatively basic rifle, but by the time he begins work the project has

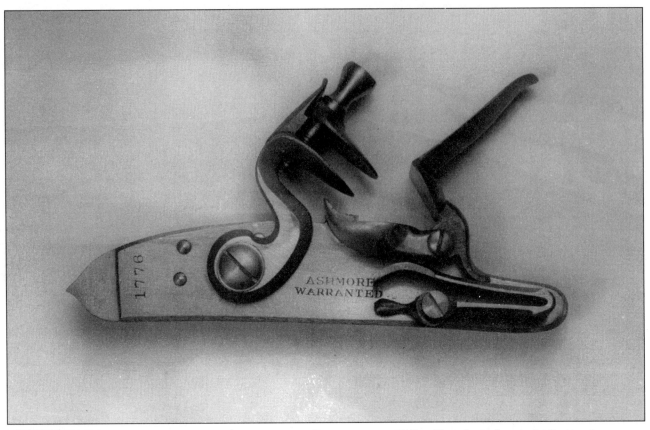

Dixie Gun Works, Mountain State Muzzleloading Supplies, Tennessee Valley Manufacturing and other parts suppliers now catalog an extensive variety of flint and percussion locks for the custom muzzleloading riflemaker.

become something quite different. Another recommendation: Before contacting a custom rifle maker, take time to study the various designs. A gun that may look fine in the hands of one shooter could prove far too awkward or clumsy for another to shoulder and shoot, or its stock could have a drop much too low (or high) for comfortable shooting. Also, don't make feature changes that don't fit the design or style. Show up at a shoot or an historical reenactment with a gun full of mismatched parts and you're sure to attract disapproving stares from knowledgeable shooters.

MODERN CUSTOM GUNS

Not many custom muzzleloading riflesmiths are currently working with any of the modern in-line percussion ignition systems. Most manufacturers of these guns are pretty stingy with the modern in-line or barreled actions. A custom builder who wants something special done with one of these guns has little option but to buy a factory rifle and then customize, whether it's a restocking job, a total rework, or perhaps a totally different barrel for better accuracy with a certain projectile. Modern Muzzleloading offers some custom work on its Knight rifles but avoids offering barrel lengths other than the standard 22' and 24". However, the company's "special order" shop does offer stocks it will shorten to pull lengths less than the standard 14¼". Rifle owners can also purchase one of Knight's LK-93 Wolverines in .36 caliber or an MK-85 in .45 caliber. The

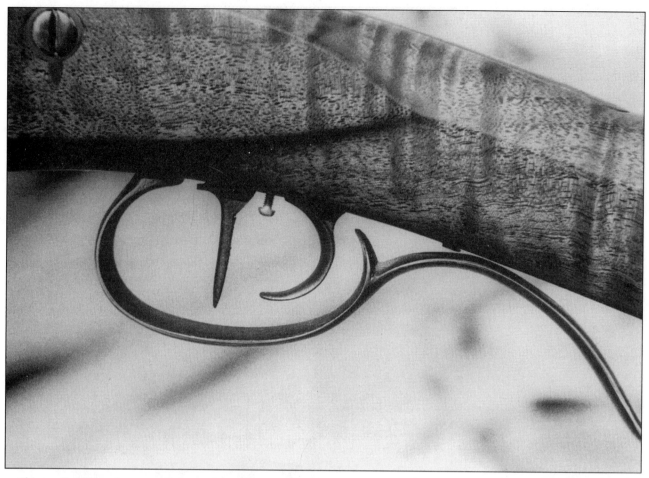

The availability of components, such as these authentically styled Hawken double-set triggrs, allows custom makers to concentrate on style, fit and finish.

Modern Muzzleloading offers a "special order" version of the Knight MK-85, known as the Grand American, featuring a laminated thumbhole stock and select barrel.

The first step in becoming a muzzleloading riflemaker is to assemble several kits currently available. A kit like this Thompson/Center Hawken rifle can be assembled and finished in a matter of hours.

company also offers a special edition of the MK-85 known as the "Grand American," featuring a laminated thumbhole stock. The company will also tailor the load to whatever bullet the shooter desires. It will test-shoot barrels until one is found that can place that particular bullet inside of an inch at 100 yards.

The Remington Custom Shop also offers customized work on its Models 700ML and MLS, such as shortening a stock for non-standard length of pull, or stocking the muzzleloader with a modernistic laminated thumbhole stock. When looking for a production muzzleloader with something other than standard features, though, be ready to fork out some cash.

TRY BUILDING A KIT

One way to end up with a muzzleloader that's different from the mass-produced copies is to buy a kit and assemble it yourself. Most of the so-called kit guns now available require easy assembly. Most of the difficult work, such as full inletting for the lock and triggers, has already been done. Even when the builder is required

The author built this custom Hawken entirely from commercially available component parts.

a third of the cost of a factory finished rifle by sanding the stock and finishing out the brass hardware themselves. With little effort, anyone can duplicate the quality of a factory-finished muzzleloader. With a kit and some extra time, the contours found around the lock can be dressed up, a little more style can be added to the shape of the cheek piece, or the flat contours of a factory-shaped and sanded stock can be rounded out. All these refinements can give even a mass-produced muzzleloader a more customized look. Some kit builders go the extra distance and replace trigger guards, side plates or patchboxes with hardware available to the custom riflemaker.

Success with a kit can encourage some black powder shooters to take on the job of building a true custom rifle. A word of caution, though: Don't bite off more than you can chew! Building a custom muzzleloading rifle from component parts means a lot of work for someone who's never done it. A considerable outlay of cash is also required for the component parts needed to produce a high quality, accurate muzzleloader.

Tennessee Valley Manufacturing offers the perfect "kit" for those who want to build their first custom muzzleloader. The company sells components for building any of the southern or Tennessee mountain rifles discussed earlier in this chapter. These guns come with the stock already channeled and the ramrod hole already drilled. The stock is about 90 percent shaped and inletted for the lock, triggers, trigger guard and butt plate. Some metal work, such as installing the breech plug and dovetailing cuts for the sights, has already been done. While this project

to make minor adjustments for the fit of these parts, it's usually not much more than scraping away some extra wood from inside the inlets.

Building a rifle from a kit usually involves sanding the stock and polishing the butt plate, trigger guard and other pieces of hardware. Thompson/Center's Hawken rifle kits come with the barrel, lock and trigger assembly already finished. Still, shooters can save nearly requires considerable work by the novice gunmaker, it can with care result in a handsome custom rifle. Best of all, once the work is done the owner can boast, "I built it myself!"

Tennessee Valley Manufacturing, Dixie Gun Works, Mountain State Muzzle-loading Supplies, and a number of other companies offer catalogs filled with components for the custom muzzleloading gunmaker. Dixie's latest catalog offers more than 50 different locks, nearly 100 different trigger guards, dozens of butt plates, and thousands of other parts for building authentically styled muzzle-loaders from the past. *But before jumping into such a project, a little more time devoted to research can pay big dividends in both time and money.*

A NEW APPROACH TO HUNTING

Like many of today's muzzleloading hunters, Mary Beth Hook is new to the sport. Many of her friends in southern Iowa hunted whitetails, and the thought of hunting deer intrigued her. She had also developed a taste for properly prepared venison, which offered even more encouragement to hunt. But before making a hasty decision, Mary Beth did her homework. She learned that as many as 150,000 shotgun hunters participated in either of Iowa's two general gun seasons. The thought of sharing the deer woods with all those people was unappealing. On the other hand, she knew it would take more time to master a hunting bow than she cared to expend. Muzzleloading, she decided, seemed like the ideal solution. Fewer than 20,000 hunters take part in Iowa's muzzleloader season, making it the least crowded and, at three weeks, the longest of Iowa's gun deer seasons.

With the help of some experienced muzzleloading hunters, Mary Beth set out to select a rifle she felt was compatible with her needs. The traditionally styled "side-hammer" reproduction rifles didn't appeal to her. They were too heavy and awkward for someone who had never handled, much less fired, a frontloader.

First-time black powder hunter Mary Beth Hook enjoyed success thanks to an improved modern rifle design, scope sight and modern projectiles.

about 90 yards. The deer went down on the spot, and with it the sport of muzzleloading had acquired another lifelong follower.

For Mary Beth Hook, it was the uncrowded hunting conditions and lengthy season that convinced her to pick up a muzzleloader for the first time. In many states the special muzzleloader deer and other big game seasons have brought millions of new shooters and hunters into the sport, many of whom turned to muzzleloading for the same reasons that attracted Mary Beth. Simply put, few hunters meant more time to put a whitetail in her sights. For whatever reasons, hunters continue to turn to muzzleloading in record numbers.

At present, only a few states still do not have a muzzleloading big game season, especially in areas where the white-tailed deer is hunted. Since the 1960s, with whitetail populations literally exploding, a growing number of state game departments have discovered muzzleloading hunts to be a great way to add to the harvest. The muzzleloading seasons held in those states where hunters are allowed to tag additional or bonus deer have become extremely popular. But even where muzzleloading simply provides the hunter with more time afield, deer hunting continues to attract new frontloading hunters each fall. Today's black powder shooters, in short, are deer hunters driven by a strong desire to hunt whitetails during a special season. They also tend to lean more toward a modern in-line percussion ignition rifle than a traditionally styled copy of a muzzleloader from the past.

Only 20 years ago, the modern muzzleloading hunting rig and load used by a novice like Mary Beth Hook would have been illegal in most states. Back then, the modern telescopic sight mounted on her rifle would have been legal in fewer than a dozen states; but now scopes are allowed during special muzzleloading seasons in more than half of the states. When it was first introduced in 1985,

Hundred-yard accuracy encourages shotgun hunters to head for the deer woods with a modern, scope-sighted muzzleloader.

Eventually, she settled on one of Tony Knight's light .50 caliber in-line percussion Wolverine rifles with a synthetic thumbhole stock. This six-pound muzzleloader performs well with a 90 grain charge of Pyrodex "Select" and a saboted 250 grain Barnes Expander-MZ. Mary Beth next had a 2 to 7 power Nikon variable scope mounted on her rifle and began practicing diligently at the shooting bench before heading off to the deer woods. By the time muzzleloader season opened in late December, she could keep hits inside of two to three inches at 100 yards. It all paid off on the third afternoon of the hunt when she connected cleanly with a big doe at

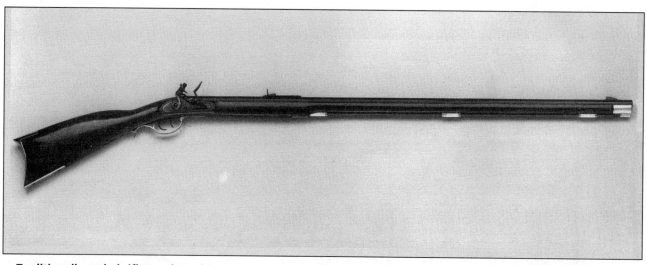

Traditionally styled rifles such as this Navy Arms "Pennsylvania" longrifle appeal to muzzleloading shooters who seek to relive history.

Knight's in-line percussion rifle was not allowed in eight or nine states. Now, only one state—Pennsylvania—does not permit hunters to use this system. Hunters who do take part there in the December muzzleloader whitetail hunt must use a rifle of flintlock ignition, and it must be loaded with a patched round ball. In the rest of the country, muzzleloading hunters have turned to saboted bullets, which can deliver three to four times the knockdown energy of a round ball; yet little more than a decade ago these saboted bullets were illegal in nearly a dozen states.

Muzzleloading has indeed matured into a true hunting sport. For the most part, today's black powder hunters aren't all that concerned about re-creating past hunting methods. Instead of attaching ties to the past, they simply want an opportunity to kill deer and other big game with a muzzleloader, and to do so as cleanly as possible. They take advantage of modern technology to help them harness all the accuracy and knock-down power a muzzleloading rifle can muster. Most of the best-selling muzzleloading rifles over the past decade were built with modern in-line

Comfortable to shoot and light in weight, modern design rifles like the Thompson/Center thunder Hawk appeal to contemporary black powder shooters and hunters.

Several manufacturers now offer popular rifle models packaged with everything needed to start shooting, including complete instructions. Shown is the Thompson/Center Thunder Hawk Value Pack.

percussion ignition systems. Generally speaking, these guns display lines that are not much different than most centerfire cartridge deer rifles. These "New Wave" muzzleloaders also feature modern safety systems and receivers that have been drilled and tapped for scope installation. But what appeals most to many muzzleloading hunters are the features and handling characteristics of a modern rifle.

The modern era of muzzleloading has ruffled the feathers of many traditional muzzleloader fanciers. They feel strongly that special muzzle-loading seasons should be reserved for those who shoot and hunt with traditionally styled side-hammer frontloading rifles. Over the past decade, though, these black powder shooters have become a minority, and yet they still represent the bulk of the membership of many state muzzleloading

associations where muzzleloading hunting regulations have been instituted. One of the biggest differences between buckskin-clad muzzle-loading buffs and their modern black powder counterparts is the use of scopes. Traditionalists argue that a scope has no business aboard a front-loading deer rifle, even though telescopic sights have been around since the early 1800s. On the other side, serious big game hunters feel that a scope, whether on a muzzleloader or a modern rifle, enables them to place more humane shots. Others argue that magnified optics encourage hunters to attempt shots that are beyond the rifle's effective range. Their detractors claim that such arguments are far from the truth. It's like saying because the speedometer on your car goes to 100 mph you'll always be speeding. Truth is, if a desirable buck is standing at 125 yards, most

Thompson/Center Arms includes a very detailed instructional video with many of its muzzleloaders, considerably speeding up the learning process for beginning black powder shooters.

black powder hunters will attempt the shot, whether or not their rifle is fitted with open or telescopic sights. The hunter who takes the time to align his scope properly has a much greater chance of putting his shot where it needs to go for a clean kill. Since the early 1970s bowhunters have witnessed similar disputes. When the first compound bows appeared on the market, longbow and recurve shooting purists hated the new mechanical contraptions. The opposition to new bow making technology prevented the compound from becoming legal in a number of states for more than a decade; even so, more than 95 percent of bowhunters today hunt with a compound bow.

Ballistically speaking, modern scope-sighted in-line percussion hunting rifles offer no advantages over more traditionally styled rifles. Stuffed with the same load, a modern in-line muzzleloader and a traditionally styled front-loader with the same length barrel will produce the same muzzle velocity, muzzle energy, and down-range ballistics. The advantage of the newer system is improved ignition, often better accuracy, and the improved safety of a modern firearm. What traditional muzzleloading shooters oppose so emotionally is the modern appearance of the in-line guns. But if today's black powder shooters and hunters weren't debating the political

Young and new muzzleloading hunters alike take to modern in- line rifles quicker and easier than they do the traditional designs. The author's son, Adam Bridges, took his first black powder buck at age 12.

correctness of modern in-line muzzleloaders, they would still be squabbling over other issues, such as round ball vs. conical, Kentucky longrifles vs. short-barreled Hawken rifles, or even flintlock vs. percussion ignition. To some degree, they still argue over these matters.

As long as whitetail and other big game populations continue to increase or stabilize at high herd levels, the muzzleloading seasons should enjoy a bright future; that is, if black powder shooters give them a chance to develop. Tolerance of each others' needs and desires can

only help build the ranks of muzzleloading shooters and hunters. Modern-in-line percussion rifles have brought hundreds of thousands of new people into the sport, greatly influencing game departments in the establishment of new or expanded muzzleloading seasons.

Pennsylvania's muzzleloading season represents a classic example of what can happen when the traditional mindset is allowed to prevail. While the number of muzzleloading hunters in other states has increased dramatically, Pennsylvania's has suffered a serious decline. It is the only state, moreover, where participation in a special muzzleloading season has experienced such a reversal. Only about half as many muzzleloading hunters there now head for the deer woods compared to the early 1980s, when as many as 140,000 black powder shooters went after whitetails. New management programs, the structures imposed by the different seasons, and imposed bag limitations partially explain the drop in muzzleloading hunters in Pennsylvania. But many black powder hunters complain that strict traditionally-oriented regulations have turned hunters away from the December muzzleloader hunt. They're required to hunt with a problematic flintlock ignition muzzleloader, a patched round ball projectile, and hard winter weather. Small wonder that the deer harvest is so low. And how many others are lost to poor hits because of the hang-fire of a flintlock ignition system, or the inefficiency of a patched round ball?

Let's take a look at another state—Virginia—where progressive muzzleloading regulations have attracted a growing number of new black powder hunters. Virginia established its first statewide muzzleloader deer season in 1990, allowing hunters to use the old frontloading rifles of their forefathers. The regulations at the time required the use of a traditional side-hammer muzzleloader loaded with a patched round ball. A percussion ignition system was allowed; otherwise, the regulations were nearly as restrictive as Pennsylvania's. Only about 20,000 hunters took part in each of the first two seasons. Soon regulations began to change, allowing the use of a broad range of muzzleloading guns and more effective conical hunting projectiles. With the Virginia deer herd on the rise, the game department needed hunters to harvest more deer, whether with a modern gun, a bow or a muzzleloader. Black powder hunters in Virginia can now head afield with as modern or traditional frontloading rifle as they wish. Everything from an early flintlock loaded with a patched round ball to a modern in-line percussion rifle fitted with a telescopic sight and loaded with saboted bullets are allowed. Today, more than 100,000 muzzleloading hunters account for slightly more than 20 percent of all whitetails harvested. And instead of just one muzzleloader season, Virginia hunters now enjoy two each fall—one held before the modern gun season and another after.

Change, of course, never comes easily, especially with muzzleloading regulations that carry such heavy emotional and political baggage. Attracting new participants to the sport goes hand-in-hand with gaining new hunting seasons. When participation drops, as in Pennsylvania, or when hunters fail to harvest enough game for the season to be considered a management tool, there is always the risk that a muzzleloading season will be lost. But when any muzzleloading season is lost, it becomes even harder to retrieve than when it was established in the first place. Regulations based purely on the aesthetics of a muzzleloader, rather than performance and overall public appeal, invite risks. We know that antiquated regulations won't change without public demand. In Virginia, for example, black powder hunters have let lawmakers and game department officials know their feelings. As a result, change took place and hunters now enjoy some of the finest muzzleloader hunting in the country.

The new Longhunter Society muzzleloading record book has created a growing interest among black powder users in trophy hunting with a muzzleloader.

Fortunately, hunting with muzzleloaders continues to mature as a true hunting sport, with regulations slowly changing to reflect the desires of today's hunters. As a result, the sight of modern in-line percussion hunting rifles and telescopic sights becomes ever more commonplace during the special muzzleloader seasons. The great thing about these progressive regulations is that they don't prevent a person from hunting with a flintlock, patched round ball and traditional open sights. It's strictly a matter of choice. As for the new muzzleloading seasons, they have become something of a happy middle ground. On one side are those dedicated bowhunters who would never consider hunting with a modern firearm during a crowded general season, but who have turned to muzzleloading in order to take advantage of the second season opportunity. On the other side, there are the dyed-in-the-wool gun hunters who refuse to sling sharpened sticks at deer, but who will pick up a frontloading rifle to cash in on another season. The smart hunter is the one who takes full advantage of all three seasons.

During the general firearms deer seasons, nearly one-third of the white-tailed deerhunters in this country must be content to hunt with a modern shotgun and slugs or a muzzleloading rifle. Fortunately, today's breechloading slug deer guns and sabot-style slugs are far superior to the guns and loads used during the early 1960s and 70s. But most still have a maximum effective range of 100 to 125 yards at best. As a result, a growing number of whitetail hunters are turning to super-accurate muzzleloading rifles that can extend this range another 25 to 50 yards. Many modern in-line percussion rifles can not only print powerful saboted bullets inside of two inches at 100 yards, they

This future black powder hunter has discovered he can hit the target with a modern in-line muzzleloader and saboted bullets.

can be sighted in for a "dead on" hold out to 150 to 160 yards.

Still another reason for renewed interest in hunting with a muzzleloader has been the establishment of a new record book for North American big game trophies taken with muzzleloading guns. This new book (compiled by the Longhunter Society, a record-keeping arm of the National Muzzle Loading Rifle Association) has caught the eye of serious trophy hunters because of the reasonable minimum qualifying scores that have been established for various North American big game species.

Bowhunters who aspire to make the Pope & Young archery record book must take a whitetail buck that nets 125 or more points after deduction for abnormal tines or variations in tine lengths. By comparison, the modern gun hunter who seeks recognition in the Boone & Crockett record book must take a buck that nets 170 points or more. The minimum qualifying score to place a typical whitetail buck in the muzzleloading record book is just 130 points. Today's deer hunter can spend a lifetime in the woods without ever once spotting a buck that qualifies for the Boone & Crockett record book, whereas taking a buck of decent size with a bow can be a real challenge. Simply put, the deerhunter has a better shot at making the record book when hunting with a muzzleloader than with either a bow or a modern firearm.

Following are The Longhunter Society's minimum qualifying entry scores for all North American big game species. Scoring is in accordance with the Boone & Crockett Club scoring system. For more information about The Longhunter Society record book and the big game record-keeping arm of the National Muzzle Loading Rifle Association, write: P.O. Box 67, Friendship, Indiana 47021.

In summation: Hunting with a muzzleloader isn't for everyone. Many modern gun hunters still feel they need the quick, added firepower of two or three additional shots, while many black powder shooters are content to engage in plinking or formal target competition with their frontloading guns. But it has been the lure of the new muzzleloading seasons that is generally credited with bringing most of today's black powder burners into the sport. These special "third seasons" present new and exciting opportunities for hunters who can't seem to get in enough time during the archery an general firearms seasons.

SPECIES	MINIMUM ENTRY SCORE
Black Bear	.18
Grizzly Bear	.19
Alaska Brown Bear	.21
Polar Bear*	.22
Cougar (Mountain Lion)	.13
American Elk (Wapiti) Typical	.255
American Elk (Wapiti) Non-Typical	.265
Roosevelt Elk (Wapiti)	.225
Mule Deer Typical	.146
Mule Deer Non-Typical	.175
Columbia Blacktail Deer	.95

SPECIES	MINIMUM ENTRY SCORE
Sitka Blacktail Deer	75
Whitetail Deer Typical	130
Whitetail Deer Non-Typical	160
Coues Whitetail Deer Typical	70
Coues Whitetail Deer Non-Typical	75
Canada Moose	145
Alaska-Yukon Moose	180
Wyoming (Shiras) Moose	125
Mountain Caribou	280
Woodland Caribou	230
Barren Ground Caribou	320
Central Barren Ground Caribou	275
Quebec-Labrador Caribou	320
Pronghorn	63
Bison	92
Rocky Mountain Goat	41
Muskox	80
Bighorn Sheep	136
Desert Sheep	125
Dall's Sheep	132
Stone's Sheep	132

*Note: The polar bear is eligible only when taken and possessed in compliance with the Marine Mammals act and other applicable regulations

MUZZLELOADERS AND WHITETAILS

Some aficionados of the muzzleloading sports like to take credit for the creation and expansion of the muzzleloader whitetail seasons we all enjoy. One side argues that these seasons allow hunters who are historically inclined to enjoy what it was like to go after big game with an old-fashioned smokepole. On the other side, the modern in-line percussion rifle-shooting crowd claims that without their involvement and the growth of muzzleloading hunter numbers, we wouldn't have the expanded seasons most states have adopted. Neither side is entirely right...or wrong.

Without the early interest in muzzleloading during the 1960s and early 1970s, it's unlikely that many game departments would have established muzzleloader seasons in this country. As the traditionalists argue, most of these new seasons were set up to give hunters an opportunity to take a whitetail with an old style muzzleloader.

Well-known black powder hunter Jim Shockey was drawn to muzzleloading by the lure of the special muzzleloader whitetail seasons and the performance of modern in-line muzzleloading rifles.

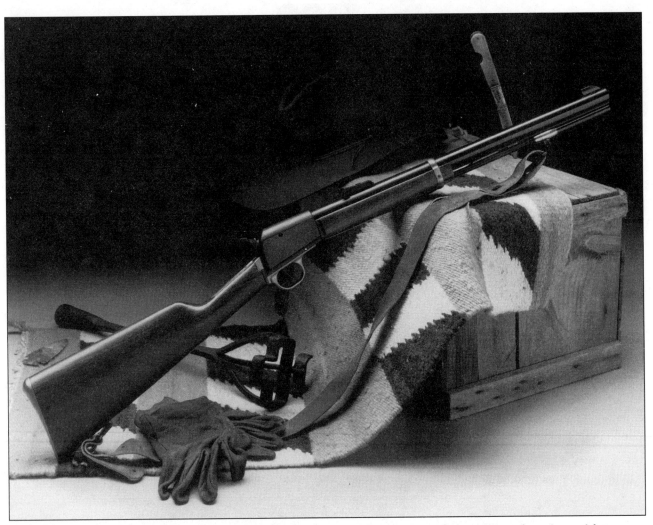

Short, fast-handling, carbine-length muzzleloaders like the Thompson/Center Scout are favorites with tree stand hunters.

It wasn't until after relaxed regulations had allowed more and more modern-looking front-loaders in the deer woods that the number of muzzleloading hunters began to grow. With that growth have come expanded hunting opportunities for traditional and modern black powder burners alike.

A few decades ago, most muzzleloader hunters who slipped silently through whitetail cover in the hope of downing a big buck were the same people who relished historical links to their prized traditionally styled muzzleloaders. A growing number now hunt with bows, modern firearms and the new-wave in-line frontloaders. When these modern hunters sight in on a whitetail buck with a scoped in-line rifle, they are not thinking about Davy Crockett or Daniel Boone. They are out to hunt deer, and they want a muzzleloader that kills a big buck cleanly at a sensible hunting distance.

In many states, the lure of special muzzleloader seasons is the opportunity to tag an additional deer or two. But even in those states where muzzleloader seasons don't allow the tagging of bonus whitetails, they are still popular because they offer additional hunting time for die-hard deer hunters who don't get enough hunting time during the archery and modern gun seasons. A growing number of states are now scheduling two special muzzleloader hunts each fall. Depending on where one lives and hunts, these seasons provide an extra month or more of hunting.

EAST AND WEST, NORTH AND SOUTH

Before you can hunt whitetails, you have to find them. So many variables exist in different regions of the country that it's impossible to cover them all. From east to west and north to south, prime whitetail habitats can be as different as night and day. The muzzleloading deer hunter of upper New England may be faced with hunting huge, roadless tracts of timber, while the Midwestern whitetail hunter must spend hours hunting in 40-acre woodlots surrounded by miles of open crop land. Meanwhile, down south, a deer hunter must find a way into the heart of a swamp to uncover an old buck, while the western hunter spends hours glassing the edges of creek-bottom hay fields before a whitetail wanders close enough to come within range of a muzzleloader.

Determining where a hunter should look includes factors like the availability of good feeding and bedding areas, the impact of local agricultural practices and land development, the extent of protected refuge areas, the impact on deer of a wet or dry season, and much more. Muzzleloading hunters who are new to an area should become regular visitors at their local muzzleloading shop; sooner or later they'll run into fellow muzzleloader whitetail hunters who agree to share their choice hunting spots.

Here we will look at hunting's three prime periods. Not every state offers dedicated black powder hunters an opportunity to hunt three times each fall. The first of these is referred to as the "early season," which means muzzleloaders

are scheduled to hunt before the start of the modern firearms season. In most states, the early season usually takes place sometime during October or early November. The farther west one travels, the earlier the hunting seasons. In several states west of the Mississippi River, these early seasons occur in September.

One advantage of an early season for muzzleloaders is the chance to hunt the elusive whitetails before they've been pressured by an army of orange-coated hunters during the general gun season. In those upper Midwest and New England states where early seasons are held, the weather offers crisp, cool mornings and warm afternoons.

The early muzzleloader season in Saskatchewan, Canada, occurs at the beginning of the rut. Gary Clancy relies on rattling and grunt calls to entice big bucks within muzzleloader range.

Early seasons in the South, however, can be downright hot, with temperatures soaring into the 90s. By contrast, when the black powder hunter heads north into Canada for a late October muzzleloader hunt, the snow can fly and temperatures may drop below zero.

When temperatures are on the warm side, early season hunting can be tough, especially during years when an abundant mast crop covers the ground with white oak acorns (the whitetail's favorite food). Often, whitetails will feed lazily all evening on the woods floor within a few hundred

Adam Bridges covers an escape route leading from heavily hunted woods. This tactic, coupled with his deadly accurate scope-sighted in-line muzzleloading deer rifle, have rewarded Bridges with several record book whitetails.

yards of where they bed down the next morning. This makes it difficult for hunters to slip in and get on stand without spooking the wary whitetails. Early muzzleloader seasons that occur at the end of October or during the first week of November come at a time when whitetail bucks in many parts of the country begin to feel the urge of oncoming rut. When cold snaps coincide with this time of season, bucks often get antsy and begin to travel, establishing their territory boundaries. Experienced muzzleloading trophy buck hunters feel this is the best time of the year to hang their tags on a real wall hanger.

Gary Clancy, a well-known outdoor writer and whitetail expert, takes full advantage of such early season opportunities. One of his favorite hunts each year comes during the month-long October muzzleloader season in Saskatchewan, Canada. By late October, the temperatures there have begun to drop, while the necks of mature whitetail bucks start to swell—a prime opportunity to down whitetails fit for the record book. The weather this far north can be brutal at this time of the year, however, so Clancy prepares well. When a trophy buck comes into his rattling or calls on a grunt tube, he's ready with a scope-sighted in-line percussion rifle loaded with a hard-hitting saboted bullet.

HUNTING THE RUT

The whitetail breeding period may be a great time to be in the deer woods, but it's also the most crowded period for hunting. In both Michigan and Pennsylvania, a million or so whitetail hunters are afield during the trophy class of the modern gun season. For those who want to hunt whitetails, this is definitely not the time to be huntin—rut or no rut. That doesn't mean the firearms seasons aren't also a great time to muzzleload for whitetails. With so many hunters moving

Scopes are allowed during more than half of the special muzzleloading whitetail seasons now held in the U.S. and Canada.

in and out of the woods, or poking around looking for big buck hideouts, deer are constantly on the move. In many states as much as 70 percent of the annual harvest is taken during the first two days of the modern gun season. When hunting pressured whitetails, it's best to forget about positioning a stand along normal trails, a rub or scrape line, or in a known feed area. Once the woods are invaded on opening morning, it's doubtful that many whitetails will be found following anything close to a normal daily routine. Instead, hunters should concentrate their efforts on secluded pockets of heavy cover where deer might seek sanctuary from heavy hunting pressure.

Adam Bridges, the author's son, has developed a knack for determining how whitetail bucks evade hunters. One of his favorite stands overlooks a tangle of multifloral rose and blackberry briars close by an open pasture. Thick cover leads to this impenetrable thicket from a heavily wooded ridge almost a half-mile away. Before gun season opens, only an occasional deer track can be found within 100 yards of the thick cover, but once hunters move into the hardwoods on the ridge above, a dozen or more deer will take refuge in the cover on opening morning. A strategically located tree stand 25 feet up an oak tree allows Adam to cover both routes into the tangle of briars. This setup has rewarded him with several muzzleloader record book bucks during Missouri's general firearms season in mid-November.

Those who are fortunate enough to hunt a

large tract of privately owned land, where hunting pressure is at a minimum, can take full advantage of the rut to put a trophy buck in their sights. Older bucks, which are often nocturnal at other times of the year, will occasionally drop their guard in search of hot does. The muzzleloading hunter who knows how to rattle and use a grunt tube can coax otherwise elusive bucks to within easy muzzleloader range. From the whitetail's northernmost range in Canada to southern Alabama, Florida and Texas, more than two

Larry Weishuhn hunts along a water course during a warm early muzzleloader season.

months can separate the earliest to latest rut activity. Generally speaking, the rut gets underway in late October to early November in the far North; but in late January and early February in the deep South it can still be at its height.

Throughout the Midwest and along the East Coast, modern gun hunters in many states are restricted to hunting with a modern shotgun loaded with either rifled or saboted slugs; in most areas, they can elect to use a muzzleloading rifle. Thanks to the deadly accuracy of modern in-line percussion rifles, these hunters can leave their pump and semi-auto quail guns at home and pack a muzzleloader during the "shotgun" seasons. Many of these rifles can print $1^{1}/_{2}$- inch groups at 100 yards; and when topped with a good scope and loaded with a saboted bullet some even shoot flat enough to hit 150-yard shots. Not many modern shotguns and slug loads can match that kind of performance.

HUNTING THE LATE SEASON

The basic definition of a late muzzleloader season, as we've seen, is any season that takes place after the close of the general firearms deer hunt. So long as muzzleloading is used as a tool to keep whitetail populations in check, the number of states promoting early and late muzzleloading seasons will continue to grow. Where only a single muzzleloader season is scheduled, though, it's usually a late season affair during mid-December or early January. Throughout the Midwest and upper New England states, December is the month when moderately cold temperatures begin to plunge to below zero and stay there for weeks on end. With three or four weeks often separating the close of the modern gun season and the start of the late muzzleloader season, the difference in the weather conditions can be like night and day. Even in the South, where temperatures rarely go

The Thompson/Center in-line rifle breech cover is a simple but effective way to keep rain and snow away from the capped nipple.

below freezing, the winter months often mark the start of a rainy season that dampens the spirits of a late season muzzleloader deer hunter faster than sub-zero temperatures and deep snow.

On the other hand, frigid temperatures and a prolonged snow cover can often contribute to a successful hunt, for by then the rut has wound down and most breeding activity is over. An old whitetail's thoughts turn then to survival, which means most deer will not stray far from a good food source. In farm country, this usually means a corn field.

Larry Weishuhn, a noted deer biologist and outdoor writer from south Texas, manages several large ranches for trophy whitetail bucks and has taken many deer close to home. But when it comes to getting a crack at a true trophy buck, Larry can't resist making at least one trip each year to northern Missouri or southern Iowa, home to some of the country's largest whitetails. The late muzzleloader seasons held in each of these states allow him to hunt for a real trophy long after the modern gun seasons have closed in most states.

Genetically, deer found along the Iowa-Missouri border are basically the same, while bucks living north of the border tend to be larger for the simple reason that Iowa allows only shotguns and slugs or muzzleloaders during the regular gun season, whereas Missouri is a centerfire rifle state. The limited range of shotguns and muzzleloaders means that more bucks reach old age. Unfortunately, Iowa offers

The Traditions Buckskinner Carbine combines traditional styling and a sabot-shooting, fast-twist barrel for whitetail hunters who want the best of both worlds.

only a limited number of non-resident deer tags, and when he doesn't draw Larry Weishuhn heads south across the border into northern Missouri, where deer tags can be purchased across the counter.

During one late Iowa season, Larry and I hunted together, an experience we'll never forget. Temperatures of -10° to -15° and wind chill factors of around -35° greeted us each morning as we headed out into the pre-dawn darkness for a long, bone-chilling wait on stands. What gave us the will to stick it out until mid-morning was the fact that we were seeing lots of deer. Hardly a morning passed during our six-day hunt that we

didn't spot 30 or 40 whitetails. But we were each looking for something special and kept on passing up easy shots. Finally, on the last day of the hunt, we led several short drives with the help of some local hunters. Before the day ended, we each had seen nearly 100 deer within 75 yards. With less than an hour of daylight left on that last day, I took Larry to a hayfield where the night before I'd glassed five good bucks. We were easing along a snow-covered logging road when suddenly Larry froze. Slowly easing the slung rifle from his shoulder, he took aim on a shadowy figure 60 yards down the side of the ridge. When he fired, the widest eight-pointer I've ever seen hit the

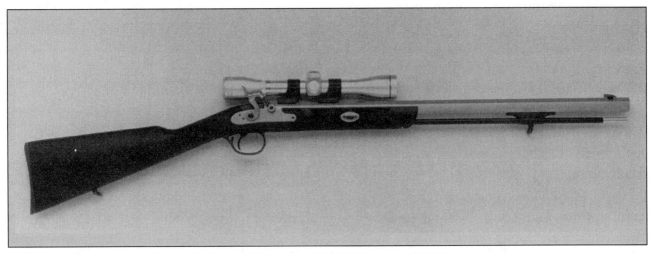

The Traditions Deerhunter can be fitted with an off-set base for easy installation of a scope.

The .45 caliber 260 grain Speer jacketed hollow-point shoots effectively out of most fast twist barrels when loaded with a plastic sabot.

ground. When the wounded deer tried to regain its footing, Larry put in the finishing shot on a record-book buck with a 26-inch inside spread and main beams measuring 31 inches in length. Later, after Larry had headed home to south Texas to thaw out, I dropped another huge eight-point weighing 275 pounds.

GUNS AND LOADS FOR WHITETAILS

The one thing that Larry Weishuhn, Gary Clancy and Adam Bridges all have in common is their preference for a modern, scope-sighted in-line percussion rifle (as opposed to a more traditionally styled, open-sighted frontloader). These serious big buck hunters demand a rifle and load that will down even the largest whitetail buck all the way out to 150 yards. Of course, many good bucks are still taken each year with traditionally styled muzzleloading rifles and projectiles. Any accurate .50 or .54 caliber muzzleloader loaded with 80 to 100 grains of the appropriate granulation of black powder or Pyrodex and a patched round ball will down even

large bucks so long as the shooter knows when not to shoot. A close range projectile like the round ball loses velocity and energy too quickly to be effective at 100 yards. The answer in that case is to keep shots inside of 75 yards.

Heavy lead conicals, such as those made by Hornady, Buffalo Bullet and Thompson/Center will deliver better knockdown power at 100 yards, but they also require a faster rate of rifling twist for stabilization and accuracy than do the patched round balls. They also need a little more powder to get them rolling along at acceptable velocities. When loading a 350 to 450 grain hunk of lead in a .50 or .54 caliber hunting rifle, 90 to 110 grain charges of FFg black powder or a volume equivalent of Pyrodex "RS/Select" normally produce the best performance. Even the border-line .45 caliber rifles can be turned into potent whitetail medicine when stuffed with a 200 to 300 grain conical bullet and 70 or 80 grains of powder. Downrange at 100 yards, these big bullets can strike a whitetail with three times the energy of a patched ball fired from the same rifle.

Looking for the flattest shooting load you can stuff through the muzzle of a frontloading rifle? Concentrate on working up an accurate load incorporating a modern saboted bullet. Most have been designed to expand and transfer energy at impact velocities of 1,200 to 1,700 f.p.s., which is exactly the same velocities produced by .50 or .54 caliber muzzleloading rifles with an 80 to 100 grain charge of black powder or Pyrodex. These conical bullets require a fast rate of rifling twist for best accuracy. If you're looking for a load that prints well out to 150 yards, concentrate on mid-weight bullets—for example, the 260 grain Speer .45 caliber jacketed hollow point, or the 240 grain .44 or 250 grain .45 caliber Hornady XTP jacketed hollow point bullets. These produce less drop after 100 yards than do heavier bullets. In fact,

The Knight LK-93 Thumbhole Wolverine, complete with scope and mounts, weights only about seven pounds.

sighted into hit dead on at 100 yards with 100 grains of Pyrodex "Select," the 260 .45 Speer will drop only 5 to 6 inches at 150 yards, depending on barrel length and velocity.

HOW TO AVOID FOUL WEATHER MISFIRES

Extreme cold, wet weather can often have an effect on how a particular load shoots. More important, adverse weather and temperatures can hamper ignition and affect rifle functions. With a few simple precautions, muzzleloading whitetail hunters can eliminate many of these problems in the field, no matter how cold or how wet the weather may be. Most misfires (or hang fires) are due to oil, cleaning solvents or moisture in the ignition system itself. Before loading a rifle for a day's hunt, therefore, take time to snap two or three caps on the ignition system. The idea is to clear and burn anything in the flash channel of the nipple or breech area of the rifle. Hold the muzzle close to a leaf or blade of grass when snapping the caps; if it moves that means the ignition system is clear. Once you're certain the

nipple and channel leading to the barrel are clear, then load the rifle.

Most projectiles—whether a tightly patched ball with a lubed patch, a well-greased conical, or a tight-fitting sabot and bullet combination—tend to fit the bore tight enough to keep moisture at the muzzle end of the barrel from reaching the powder charge. You can also place a thin latex "muzzle mitt" over the end of the barrel, or seal it with a few short strips of vinyl tape. The cone of most nipple designs features a relatively sharp taper. When a hunter takes time to seat a cap on the nipple properly—either by exerting extra pressure with the capper, a thin slat of wood, or an accessory tool made specifically for that purpose—the fit of the cap is often enough to keep the ignition system fairly moisture-free. Several companies offer tight-fitting vinyl rings that can be slipped around the nipple for extra protection. Another effective approach is to rub a light coat of beeswax or bowstring wax around the flange of the cap after it's been seated on the nipple.

When temperatures drop below zero, the

Uncle Mike's Cap Guard is a simple plastic sleeve that fits snugly around the base of the cap, forming a weatherproof seal with the cone of the nipple.

mechanics of a muzzleloading hunting rifle can get sluggish, or not work at all. Hunters too often try to remedy the problem by dousing the gun's working parts liberally with oil, which can do more harm than good. Instead of smoothing and loosening up the action, too much oil can create even more sluggishness. A better approach is to clean excess oil from all working surfaces, using plain old rubbing alcohol or a special gun degreaser. After wiping the surfaces dry with a soft clean cloth, follow up by going over the surfaces with a cloth that's been lightly sprayed with a protective lubricant. When it comes to oil and graphite greases in a muzzleloader lock or action

during cold weather, less is definitely better. Also, before heading out on a cold weather hunt with the same load that performed well during warmer weather, check its accuracy using a rifle that's been sitting around an hour or so. Don't be surprised if it impacts quite differently. You'll find also that it takes more effort to start and seat the projectile.

If a rifle hasn't been fired during the course of a day's hunt and you plan to hunt the next day with the same rifle and load, don't bring the gun from out of the cold into the warmth of your home or hunting camp. Even with an outside temperature in the 40s, condensation can quickly form on the metal surfaces of a barrel and action

Muzzleloader hunting late in the season often means braving the worse weather of the year. Once the temperatures drop below zero, hunters need to know how their rifles will load, shoot and function.

that have been exposed to a warmer climate. That applies as well to the internal surfaces of the barrel and the flash channel of the ignition system. Remember, condensed ̶ture in the ignition system has caused many a misfire. Instead of bringing a gun inside, leave it in the trunk of a car or in an unheated out-building. *You can then hunt with confidence the next day, knowing that your rifle will fire when the first opportunity arises.*

MUZZLELOADING FOR PRONGHORN AND MULIES IN OPEN COUNTRY

The Longhunter Muzzleloading Big Game Record Book has caused many a black powder hunter to think about trophy hunting for the first time. In addition, the big game record-keeping program of the National Muzzle Loading Rifle Association is attracting serious trophy seekers from the ranks of bowhunters and modern firearms hunters. To understand why, consider the minimum qualifying scores that now make trophy hunting with a front loading gun so attractive to hunters who seek entry to *The Book*. Since whitetails are the favorite big game animal among muzzleloading hunters, it stands to reason that more whitetail bucks make it into the muzzleloading record book each year than any other species. Which is not to say it's easy to take a typical whitetail buck in order to meet the 130 minimum points required by The Longhunter Society. It's because the sheer number of hunters who go after this great game animal with a muzzleloader has grown so fast that more and more new entries are inevitable.

Pronghorns make a challenging muzzleloading trophy. The patient black powder hunter will find it's not all that difficult to get within range of these open country dwellers.

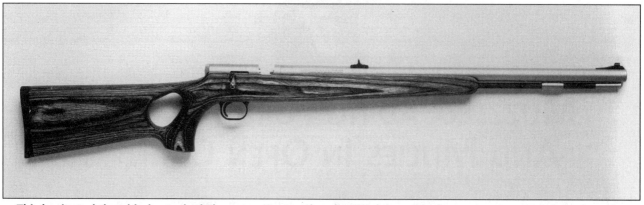

This laminated thumbhole-stocked Thompson/Center Thunder Hawk is an ideal open country pronghorn or mule deer rifle. With heavier hunting powder charges behind a saboted bullet of 240 to 260 grains, accuracy and trajectory at 150 yards allow the hunter to place his shot effectively.

For those whose goal is a trophy worthy of entry into the muzzleloading record book, species are available with less rigorous qualifying scores. Any of the caribou subspecies, for example, offer ample opportunity to harvest a "book" trophy. Any bull with long main beams, a few long upper points, plus decent bez and shovel points should meet minimum requirements. A muzzleloading hunter who can hold off for a 300- or 400-pound bruin will find that taking a record-book black bear isn't all that difficult, either. In short, muzzleloading hunters who have the time and money to track down most North American big game species will discover that taking record-book trophies isn't all that difficult. Unfortunately, most of us lack the resources to pick up and take off for the Northwest Territories or Alaska, or even a guided hunt for western elk in the fall.

On the other hand, for those who seek a challenging game animal that offers plenty of opportunities for a trophy and a chance of getting into the Longhunter record book, the pronghorn of the American West may be the answer. In terms of availability, transportation and other expenses, opportunities to hunt without a guide, among other good reasons, the pronghorn belongs at the top of the list. That doesn't mean a trophy class pronghorn antelope is a pushover. When members of the famed Lewis & Clark expedition, armed only with their flintlocks, first encountered this dweller of the open plains, they soon classified the pronghorn as impossible to hunt. Fortunately, today's hunter who takes the time to put together a modern in-line percussion rifle will have much better results, especially with a good scope (where regulations allow its use). Only a few such hunts, however, are held in New Mexico, Arizona, Colorado, Wyoming and a handful of other states. Some take place in areas where centerfire rifle hunting is not allowed, which

This scoped modern in-line Knight MK-85 Grand American rifle, coupled with a flat-shooting saboted bullet, are a perfect combination for 150-yard shots common in pronghorn and mule deer country.

Tom Fegely relied on a saboted .45 caliber Speer pistol bullet to drop this tall-horned Wyoming 4x4 on the spot.

means pronghorns have an opportunity to mature into 16-inch plus trophies that qualify for the muzzleloader book and Boone & Crockett as well.

Getting drawn for one of these tags can be difficult, though. In New Mexico and Arizona, for example, 20 to 30 applications for each available permit are not uncommon. Much of the hunting there is conducted on public lands administered by the Bureau of Land Management or the National Forest Service, so hunters needn't pay trespass fees. Hunts held on private lands, however, usually require additional access fees. In New Mexico, landowners receive a percentage of the tags, which are then sold to hunters and outfitters for around $750 to $1,000. Wyoming issues resident and nonresident hunters more than 100,000 pronghorn tags annually. Plus, nearly 70% of the entire state is public land open to hunting. Permits left over after the draw are sold

on a first-come, first-serve basis. Wyoming also schedules several early muzzleloader hunts for pronghorns, but during the general seasons muzzle-loading hunters must compete with the long-range centerfire crowd, especially on public land open to everyone. With high pronghorn populations across the state offering opportunities for every-one, patient black powder hunters who can weather the first two or three days of the season opener will find that most modern gun hunters have filled their tags and left the area. There are always a few bucks remaining; moreover, the hunter with the patience to wait until the second half of a season will most likely enjoy a quality hunt.

Ted Schumacher, owner of Lone Wolf Outfitters (Buffalo, Wyoming), leases some private lands between the towns of Buffalo and Gillette, where his clients have consistently taken impressive record book class bucks, most of them with scope-sighted in-line percussion rifles and flat-shooting saboted bullets. Among them was outdoor writer Tom Fegely, who booked his first muzzleloader pronghorn hunt with Schumacher a few seasons back. Before heading for the open country of Wyoming, Tom's black powder hunting had been restricted entirely to whitetails in habitats where shots were seldom fired more than 60 or 70 yards. Shots taken at western pronghorns are generally closer to 200 yards.

Fegely soon learned that it takes a patient, skilled hunter to slip within 150 yards. On the fourth day of Tom's hunt, he managed to crawl on his belly to within 140 yards of a 14-inch horned buck. Using a fence post for a rest, he then placed a deadly shot with his .50 caliber MK-85 Knight Hawk. Tom had relied on "spot and stalk" techniques to take his prize buck (which qualified for the record book). Knowing he'd be faced with long range shooting, he had earlier mounted a 3-9x Nikon scope on his rifle, then sighted it in with

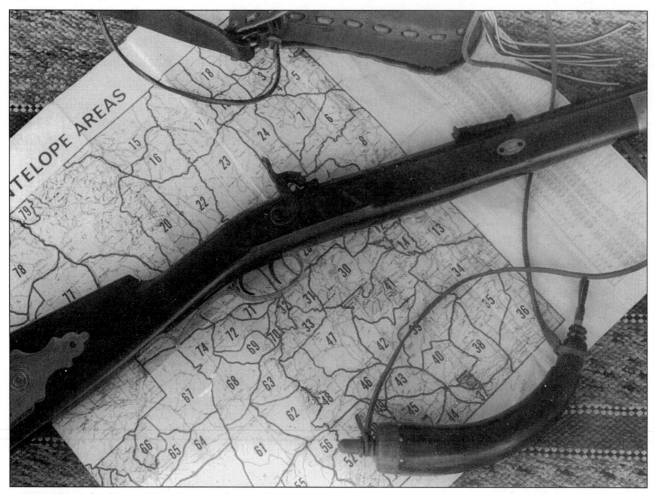

Wyoming is broken up into dozens of pronghorn management zones, with seasons opening as early as August or as late as November.

a 100 grain charge of Pyrodex "Select" and a saboted 260 grain Speer .45 caliber jacketed hollow-point bullet. At 100 yards, his rifle printed three shots inside of 1½ inches, impacting about 2 inches high. At 150 yards, his load hit less than four inches low, allowing him to hold almost dead on out to that range. His shot caught the buck perfectly, dropping it on the spot. Barely an hour after dropping the antelope, Fegely took a nice 4x4 mule deer buck at slightly over 100 yards with the same rifle and load. A few days later, I was hunting mule deer less than 20 miles from where Tom had taken his pronghorn and mule deer buck. Shooting the same bullet and powder charge out of my .50 caliber Knight

"Grand American," I took an exceptional 5x5 buck at just over 150 yards. That buck never knew what hit him.

In Wyoming, good mule deer can often be found in the same areas as the pronghorn, and in places where the open seasons for both species coincide, giving black powder hunters a double opportunity to take home a muzzle-loader trophy. The same loads that perform well on whitetails will do so on pronghorn and mule deer—provided they group out to 150 yards with enough accuracy to justify taking shots at that distance. In really arid pronghorn and mule deer country, the patient hunter who can sit in a blind for days on end is likely to get

The author used an open-sighted .45 caliber Mowrey rifle to take this nice buck at about 100 yards.

where regulations require the use of open sights. Hayfields are also lush oases in the midst of stark habitats, often attracting pronghorns and mule deer like a magnet. Several years ago, on a hunt with Tom McIntyre of Sports Afield, I spent considerable time at the range testing the 100- yard-plus accuracy of the rifles and loads we planned to use on the hunt. Tom was shooting 100 grains of FFg black powder behind a 250 grain Barnes Expander-MZ out of his .50 caliber. Knight MK-85. I was using a lightweight Knight LK-93 thumbhole Wolverine model, loading the .50 caliber in-line rifle with 90 grains of Pyrodex "Select" and a saboted Speer .45 caliber jacketed hollow point. Both rifles were sighted a little high at 100 yards, about dead on at 125 and only 3 inches low at 150. At the longer range we both kept shots inside $2^1/_2$ inches.

At the time, we were hunting a 400-acre hayfield about 15 miles west of Gillette. Earlier, we had scouted the area and glassed five or six good bucks, any one of which would make the muzzleloader record book. We took stands about a half-mile apart, and come afternoon I decided to take advantage of some knee-high grasses bordering the hayfield and crawled to within 75 yards of a tall, straight-horned 14-incher. It was an easy shot for my scoped in-line rifle. I then moved Tom to a drainage ditch in the center of the hayfield, then drove to a water hole at the opposite end. As I neared the small pond, a band of pronghorn stood nervously watching from 200 yards away. I had just gotten out of my truck to wash off my knife and hands when the animals pranced to the middle of the wide open field, close to the ditch where I had left Tom. A cloud of white smoke appeared from the high grass growing

a much closer shot. Windmills dot much of the Bureau or Land Management properties, providing water holes for grazing stock and wildlife. Early in the morning and late in the evening are great times to be waiting for a mule deer buck to visit these water holes, while for pronghorns this can occur at almost any time of day. The hunter who conceals himself in a shallow pit blind (or one made from mesquite or sagebrush) can get shots as close as 20 or 25 yards. This technique is a favorite of bowhunters and works equally well for muzzleloading hunters. It's a great way to get within range in those areas

When hunting antelope, hunters may need a rest similar to this modern set of cross sticks.

This chunky Wyoming buck taken by the author had a live weight of around 300 pounds, but still went down with one good hit by a saboted 260 grain .45 caliber jacketed hollow-point bullet.

One clean 100-yard shot dropped this 32-inch Utah mule deer buck for black powder hunter Aly Bruner. He used a .50 caliber UFA "Teton" rifle loaded with 100 grains of FFg black powder and a 450 grain pure lead Buckskin Bullet Company hollow-point conical.

Moving pronghorns, which have been clocked at over 60 m.p.h., are no target for the muzzleloading hunter. Patience will eventually bring the hunter close to a standing still target.

along the ditch, and a moment later I saw a 15-inch horned record book buck hit the ground. Tom McIntyre had just tagged his first muzzleloader pronghorn at about 130 yards.

Pronghorn are relatively frail animals, weighing 125 pounds tops. Their major defenses are exceptional eyesight and tremendous speed. Experts often claim that a pronghorn's eyesight is the equivalent of 6x binoculars, but once you've hunted them, you're likely to say that it's closer to 10x binoculars. Little, if anything, escapes their attentive stares, and at the first sight of danger they will race off to safe country at speeds approaching 60 m.p.h. So whether you try stalking a good buck or prefer to play the waiting game at a popular water hole or hayfield, a trophy pronghorn buck will test your skills, patience and shooting ability. Remember, it doesn't take a cannon to down a good buck; in fact, loads that can take a whitetail effectively are considered over-kill. But if you happen to be hunting mule deer on the same hunt, the extra punch will come in handy. In some parts of the West, mule deer grow big, often topping 300 pounds live weight. *Most, though, are about the same size as big Midwestern whitetails, so the same rifles and loads that work well on these will double nicely for mule deer.*

8

FRONTLOADER ELK

Sooner or later, most whitetail hunters dream about a western elk hunt. The sight of a big bull elk tipping his head back and filling the crisp autumn morning air with a high-pitched bugle is enough to send cold chills running up the spine of any hunter worth his salt. And the sight of a fine 6x6 rack on anyone's den wall is evidence that the owner has met one of hunting's most taxing challenges. To do so with a muzzleloading rifle makes the reward even sweeter.

Fortunately, elk populations throughout the Rocky Mountain states have never been greater, nor have the hunting opportunities. Colorado,

Idaho, Oregon, Montana and a few other states now have burgeoning elk populations; in fact, the big animals have become so plentiful they're becoming nuisances. A few hungry elk can totally destroy a winter's hay supply practically overnight.

To help keep the growing elk numbers in check, a number of western states now conduct special muzzleloading seasons. This not only provides the game departments with an additional management tool, it offers the black powder hunter a unique opportunity. The September muzzleloader elk season held in Colorado ranks among the most popular of these hunts. With the

During the rut, shots at bulls can be as close as 15 to 20 yards. Open sights could prove more an advantage than a disadvantage.

Gerry Blair poses with a huge 7x7 Arizona bull which at the time held the muzzleloading world record.

Division of Wildlife will announce right up front that it will take three, four or five preference points even to be eligible for the draw. Still, hunters submit applications year after year, trying to build the preference points needed to obtain a permit four or five years down the road.

In Arizona, serious trophy-minded elk hunters know that their best shot at taking a prize bull is during the special muzzleloader hunts held in some of the management units. The odds of getting drawn for one of these coveted permits can go as high as 100 to 1; but getting drawn is about as close to having a shot at a 6x6 or 7x7 bull as a black powder hunter can get. Each season these units produce some truly magnificent bulls, including the current muzzleloading world record taken just north of Flagstaff during a hunt in September of 1990. Not long ago, outdoor writer Gerry Blair was hunting with several friends near his home in Flagstaff. Gerry's "home court" advantage had allowed him to scout the area where several good bulls had been spotted in a huge burn, where the pinions and junipers had not reforested. When given a choice, elk prefer to feed on grasses rather than leafy brush. Before the rut, Gerry realized that a large number of cows were feeding regularly on the lush grass growth of the old burn. He also knew that once the rut was underway, the bulls would go wherever the cows went. During his first day in the area, Gerry had gotten a glimpse of a huge 7x7 bull, and at that moment he knew he could never be content to hang his tag on anything less.

Early on the fifth morning of the hunt, Gerry got his chance. At daybreak, the barks and chirps of cows had squeezed a low, throaty chuckle out of the battle-smart veteran. Gerry proceeded to fill the morning air with seductive cow talk, and a few minutes later the tips of the bull's towering rack appeared over the conifers. Suddenly, the huge elk

highest elk population of any Rocky Mountain state, Colorado offers tags for the October general gun season right over the counter. But for the special muzzleloader season that begin in mid to late September, Colorado issues fewer than 20,000 bull tags. Competition for these is consequently fierce with as many as 50,000 applications rolling into the Division of Wildlife in pursuit of a tag. As in other states, Colorado is broken up into numerous management units. In some of the better trophy units, a dozen or more applications may be received for each available permit. And in some of the best units, the stepped out into the open, barely 100 yards away, coming straight on and slowly closing the distance to 50 yards, then 40 yards. Finally at 20 yards the bull stepped broadside, offering Gerry the perfect shot. Holding slightly to the rear of the shoulder, he eased back on the trigger. The saboted 260 grain Speer jacketed hollow point, pushed by 87 grains of Pyrodex "RS", caught the rib cage perfectly. The thousand-pound elk traveled less than 100 yards before piling up. Gerry Blair's muzzleloading world-record bull scored 400 points; it also netted 388 3/8 Boone & Crockett points, good enough for the No. 1 spot in The Longhunter Society record book.

Since most readers are not likely to experience the thrill of hunting moose or American bison, an elk is probably the largest member of the deer family they will likely ever get in their sights. Depending on where they're being hunted, good bull elk can weigh anywhere from 600 to more than 1,000 pounds. A few Roosevelt elk taken on several Alaskan islands and the coastal mountains of Oregon, Washington and British Columbia have even topped 1,200 pounds. It takes a lot of punch to down an animal this size cleanly. The load Gerry Blair used in his .54 caliber Knight

MK-85 to take that big 7x7 is actually on the light side. Had it not been for the close range, pin-point shot placement and the effectiveness of the modern jacketed hollow-point bullet, that bull could have been lost forever.

Some states still allow muzzleloading hunters to go after elk with a .50 caliber rifle loaded with a patched round ball. Even with heavy hunting charges, though, this can be risky. A .50 caliber Thompson/Center Hawken rifle loaded with a 100 grain charge of FFg black powder (or Pyrodex "RS/Select") and a patched 178 grain .490" soft lead round ball are good for about 1,900 f.p.s. at the muzzle and approximately 1,400 ft. lbs. of muzzle energy. Somewhere on the shooter's side of 50 yards, that energy level drops to below 1,000 ft. lbs. By the time that bullet gets to 100 yards, it hits with some 450 ft. lbs. of remaining energy. Even when the powder charge is upped to 110 grains, the remaining energy at 100 yards is less than 500 ft. lbs. That's hardly the kind of performance a hunter should count on when bringing down a magnificent animal like a bull elk. The .54 caliber rifle does a little better job when stuffed with a patched round ball—but not much better. With 110 grains of FFg black

Modern in-line rifles like this camouflaged Thompson/Center Fire Hawk are fast becoming the number one choice of serious black powder elk hunters.

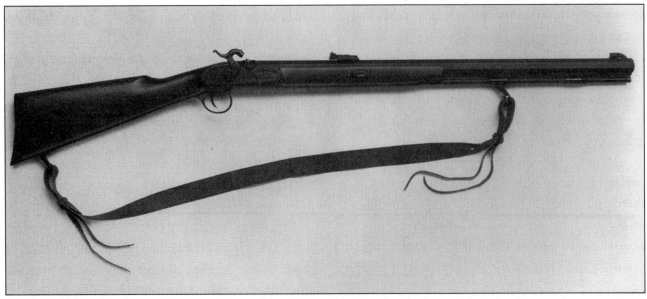

The muzzleloading hunter who is determined to take an elk with a patched round ball should concentrate on the large bore rifles, such as this .58 caliber Thompson/Center "Big Boar."

powder or Pyrodex "RS/Select" and a 230 grain .530" ball, a .54 caliber Hawken with a 28-inch barrel can produce about 1,700 f.p.s., with nearly 1,400 ft. lbs. of energy. At 100 yards, it can hit a bull elk with around 525 ft. lbs. of knockdown energy.

To serious elk hunters, the best advice is: leave the patched round ball rifles to those who seek the ultimate challenge of getting a bull within 30 to 50 yards before pulling the trigger. Those who want to take full advantage of the special muzzleloader elk hunts, and who demand all the punch a muzzleloading big game rifle can muster, should concentrate on rifles that can handle the heavy lead conical or saboted bullets. When hunting elk, I tend to favor saboted bullets of around 300 grains. When loaded ahead of 100 grins of Pyrodex "Select", a saboted 300 grain bullet will leave the muzzle of a 24-inch barreled in-line percussion rifle at about 1,600 f.p.s., generating around 1,700 ft. lbs. of muzzle energy. At 50 yards the same bullet is good for around 1,475 ft. lbs. of energy, and has more than 1,300 ft. lbs. at 100 yards. Even at 150 yards, a modern jacketed

or all-copper 300 grain slug can still drive home with close to 1,200 ft. lbs. of energy, or about four times the energy of a patched round ball fired with the same amount of powder from a .50 caliber rifle at 100 yards.

When hunting elk during the rut, patient hunters will find that shots well inside 100 yards can be quite common. Several seasons back, I was hunting the rut in one of Utah's special Posted Hunting Units. During the first three days, at least four 6x6 bulls tempted me with 150-yard shots. I was shooting a .50 caliber Knight MK-95 Magnum Elite, loaded with 100 grains of Pyrodex "Select" and a saboted 300 grain Barnes all-copper Expander-MZ. On the fourth morning, a large, elderly 6x6 elk presented the opportunity we were looking for. A bull had answered the cow calls made by my guide, Fred John. Scrambling to the edge of a high meadow, we dropped down next to a big aspen. Fred called once more and the bull answered back immediately. A few minutes later, we watched as the bull and seven or eight cows eased into an aspen thicket several hundred yards away. Fred called again, whereupon the bull came

Big heavy conical bullets, such as the Thompson/Center "Maxi Hunter" bullets, deliver massive energy levels for bringing down game as large as a bull elk.

Most experienced black powder hunters feel that a good expanding bullet, such as the Black Belt Bullet from Big Bore Express, delivers superior performance on game as large as elk.

walking into the open and bugled. My guide answered back with a low squeal on his bugle tube, ending with a series of chuckles. The big bull came on at a hard stiff-legged walk, ready to take on the bull he thought had invaded his territory. At about 50 yards, the big animal turned broadside, offering the perfect shot. I held just to the rear of the shoulder and squeezed back on the trigger. The shot was perfect. The all-copper bullet opened completely upon impact and the solid copper base kept pushing the expanded bullet on through both lungs and the opposite rib cage before coming to rest on the other side. Every ounce of energy had been transferred to the target and the 900-pound bull staggered less than 50 yards before dropping.

The following year, I managed to take another fine 6x6 bull on the same ridge, shooting one of

the .50 caliber Knight D.I.S.C. rifles loaded with two 50 grain Pyrodex Pellets and a saboted 300 grain Barnes Expander-MZ. My 15-yard shot dropped the bull right in his tracks. On the same hunt, outdoor writer John Zent also took a good 6x6 bull at just over 150 yards, shooting two of the 50 grain pellets and a 325 grain Barnes Expander-MZ out of his .54 caliber Knight MK-95 Magnum Elite rifle. The bull traveled just 20 yards after being hit through both lungs. Now, that's performance.

As this book is being written, Colorado still does not allow the use of saboted bullets during its special muzzleloader elk season. The traditionally-minded state muzzleloading organization there has kept muzzleloading somewhat in the Dark Ages, and no one at the Division of Wildlife knows anything apparently about muzzleloader ballistics or the efficiency of projectiles. They could end unnecessary game loss by legalizing saboted jacketed and all-copper bullets and making it illegal to use the patched round ball. Where regulations prohibit the use of saboted bullets, the heavy lead, bore-sized conicals deliver knockdown power superior to that of patched round balls. Big bullets like the 385 grain Hornady Great Plains bullet or the Buffalo Bullet Company soft lead conical of the same weight and design for the .50 caliber rifles, or the huge 540 grain Maxi-Hunter for the .54 caliber from Thompson/Center, for example, all hit with authority. But getting these big hunks of lead rolling at acceptable velocities calls for quantum amounts of powder.

The owner's manual accompanying each Thompson/Center muzzleloading rifle lists 120 grains of FFg black powder as a "maximum" powder charge behind the big 540 grain Maxi-Hunter bullet in a .54 caliber rifle. This load produces only 1,396 f.p.s., but it's still good for 2,337 ft. lbs. of energy. At a hundred yards, it can down a bull elk with more than 1,400 ft. lbs. of energy left over. And for the .50 caliber rifle, Thompson/Center offers a 470 grain Maxi-Hunter. With a recommended maximum powder charge of 100 grains of FFg black powder, this bullet leaves the muzzle of a 28-inch Hawken barrel at 1,416 f.p.s., with 2,093 ft. lbs. of energy.

When choosing a hunting projectile for large game, such as the elk, two opposing schools of thought emerge. The most popular one is that a bullet, to be really effective, must expand and transfer energy. The other side argues that the best performance is produced by big, heavy flat point bullets designed specifically to prevent expansion. Al Marion, a respected black powder authority from Walla Walla, Washington, strongly defends the use of special hard-cast heavy bullets for punching through heavy bones and the vitals of

This hunter used seductive cow calls to talk an old bull to within 20 yards for an easy shot with his modern in-line percussion rifle.

a big bull for a clean kill. He contends that practically all expanding bullets give inferior performance by producing large wound cavities within the first six inches of impact, then quickly tapering to little more than bullet diameter. He has designed two hard lead bullets featuring large, flat frontal areas that he claims make a more effective wound channel than do expanding soft lead conical or saboted jacketed or all-cooper bullets. Al Marion's bullets, known as the C&D Harvester (located in Hopkinsville, Kentucky) hard cast bullets, are designed to be shot with C&D's own E-Z Load sabots.

During Al Marion's penetration tests, he found that when loaded with a 100 grain charge of GOEX FFg black powder, a 335 grain Harvester hard cast bullet would penetrate ballistics clay a full 46", while the heavier 422 grain projectile plowed through 61" of the clay compound. By comparison, the 300 grain Barnes Expander-MZ penetrated just 17 1/2". Morgan Freeman, a veterinarian from Utah, is a firm believer in the performance of flat-nosed hard cast bullets. He took a 330-class bull with a 330 grain Harvester bullet that broke both shoulders and left a wound channel two inches wide through the lungs. Proponents of these bullets agree they can take elk-sized game effectively whether they are shot broadside or from any frontal or rear angle, as long as the angle of the shot takes the bullet through vital organs.

This chapter would not be complete without sharing some thoughts on flat-nosed hard cast bullets. I prefer the expanding bullet and find the saboted bullets far superior to anything else. It's difficult to beat a well-designed bullet like the 300 grain Speer jacketed soft-point flat-nose bullet or the 300 grain Hornady XTP jacketed hollow-point bullet. And now we have the new all-copper designs—the Barnes Expander-MZ and Remington Premier Copper Solid bullets—which offer both good penetration and unbeatable expansion. The 300 grain Barnes Expander-MZ I used to take that bull in Utah lost less than one grain, even though it broke a heavy rib bone upon impact and another when it punched through the opposite side of the rib cage. The recovered bullet was beautifully expanded, leaving a hole through both lungs large enough to stick both fists through. For me, there's no substitute for proper shot placement and a bullet that fully expands and transfers every ounce of energy. *But a bullet that punches out the other side and goes ricocheting its way across the countryside is simply energy wasted.*

MUZZLELOADING FOR OTHER BIG GAME

True, there are more than 24 different species or sub-species of big game walking the North American continent, but that doesn't mean black powder hunters must work up a load specifically for each animal. There are times when a lighter, flat-shooting bullet is the best choice, or when a heavy, bone-crunching hunk of lead or heavy jacketed bullet will deliver greater knockdown. But for the most part, we're talking about going after game that is either the size of an average whitetailed deer—or considerably larger than a whitetailed deer. What that means is obvious: some black powder hunters must develop two loads, one for big game and one for even larger game!

Years ago, I concluded that bringing down a frail pronghorn required a different load than the one I used to down a mountain of moose meat. A hunter shouldn't go after moose, elk or bear with a load that's barely adequate for whitetails, or so I reasoned. Fortunately, though, many of today's modern muzzleloading rifles—both modern in-line percussion ignition and traditionally styled—can deliver good hunting accuracy with two entirely different loads. One of the best shooting saboted bullets I've ever fired from a modern in-line ignition rifle is the 260 grain Speer .45 caliber jacketed hollow-point. Loaded into most .50 caliber bores with a fast one-turn-in-24 to 32 inches, this sabot-sleeved projectile is capable of amazing accuracy. When loaded with 90 or 100 grains of FFg black powder or Pyrodex "RS/Select," it can deliver all the knockdown energy a modern muzzleloading deer hunter could

ask for. However, as effective as this bullet may be on whitetails and mule deer—even big bucks that top 300 pounds live weight—it's hardly the choice for thicker skinned and heavier boned elk or moose.

Most of the fast-twist barreled muzzleloaders that perform so well with the 260 grain Speer .45 jacketed hollow-point can shoot with the same

The black bear is a popular trophy species for muzzleloading hunters. This big boar was downed with the same powder charge and load hunters use to hunt whitetails with an in-line percussion rifle.

The author shot this half-ton Alaskan moose with a single 300 grain saboted bullet.

accuracy using Speer's 300 grain .45 caliber jacketed flat-point soft-nose bullet. Moreover, when loaded with 100 or 110 grains of black powder or Pyrodex, this bullet will deliver the extra punch needed to bring down larger game. It's not just the extra 40 grains that make this bullet more suited for moose than the lighter 260 grain hollow-point. Its flat soft-nose design translates into slower expansion, so the 300 grain Speer .45 can plow through heavy bone without being seriously deformed or fragmented. The controlled expansion and deep penetration of this bullet make it a far better choice for bigger game topping 500 or 600 pounds. That doesn't mean

there is no expansion. Several bullets have been recovered from elk or moose with mushroomed noses rolled back to .600" or .650". Usually, these bullets are found just under the hide of the opposite shoulder—a sign that the bullet has done everything a hunter could ask of a projectile, i.e., every ounce of energy has been transferred to the game. And yet, that same bullet has passed completely through muscle tissue, shoulder or rib bones and vitals of an animal—a path measuring two feet or more from one side of the chest cavity to the other. Black powder hunters who argue that "pistol" bullets are too weak for use on big game have never hunted with the 300 grain .45 caliber Speer jacketed flat soft-point bullet. It's an excellent bullet for moose, muskox or American bison, but a little too tough for caribou.

The challenging part of a caribou hunt is to locate a record book class bull and then get within 150 or 175 yards of the animal. Caribou are not particularly hard animals to put down. And even though a really large trophy class bull may top 400 pounds, heavily constructed bullets like the 300 grain .45 Speer can zip right through the vitals with no significant expansion. During one hunt in the Northwest Territories, I used the 300 grain Speer to take a nice bull at about 175 yards. The bull was angling away from me, so I placed the shot slightly to the rear of the last rib. The caribou went down on the spot. Later, while boning out the carcass, we found the exit hole. It was no larger than the entrance wound and was located just in front of the opposite front shoulder. The bullet had not expanded at all, thanks to the accuracy of the rifle and a load that allowed me to place that bullet squarely through the vital organs of the chest cavity for a clean kill.

On another hunt, where I relied on the same 110 grain charge of Pyrodex "Select" and 300 grain saboted Speer bullet, I was able to take an

This caribou was taken at 200 yards with a scoped .50 caliber Knight MK-85 "Knight Hawk."

Alaska moose. My shot went squarely through the chest cavity at 65 yards, causing the 1,200 pound animal to stagger some 50 yards before collapsing. The nose of the recovered bullet had flattened to about .600". Bullets of 300 to 325 grains do, in fact, retain energy more efficiently at 150 to 175 yards than bullets of 250 grains or so. If caribou is your goal, then a jacketed hollow-point bullet of around 300 grains will probably do a better job than a lighter bullet. But if your sights are set on moose or a big coastal grizzly, you may want to work up a load around a flat soft-nose bullet design like the 300 grain Speer.

I own a .50 caliber Knight MK-85 that is a classic example of an effective two-load rifle. Over a ten-year span, this rifle has fired between 6,000 and 7,000 saboted bullets, most of them the 260 grain Speer jacketed .45 caliber hollow-point. With a 100 grain charge of Pyrodex "Select," this rifle consistently prints a saboted .45 bullet inside $1\frac{1}{2}$ inches at 100 yards. With a slightly heavier 110 grain charge of Pyrodex "Select" behind a saboted 300 grain Speer .45 caliber jacketed flat soft-point, the rifle will perform about the same. These two different loads will impact on a 100-yard target less than two inches apart. In fact, a six-shot group fired with three Speer 260 grain hollow-point and three 300 grain flat point jacketed bullets will still print inside $3\frac{1}{2}$ inches. With this rifle, a good scope and my two favorite loads, I can head out for whitetails or moose, sheep or mountain goats, with full confidence.

Black powder hunter Jim Shockey takes an entirely different approach. He uses the same rifle and load for everything, whether he's going after Dall sheep, mountain caribou, moose, muskox, pronghorns or his favorite big game animal, the whitetail. It's not that Jim feels he needs the extra firepower; he simply likes shooting the same bullet and powder charge for all big game hunting, no matter the season. Before the fall season gets underway, Jim will shoot his rifle and load extensively at all ranges—50, 75, 100, 125 and 150 yards. He knows the point of impact at all hunting distances and where exactly he must hold to put the bullet where it needs to go.

For several years, Jim Shockey relied on the Knight 310 grain saboted lead bullet for his hunting. Loaded ahead of 100 grains of Pyrodex "Select," this bullet is pushed from the muzzle of his .50 caliber Knight MK-85 at about 1,500 f.p.s. and develops around 1,500 ft. lbs. of muzzle energy. At 50 yards, the all-lead projectile is good for about 1,400 ft. lbs. of energy; and at 100 yards

Muzzleloading trophy hunter Jim Shockey shows off a mountain grizzly taken with his modern in-line percussion rifle and saboted bullet.

Not many hunters will invest the time and money needed for a muzzleloading hunt without arming themselves with the most efficient rifle and load possible.

his frontloader. But often it has flown right through whitetails without much, if any, expansion, often causing a lengthy tracking job. He has since remedied the problem by switching to a saboted all-copper 300 grain Barnes Expander-MZ bullet, which supplies the expansion needed for taking smaller big game cleanly while maintaining the deep penetration needed to bring down much larger game. When Jim first tried to make the switch to the all-copper Barnes bullet, though, it wasn't as accurate as he wanted. He discovered that his problems lay instead with an older Knight MK-85 rifle whose barrel was rifled with a one-turn-in-32 inches rifling twist—too slow for stabilizing the long all-copper bullets. The rifle did a nice job with the shorter 250 grain Barnes Expander-MZ, but it tended to throw the longer, heavier 300 grain bullet all over the target paper. The problem was cured by switching to a more recent Knight MK-85 rifle with a Green Mountain barrel featuring a faster one-turn-in-28 inch rate of twist. Loaded with two 50 grain Pyrodex Pellets and a saboted 300 grain Barnes Expander-MZ, Shockey's rifle consistently prints sub 2-inch groups at 100 yards. Sighted to hit dead on at 100 yards, Jim's rifle and load now hit just 6 1/2 inches low at 150 yards. It's a one-load rifle that is deadly on all North American big game, whether a 100-pound pronghorn, southern whitetail, or a one-ton moose or buffalo.

Caribou, mountain goat, and any of the North American wild sheep can be extremely difficult to get within effective muzzleloader range. When the hunter does get a decent shot, it's often at ranges approaching 200 yards, which is the limit for even the best rifle and load. To bring down any big game animal cleanly, shot placement is critical, especially with a muzzleloading rifle. Once a projectile passes the 150-yard mark, velocity and

it can still hit a big game animal with around 1,300 ft. lbs. At 150 yards, it will plow home with close to 1,200 ft. lbs. of energy left over. This load has enabled Jim to put more big game in the muzzleloading record book than any other muzzleloading hunter today, a list that now includes black bears, grizzlies, Alaska brown bear, moose, caribou, muskox, Dall and Stone sheep, mountain goat, pronghorn, mountain lion and plenty of whitetails.

The big Knight bullet has performed nicely on most of the bigger animals Jim has harvested with energy begin to nosedive. Once the bullet begins to slow down, it also begins to drop in a hurry, making it even more difficult to place a bullet on the intended target. Once shots get out past 150 yards, most hunters lose their ability to judge distances. Imagine a caribou standing at exactly 200 yards while a hunter estimates the distance at 175 yards. Some projectiles could hit as much as 10 inches low, resulting in a poor hit and possibly a lost animal. Loaded with 110 grain of Pyrodex "Select," a saboted 300 grain Speer .45 caliber jacketed flat soft-point bullet will drop six inches at 100 to 150 yards; and from 150 to 200 yards it will drop another 13 inches. At that distance a miscalculated shot could impact much too high or low to be effective.

Heavy lead conical bullets, such as the Hornady Great Plains or Thompson/Center Maxi-Ball, are even worse when it comes to excessive drop at long range. When loaded with maximum or near maximum recommended powder charges of 110 to 120 grains of FFg black powder or Pyrodex "RS/Select, these 350 to 450 grain hunks of lead start to drop as soon as they slow down. A 370 grain Maxi-ball propelled by a 100 grain charge of FFg leaves the muzzle of a 28-inch barreled .50 caliber Thompson/Center Hawken at just over 1,500 f.p.s. Sighted dead on at 100 yards, the big slug drops about 7 3/4 inches at 150 yards. At that distance, velocity has dropped to about 1,100 f.p.s. and gravity has begun to pull the bullet down. By the time it reaches 200 yards, the bullet has dropped more than two feet.

One handy accessory for big game muzzle-loading hunters to own, by the way, is a modern laser rangefinder. Bushnell has several models priced low enough to fit almost any big game hunter's budget. The Yardage Pro 800, for example, instantly reads distances out to 800 yards, while the Yardage Pro 400 is good for distances up to 400 yards. Both are accurate to within one yard. The hunter simply centers the target in the viewfinder, pushes a button and gets an instant reading.

Black powder hunters are now traveling to all corners of the globe after species that were once reserved for the centerfire shooting elite only. The new Longhunter Society record book for trophies taken with a muzzleloader has sparked new interest in hunting almost every species of big game with a modern muzzleloader, especially with an in-line hunting rifle and saboted projectiles. *Together, they make it easy to deliver the performance needed to get the job done—no matter what they're hunting.*

SELECTING THE RIGHT HUNTING PROJECTILE

It's unfortunate, but many muzzleloading shooters buy a frontloader for looks alone, without giving much thought to the type of projectile they intend to load and shoot. For some, the style of a muzzleloader may be of primary importance. However, if performance with a particular projectile is more important than the aesthetics of the rifle, looks may have to take a back seat to the rate of rifling twist found in the bore. Generally speaking, it takes an entirely different bore to get the absolute best accuracy with either the patched round ball or a conical bullet. Before the modern in-line percussion muzzleloading rifle became popular, black powder shooters debated over such personal preferences as type of sight, variances of traditional ignition systems, even the accessories used to load and fire a traditionally styled muzzleloader. But none stimulated more heated arguments than the projectiles preferred by the muzzleloading fraternity.

Through the 1970s and into the early 1980s, two different lines of thought developed over how to select a projectile and a rifle designed to shoot it with accuracy. One school insisted that the patched round ball be considered the only true traditional projectile for muzzleloading rifles. The other claimed to rely on the heavier bore-sized lead conical bullets for the knockdown energy needed to down big game cleanly. Black Powder shooters now enjoy a third choice: the plastic-saboted bullets that perform so well out of the newer guns. Which is the right one for your rifle? And which rifle will produce the best accuracy from that particular projectile? The following pages will examine all three projectiles, along with the rifles that perform best with each one.

THE PATCHED ROUND BALL

Accuracy with a patched round ball is based on a paradox: an undersized projectile spun by rifling that it never touches. Transferring the spin of rifling grooves to the projectile is a vitally important job of the patching. And since the patching plays such a critical role in obtaining optimum performance with a round ball, it follows that not just any material will fill the bill. Likewise, the ball cannot be cast or swaged from just any source of lead. It must be pure soft lead

Dave Ehrig (Pennsylvania's "Mr. Flintlock") traveled to Missouri to take this buck with a modern scope-sighted, in-line rifle and a saboted all-copper Barnes Expander-MZ bullet.

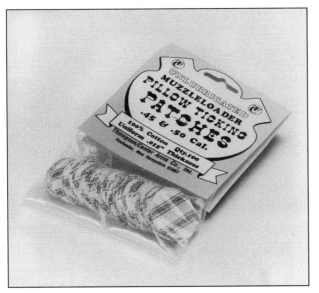

Patching plays a crucial role in obtaining optimum accuracy from a patched round ball. The type of material, the weave, the thickness and how the patch is lubricated all can affect accuracy.

in order for the weave of the patching material to grip the bullet's smooth, round surface.

The best accuracy with a round ball is usually obtained from a barrel that's rifled with grooves of .008" or .010" depth, and which spiral with a slow one-turn-in 60" to 72" (depending on caliber). The deep grooves allow shooters to use a ball diameter close to the actual land-to-land measurements of the bore while still using relatively thick patching material. This material is easily compressed between the rifling lands and the soft lead ball, while any excess material is forced into the deep grooves, providing a good grip on both ball and rifling. With a muzzleloading rifle whose bore has grooves that spin with a much faster rate of rifling twist, the ball may have a tendency to "skip" or "strip" the lands, i.e., ball velocity is so fast it won't spin properly. The faster the rate of rifling twist, the more likely this condition will occur, especially with the heavy powder charges used by hunters.

Most reproduction muzzleloading rifles today feature "button" rifling, whereby the grooves are produced by pulling a hardened button, or broach, through a barrel blank that has been drilled, reamed and polished. As it is pulled through the blank, the slightly over-sized button turns, producing the desired rate of rifling twist. Muzzleloading rifle manufacturers can, to some extent, control the rate of twist with this rifling method, but the depth of the grooves is another matter. The button-rifled grooves, once they've been compressed into the softer barrel steel, will rarely measure more than .005" in depth, leaving little room for the thick patch material. True round ball rifles featuring cut-rifled or hammer-forged barrels with .008" to .010" deep grooves are commonly loaded with a round ball that's just .005" smaller in diameter than the caliber of the rifle. Patching of .018" to .020" thickness insures a tight fit, while loading remains relatively easy. Manufacturers who use button rifling often recommend a round ball that's .010" smaller in diameter than actual bore size. This works out to the following comparisons:

No muzzleloading projectile is a brush buster. Even when shooting a heavy, slow-moving conical bullet, the muzzleloading hunter needs to pick his shot when shooting in cover like this.

Diameter	Caliber
.310"	.32
.350"	.36
.390"	.40
.440"	.45
.490"	.50
.530"	.54

These ball diameters load easily into button-rifled barrels, yet they remain capable of producing exceptional accuracy.

A thick or heavy patch isn't necessarily stronger than thinner material. What dictates strength is the type of material and the weave of the cloth. Experienced black powder shooters who prefer the patched round ball tend to favor tightly woven fabrics, such as linen or cotton pillow ticking. Equally important is the lubricant used on the patch material. Not only will a good patch lube reduce the amount of friction on the cloth during loading and shooting, it will help prevent the heat of the powder charge from burning through the patch. It will also help keep the powder fouling from drying out quickly, making fast reloading much easier.

Many black powder shops sell round balls cast from lead of dubious origin. A quick check will indicate whether they are made of lead of sufficient softness and purity so as to produce good accuracy. Simply press a thumbnail into the surface; if the nail inscribes the surface, the lead is reasonably pure. Some round ball shooters still cast their own round balls, relying on quality molds from companies like Lyman, Lee Precision and RCBS to ensure precise ball diameters. For those who choose to cast their own round balls, a word of caution: as little as two to three percent tin and antimony in the mix can result in lead that's too hard for the patch to grip. Shooters who

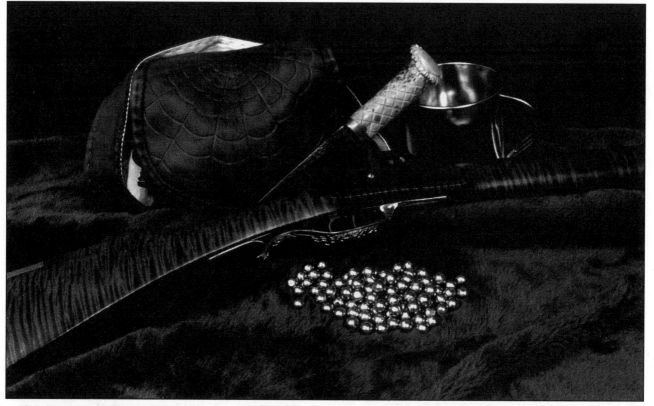

The slow rate of rifling twist common to many traditionally styled muzzleloaders dictates that such rifles produce best accuracy with a patched round ball. The rifle shown is the "Silver Classic" from Mountain State Muzzleloading Supplies.

shoot less than a few hundred rounds a year should rely more on the excellent swaged round balls available from Speer, Hornady or Buffalo Bullet Company. They offer a wide range of diameters along with a guarantee that their product is made of pure virgin lead and is the exact diameter desired.

In the hands of a good shooter, a loaded round ball rifle can be deadly accurate. In fact, it is today the most widely used projectile in muzzleloading target competition. As a hunting sphere, though, the round ball has serious shortcomings. Being perfectly round, it loses velocity and down range energy levels quickly. For example, it will hit a big game animal at 100 yards with only about a third of the energy generated at the muzzle.

The Thompson/Center "Hawken" rifle, one of the most popular muzzleloading guns ever made, features a bore with a one-turn-in 48 inches rate of twist. Experts will claim this is not an ideal rate of twist for either a patched round ball or an

elongated conical bullet, although they concede it does an acceptable job with both types of projectiles. Loaded in front of a 100 grain charge of FFg blackpowder, a 177 grain .490" round ball leaves the muzzle of the Hawken's 28-inch barrel at about 2,000 f.p.s. and slightly more than 1,600 ft. lbs. of energy. Down range at 100 yards, this same projectile hits the target with only 450 ft. lbs. of energy left over. Loaded ahead of a powder charge of equal weight, Thompson/Center's "Maxi-Ball" conical bullet exits the muzzle of the Hawken at only 1,500 f.p.s., but it generates a whopping 1,900 ft. lbs. of muzzle energy. At 100 yards, the bullet will smack a whitetailed deer with 1,100 ft. lbs. of energy.

As dismal as the patched round ball ballistics may seem, these spheres of soft, pure lead have accounted for plenty of game over the years. For .32 and .36 caliber small game rifles, it's the absolute best choice. And when propelled by light

The late Turner Kirkland, founder of Dixie Gun Works, took this Botswana bull elephant with patched round ball loads. He was shooting an original four-gauge percussion double rifle loaded with 300 grains of FFg behind each of the 1,030 grain balls needed.

15 to 30 grain powder charges, these tiny lead balls cause much less meat destruction than do the hard-hitting conical bullets. Loaded with a hefty 80, 90, or 100 grain charge of FFg black powder or Pyrodex "RS/Select," an accurate .50 or .54 caliber muzzleloading rifle can down deer and other big game with a patched round ball. At 30 to 50 yards, a round ball pushed from the muzzle by a heavy hunting powder charge maintains an energy level of 800 to 1,000 ft. lbs., which many experts feel is required to take big game cleanly. At such close range, a soft lead ball is generally flattened upon impact into a disc that's half again the ball's original diameter. Properly placed to the rear of a big buck's front shoulder, a round ball can deliver a potent wallop at distances of less than 50 yards. More often than not, the flattened ball will not exit the other side, transferring every ounce of energy to the target. The result is quite often a good, clean kill.

When loaded with a patched round ball, the once popular .45 caliber rifles are marginally effective on deer-sized game. As muzzleloading hunters quickly learned, light 128 to 130 grain lead balls couldn't produce the "oomph" needed to get the job done cleanly. Only a few muzzle-loading rifle manufacturers still offer a .45 caliber. The top choice among serious muzzleloading big game hunters now is the .54 caliber.

For elk, moose and other big game, some round ball shooters opt for a still larger caliber. Thompson/Center lists 120 grains of FFg black powder behind a hefty 279 grain .570" diameter ball as its recommended maximum load for the .58 caliber percussion "Big Boar" rifle. This load is good for 1,595 f.p.s. at the muzzle and 1,576 ft. lbs. of muzzle energy, which is actually 200 ft. lbs. less than the muzzle energy produced by a light 177 grain round ball fired from a .50 caliber Hawken rifle with 110 grains of FFg. The weight

The .980" diameter balls recovered from Turner Kirkland's elephant flattened into discs measuring nearly 2 inches across.

of the .570" diameter ball is what prevents it from developing the proper velocity. However, any big game animal that's hit squarely with a ball this size within the effective range of a round ball load is sure to go down. The Pacific Rifle Company (Newberg, Oregon), which also believes that bigger is better, points to its .62 caliber "Zephyr" under-hammer rifle. The company's recommended load of 175 grains of FFg black powder pushes a 325 grain .600" diameter patched ball from the muzzle of the Zephyr's 30-inch barrel at nearly 1,700 f.p.s., for about 1,800 ft. lbs. of energy at the muzzle. At 100 yards this big sphere of soft lead plows home with almost 1,100 ft. lbs. of energy. It's no wonder Pacific Rifle refers to its underhammer cap-lock frontloader as "The thinking man's rifle."

During the late 1970s, Turner Kirkland of Dixie Gun Works realized a lifelong dream: hunting Africa with a muzzleloader. Several years prior, he had purchased a beautiful antique side-by-side percussion four-gauge elephant rifle built during the mid-1800s. While shooting loads comprised of 300 grains of FFg black powder behind a patched 1,030 grain round ball, Kirkland took a bull elephant with three shots from that old double rifle. The recovered .980"

The big .58 caliber rifle muskets used during the Civil War were designed to shoot an easy loading, hard-hitting, hollow-based conical bullet known as the Minie.

balls had been flattened into discs measuring nearly two inches across. Few black powder hunters will ever own or shoot a four-gauge rifle—or a .62 caliber for that matter. When it comes to generating and maintaining high levels of energy, the round ball must be rated among the worst possible hunting projectiles. In general, when contemplating the purchase of a new rifle designed specifically for big game hunting, shooters should opt for a more effective projectile than the round ball.

BORE-SIZED CONICAL BULLETS

By the early 1820s the percussion caplock ignition system had been developed and was in general use. But by 1830 few makers of fine sporting guns were still producing muzzleloaders with a flintlock ignition. This transition from flint

Two common variations of the Minie bullet used during the Civil War: the standard "old style" Minie commonly used by northern troops (left), and the Pritchett bullet (right) which southern troops often fired out of Enfield rifle muskets they carried.

Improved conical bullet rifles of the mid-1800s included the Whitworth, whose hexagonal bore relied on a mechanically fitted bullet. This Parker-Hale reproduction of the Whitworth Military Target Rifle is from Gibbs Rifle Company.

to percussion ignition was swift, indeed; but as things turned out, the percussion era itself proved the shortest. By the end of the Civil War in 1865, the muzzleloader had been all but replaced by more modern breechloading firearms. The heyday of the percussion ignition system had lasted a mere 40 years, during which some of the finest muzzleloading guns of all times had been built in this country, along with Great Britain, Germany, and other European armsmaking centers.

More to facilitate the needs of war than those of muzzleloading hunters, considerable effort was made during this period to produce a fast-loading and hard-hitting elongated bullet to replace the patched round ball. Early attempts to develop a true conical bullet—one that would perform better at longer ranges—was a bullet shaped something like an acorn. Developed in the U.S. during the early 1830s, it featured a rounded base and a sharp pointed nose. Patched much like the round ball, performance revealed a difficulty to load. There wasn't enough bearing surface for the patch to transfer the rate of rifling twist to the bullet; moreover, the sharp-pointed nose caused the bullet to cant in the bore when seated with the ramrod. Improved variations emerged slowly, however, and by the mid-1830s a growing number of hunters had made the switch to so-called "sugar-loaf" or "picket" bullets. While

most still required patching, their designs were lengthened to provide better contact with the rifling. And as the bullets became longer, riflemakers learned that a fast rate of rifling twist was needed to stabilize the longer projectiles in flight. Beginning in the mid-1840s, British and European gunmakers gradually eliminated the use of a patch altogether, designing new types of rifling and projectiles that loaded faster without having to wrap the base of the bullet with cloth or paper.

ENTER THE "MINIE"

By the time the Civil War erupted in 1861, one conical bullet stood out among all the big, hollow-based bullets: the "Minie" bullet. Named after Captain C.E. Minie, of the French Army, it played a significant role in the war, with tens of millions of the huge 500 grain .58 caliber Minie bullets fired on the battlefields, accounting for more than its share of the casualties. The diameter of this conical bullet was slightly less than actual bore size, allowing the bullet to drop easily into the muzzle. This loose fit also allowed soldiers to reload quickly and repeatedly during the heat of battle without taking time to wipe fouling from the bore.

In most of the rifled muskets used during the Civil War, pressure from exploding powder charges forced the thin skirts of hollow-based bullets into the grooves of the shallow rifling. This

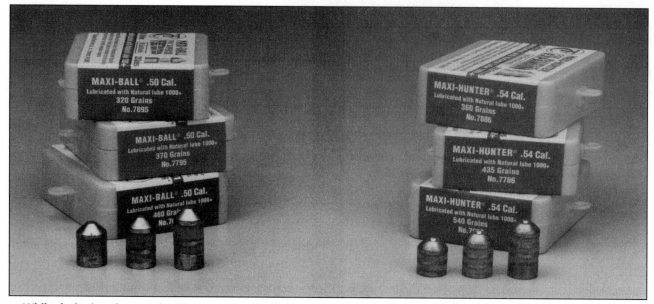

While designing the popular Thompson/Center Hawken rifle in 1970, Warren Center also designed the widely used "Maxi-Ball" (left). The company also offers a rapid-expanding conical bullet known as the "Maxi-Hunter" (right).

gave the Minie the precise bullet-to-bore fit necessary for a high degree of accuracy. Military tactics then relied on keeping a volume of lead in the air, not precision shooting. Which is not to say the big .58 caliber guns of that period weren't accurate, because many were; but rather, the outcome of battle often swung in favor of the side that kept its guns loaded and firing. A typical powder charge for a .58 caliber rifled-musket was around 60 grains of FFg black powder, enough to propel the big Minie bullets from the muzzle at about 700 f.p.s., with only a little over 500 ft. lbs. of energy. At 100 yards, the Minie struck enemy soldiers with around 400 ft. lbs. of energy, more than enough to knock a man clear off of his feet.

Despite their aerodynamic, cylindrical shape and heavy weight (around 500 grains), the original Minie designs of the early 1860s made poor hunting bullets. The thin frail skirts of their hollow-base design were easily blown or ruptured by the pressures created by the heavier powder charges. Modern high-speed photography reveals that the skirt of an "old style" Minie bullet is easily deformed or damaged when velocities

exceeded 1,100 or 1,200 f.p.s. Unfortunately, these velocities are needed to generate the 1,500 ft. lbs. of energy required to make the Minie an acceptable hunting projectile. Fortunately, today's muzzleloading big game hunter can turn to the "new style" hollow-based conicals, which perform well with heavy hunting powder charges. However, unless there's a local black powder shop available where these bullets are already cast, interested shooters will have to cast their own.

The new improved Minie designs feature a much heavier skirt, one that stands up to greater pressures but expands enough to fill the rifling grooves. RCBS, Lyman, Lee Precision and a few other makers now offer bullet molds for casting .45, .50, .54 and .58 caliber Minie bullets with heavier skirts for better performance with heavy hunting powder charges. The .54 caliber Lyman (No. 533476) 410 grain Minie is a classic example. With a maximum powder charge of 120 grains of FFg black powder or a volume equivalent of Pyrodex "RS" or "Select," this bullet leaves the muzzle of a 28-inch barrel at around 1,500 f.p.s., while churning out 2,000 ft. lbs. of

The one-turn-in-38 inches rate of rifling twist of the Thompson/Center Fire Hawk actually make the rifle a better performer with the Maxi style bullets than the one-turn-in-48 inches rate of twist Hawken barrels.

muzzle energy. Fired from rifles with a one-turn-in-48 inches or faster rate of rifling twist, the bullet has proved quite accurate.

WARREN CENTER AND THE MAXI-BALL

During the early development of the Thompson/Center Hawken (c. 1970), Warren Center was unable to develop Minie loads that would shoot well out of his new rifle. For the muzzleloader to be a serious big game hunting rifle, he knew he had to come up with an accurate conical bullet. The patched round ball had performed well from the early prototypes, true, but Center knew it would take a more potent elongated bullet to make his new muzzleloader a success. So he sat down one day and designed a bullet that became the now famous

Thompson/Center "Maxi-Ball." Its design represented the first real improvement in muzzle-loading projectiles since the hollow-based Minie bullets of the 1860s. Center's bullet was (and remains) a solid base design featuring three rifling or bearing bands, and two exceptionally deep grease grooves for holding lots of bullet lube. The bottom and middle bearing bands are basically the same diameter as the caliber of the rifle, riding easily on top of the lands when inserted into the muzzle. The bearing band at the nose of the bullet, though, is approximately .002" larger in diameter; hence, it won't drop readily into the bore. A small amount of pressure on the bullet now causes the rifling to engrave the oversized bearing band of the soft lead bullet, which is then seated easily over the powder charge with a ramrod. The "Maxi-Ball's" design ensures the bullet is set perfectly in line with the bore, while the rifling's grip on the forward bearing band keeps it in place over the powder charge when the rifle is carried muzzle down.

Even so, this precise but somewhat loose fit of the bullet is only partially responsible for its accuracy. Upon ignition of the powder charge, the weight of the bullet resists being pushed forward

The Thompson/Center Maxi-Ball maintains energy well at longer ranges and produces exceptional penetration. The expanded bullet shown was recovered from a near 300-pound mule deer buck dropped at 125 yards. The big bullet passed through both shoulder blades.

by the burning powder charge, causing the soft lead projectile to flatten somewhat in the bore. The undersized rear and middle bearing bands can then expand into the bottoms of the rifling grooves, creating a tight fit with the bore. As a result, the pressure of the burning powder charge is applied to the rear of the bullet instead of around the Maxi.

As with most modern reproduction muzzle-loading rifles, the Thompson/Center Hawken barrel features button-rifled grooves of .005" or so depth. These shallow grooves often make it difficult to obtain good accuracy with a patched round ball, but they're ideal for assuring bullet-to-bore fit with an elongated conical bullet like the Maxi-Ball. The shallower the grooves, the better the fit of the bullet at the moment of ignition. Since the length of many conical bullets is often nearly twice their diameter, it takes a relatively fast rate of rifling twist to stabilize these long projectiles in flight. Muzzleloading hunters in search of a rifle meant specifically to shoot heavy conical bullets like the Maxi-Ball should consider the Hawken's one-turn-in-48 inches rate of rifling twist. Many accurate long range percussion target rifles of the mid-1800s were built specifically for shooting bullets that often measured two to three times longer than their diameter. The rifling in some of these guns spun with rates of twist much faster than anything available today. The famed Whitworth rifles of the 1850s, for example, relied on a fast one-turn-in-20 inches when shooting a 530 grain .45 caliber bullet with a length of 1.32." A few other noted makers, notably Norman Brockway and William Billinghurst, often rifled their barrels with twists as fast as one-turn-in-14 to 17 inches in an effort to improve accuracy with the longer conical bullets.

That doesn't mean fast twists will always produce better accuracy with elongated projectiles. Truth is, some fast bores are even more finicky than are slower twists with conical bullets. The precision target rifles of the 1800s were often designed to shoot one specific bullet, so riflemakers often provided a mold along with the rifle. Rates of rifling twist ranging from one-turn-in-24 inches to 38 inches, however, generally deliver superior accuracy with conical bullets like the Thompson/Center Maxi-Ball.

Even Thompson/Center has gone to a one-turn-in-38 inches rate of rifling twist for most of its recent models. The Scout rifle and carbine models, along with the Thunder Hawk, Fire Hawk and System 1 in-line percussion models, now feature a faster rate of twist. Shooters generally find them extremely accurate with heavy lead bore-sized conicals. The Thompson/Center Maxi-Ball is available in .45, .50, .54 and .58 caliber. When loaded ahead of 80 to 100 grains of black powder or Pyrodex, the .45 caliber 240 grain Maxi bullet weight turns a .45 rifle into a potent big game rifle. Thompson/Center offers both the .50 and .54 caliber bullets in three different weights. The .50 Maxi comes in 320, 370 and 460 grain sizes, while the .54 is available in weights of 365, 430 and 530 grains. The big .58 caliber Maxi-Ball weighs in at 555 grains.

If the Maxi-Ball has one fault, it tends to over-penetrate smaller big game species, especially on close shots of 20 to 40 yards. With so much energy, the bullet punches right through small southern whitetails and western pronghorn without having time to expand and transfer energy. Often the exit hole isn't much larger than the entrance wound, causing many deer to travel a fair distance before going down after being hit by one of the heavy conical bullets. However, for the deep penetration often called upon to down big game like elk or moose, the old Thompson/Center Maxi-Ball is still hard to beat.

For maximum expansion on deer and other big game of that size, today's hunters have discovered the Thompson/Center "Maxi-Hunter" bullet delivers better knockdown. This bullet features a

The Lee Precision R*E*A*L* Bullet comes in two different lengths and weights for .45, .50 and .54 caliber rifles. The shorter length bullets often perform well out of barrels with slow twist rifling.

blunt, slightly rounded nose with a shallow hollow-point. Upon impact, it flattens or expands much easier than the old Maxi-Ball, transferring more energy to the game animal. In .45 caliber, the bullet is offered in 255 grains only, while the popular .50 caliber offers shooters a choice in weights of 275, 350, and 470 grains. The .54 caliber Maxi-Hunter bullet is available in weights of 360, 435 and 540 grains; and for .58 caliber big-bore fans, a 560 grain bullet is marketed.

Occasionally a rifle with a one-turn-in-48 inches rate of twist won't shoot effectively with a longer bullet like the Maxi-Ball and to a lesser degree with the shorter Maxi-Hunter. Too often, shooters assume their rifles won't perform well with a conical bullet, so they turn to the patched round ball without first trying one of the shorter conical bullets now available. Remember, the longer the bullet, the faster the rate of twist needed for stability in flight and acceptable accuracy. With longer bullets, the one-turn-in-48 inches rate of rifling twist is marginal at best.

The R*E*A*L* (Rifling Engraved At Loading) Bullet made by Lee Precision is offered in .45, .50 and .54 caliber, with two different weights and lengths for each. The .45 caliber REAL Bullet comes

in 200 and 250 grains; the .50 caliber is available in 250 and 320 grains; and the .54 caliber is offered in 300 and 380 grains. It features a series of slightly oversized bearing bands that are engraved by the rifling as the bullet is pushed into the bore. The longer, heavier bullets feature four bands, while the shorter and lighter bullets have three. Since the grease grooves between these bearing bands are relatively shallow, the length of either bullet for each caliber is fairly short compared to the Thompson/Center Maxi-Ball. During a pronghorn hunt in Wyoming back in 1980, I relied on a .45 caliber Squirrel Rifle (made by Mowry Gun Works) to take a beautiful 15" horned buck at about 125 yards. This light six-pound muzzleloader, which had a slow twist barrel, shot the light 200 grain Lee REAL Bullet as well as it had earlier fired a patched round ball, and with a lot more authority. Shooting 80 grains of FFFg behind the bullet with open sights, I easily kept hits inside of four inches at 100 yards.

Buffalo Bullet Company offers one of the most extensive line-ups of muzzleloading projectiles in

Ron Dahlitz, founder of Buffalo Bullet Company, began offering his popular hollow-point lead conical bullets during the early 1980s. The company now offers an expanded selection of the bullets, along with swaged round balls and a few innovative saboted bullets.

The hollow-pointed conical bullets from Buffalo Bullet Company are excellent performers on big game, large and small. The flattened and expanded bullet was recovered from a pronghorn that had been downed at over 200 yards.

the business. Among its various calibers, weights and lengths are several that perform well in one-turn-in-48 inch bores. The company claims its 285 grain (.45 caliber), 350 grain (.50 caliber) and 390 grain (.54 caliber) hollow-based, hollow-point bullets are short enough to perform well in bores rifled as slow as one-turn-in-66 inches. Like all Buffalo Bullets, this slug is cold-swaged from pure virgin lead under 50 tons of hydraulic pressure. When it drops from the die, there are no sprue marks, hidden air pockets or mold seam lines to affect accuracy. This perfectly swaged muzzleloader bullet is held to tolerances of plus or minus four-tenths of a grain, a variance better than most centerfire bullets.

The design of the Buffalo Bullet features a slightly undersized base that slips easily into the muzzle. The bullet can then be started into the bore straight with no problem. A bullet starter is needed so the oversized bearing or driving band located near the center and nose of the bullet is engraved by the rifling. Between the base, middle and front bearing bands is a knurled surface that holds a supply of bullet lube (applied at the factory).

What makes the 385 grain .50 caliber Buffalo Bullet so attractive is its hollow-point design. I had lost some good whitetails because the

Thompson/Center Maxi-Ball I used had passed through without sufficient expansion. The hollow-point nose of the soft lead conical, I discovered, produced more expansion and more transfer of energy. The bullet also ensures a better gas seal at the rear of the bullet. Unlike the Minie's thin skirt, the Buffalo Bullet is formed with a heavy skirt that stands up to heavy hunting charges. For the faster rifling twists found in most modern in-line percussion rifles, as well as a few side-hammer rifles designed to shoot modern conical bullets, Buffalo Bullet Company also offers several longer bullets. For the .50 caliber, there's a 490 grain solid-based hollow-point bullet that measure a full inch in length, as well as a similar 510 grain bullet for the .54 caliber rifle. A 525 grain hollow-based hollow-point chunk of lead is available for the .58 caliber.

Similar in many respects to the Buffalo Bullet, the Hornady Great Plains Bullet is a cold-swaged muzzleloading bullet of pure lead featuring an undersized base that slips easily into the bore of the rifle, making it easier to start. Three oversized, narrow bearing bands, plus another wider band located near the nose, are engraved by the rifling as the bullet starts down the bore. Four narrow,

The nicely knurled circumferences of the Buckskin Bullet Company conicals make them one of the best-looking projectiles currently available. This .50 caliber bullet can be loaded into a .50 caliber bore by itself, or it can be loaded into a .54 caliber rifle using one of the purple Muzzleload Magnum Products sabots.

knurled grease grooves come pre-lubed by the manufacturer. Hornady offers its big bullet in .45, .50, .54 and .58 caliber. The.45 caliber is available as a 285 grain hollow-point or a 325 grain solid-point bullet. The .50 caliber comes in weights of 385 grain (hollow-nose) or 410 grains (solid-point) and is also available with either a hollow or solid-point nose. The .54 and .58 calibers are offered in hollow-point only, weighing in at 425 grains and 525 grains, respectively.

Another company offering an excellent swaged muzzleloader bullet is Buckskin Bullet Company (Cedar City, Utah). Like Buffalo Bullets and the Hornady Great Plains Bullets, its products are swaged from cold pure virgin lead and formed in a precision die under tons of pressure. What's different is that these bullets are made one at a time on a hand-operated press. The result is a bullet of extremely high quality, and it's eye-pleasing, without the sprue mark, mold seams or other surface blemishes common to cast bullets. More important, they shoot extremely well and deliver excellent performance on big game. The company now offers a variety of .45 and.50 caliber bore-sized conicals with either a hollow or round point nose. Weights range from 260 grains to 450 grains in .45 caliber, while the .50 caliber bullets run from 305 to 600 gains. Instead of oversized bearing bands designed for a good fit with the rifling, these bullets rely on deep knurling that runs the full length of the conical's cylindrical portion. As the bullet starts into the bore, the rifling lightly engraves the knurling, providing the grip needed to keep the bullet in place once it's been seated over the powder charge. The knurling feature replaces the grease grooves found on most conicals and offers a good amount of tiny pockets for bullet lube. Buckskin Bullet markets all of its .45 bullets with either a solid flat base or a slightly cupped base, while the .50

Big Bore Express catalogs its unique Black Belt Bullet in a variety of weights for the .45, .50 and .54 caliber rifles.

caliber bullets come with a flat, cupped or deep hollow base. For deep penetration on big game animals like elk, moose or large bears, a heavier round-nose Buckskin Bullet performs well. The hollow-point version features the deepest hollow-point cavity found on any modern cold swaged muzzleloading conical bullet. This design ensures good expansion, but care must be taken lest the bullet nose is deformed as it starts into the bore.

The Black Belt Bullet made by Big Bore Express is another hard-hitting conical hunting bullet worth discussing. It also is cold-swaged, but it lacks oversized bearing bands, grease grooves or fancy knurled surfaces. In fact, the outside surface of this bullet is nothing but smooth soft lead. What makes it unique is a gas check, or Power Check, inserted at the rear of the bullet. This small plastic cup—which is slightly larger than the land-to-land measurement of the rifling— snaps onto a lead post protruding from the bottom center of the bullet. The plastic compresses easily so that the bullet can be pushed into the bore with one's finger or palm. The bullet itself is approximately .001" underbore, offering no resistance as it's seated over the powder charge.

Actually, the Black Belt Bullet is one of the easiest-to-load conical bullets available. Once it's been seated over the powder charge, the grip of the slightly overbore plastic gas check on the

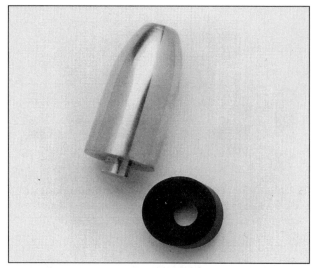

The Black Belt Bullet incorporates a plastic gas check that snaps easily onto a center post at the rear of the bullet.

rifling is strong enough to keep the bullet in place. When the rifle fires, pressure from the burning powder charge forces the Power Check's hollow base into the grooves, thus providing the necessary gas seal. Simultaneously, bullet obturation causes the soft lead conical to flatten somewhat and fully engage the rifling. Then, as the projectile leaves the muzzle, the plastic gas check drops off. This innovative conical bullet performs extremely well with rifles having a faster one-turn-in-24 to 38 inches rifling twist. In our test shots, the faster one-turn-in-28 inches rate of rifling twist consistently printed the Black Belt Bullets inside two inches at 100 yards, using mostly hefty 100 to 110 grain hunting charges of Pyrodex "Select." Because the plastic at the rear of this bullet does not envelop the projectile, it's not considered a "sabot," hence it's legal where regulations prohibit the use of saboted bullets. Big Bore Express market the bullets in .45, .50 and .54 caliber, with weights of 295, 348, 405, 444 and 520 grains available in each caliber. All five bullet weights are offered with a solid flat-point nose. The three lighter weights are available as well with a hollow-point nose. To eliminate

leading of the bore, Big Bore Express also offers a Copper Magnum version featuring a light lubaloy coating on the bullet, similar to that used on high velocity .22 longrifle ammo.

We have now reviewed some of the more popular and innovative bore-sized lead conical bullets now available to muzzleloading hunters. These and several others currently on the market give big game hunters the extra knockdown power they need to take most big game animals. Used with heavy hunting powder charges, they can deliver three or four times the energy of a patched round ball at 100 yards. With their longer, heavier design, though, comes a considerable drop at longer ranges. Before attempting shots on game out to 150 yards, it's wise to spend some time at the shooting bench until you know exactly where these big bullets hit at 50, 100 and 150 yards.

Since the introduction of the Thompson/ Center Maxi-Ball in the early 1970s, black powder shooters and hunters have come to categorize conical muzzleloading projectiles either as "Minie" or "Maxi" types, whether the bullet has a hollow or solid base. Conical muzzleloading

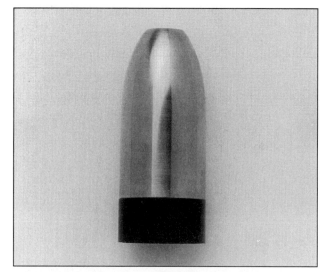

Because the plastic gas check does not surround the bullet in any way, Black Belt Bullets are not considered saboted bullets and are therefore legal where regulations do not allow the use of a sabot.

bullets should more correctly be categorized as either "slip fit" or "interference fit" in their design; i.e., whether the bullet drops into the bore without having to engage the rifling, or whether it must first be engraved by the rifling as it starts into the muzzle. The makers of muzzleloading rifles are slowly moving away from recommending the loading and shooting of "slip fit" bullet designs. It doesn't take a rocket scientist to notice that when a bullet drops into the bore without resistance it can also slide back toward the muzzle when the gun is carried down. A bullet that slides forward only a few inches can create a dangerous situation, one that could cause the barrel to burst.

Even when loading and shooting conicals of "interference fit" design, shooters should know that the bullet can be jarred off the powder charge. The bullet may have fit snug when it started into the muzzle; but lead has no memory, and once the rifling has cut or engraved an oversized bearing surface, the fit only becomes looser as the conical is pushed down the bore with a ramrod. A hard thump at the muzzle, perhaps caused by a hunter jumping from a log, steep bank or other obstacle, can easily dislodge a loose-fitting projectile from the powder charge. The lesson is simple: when hunting with bore-sized lead conical bullets, stop several times during the course of the hunt to slip the cap from the nipple, drop your ramrod down the bore, and check to make sure the bullet hasn't moved forward.

SABOTED BULLETS

Modern technology continues to play a leading role as blackpowder hunters try to make their frontloading rifles perform more like a modern centerfire rifle. The fast lock time, improved ignition and high quality barrels found on today's modern in-line percussion rifles have set new standards for muzzle-loaded hunting rifle accuracy.

Today's black powder shooter has three choices of projectiles: the round ball, the bore-sized lead conical, or the modern saboted bullet. Hornady Manufacturing packages all three.

Equally significant are the advanced plastic-saboted bullets preferred by modern in-line rifle shooters. Just as William "Tony" Knight worked to perfect his now widely accepted MK-85 in-line percussion muzzleloading rifle, another enterprising black powder shooter named Del Ramsey was finishing years of searching for the perfect muzzleloading hunting projectile. Owner and operator of a small plastic molding operation near Harrison, Arkansas, Ramsey had spent years testing a wide range of commercially available and custom molded muzzleloader projectiles in his frontloading hunting rifles. Eventually, he turned his attention to a wide range of modern jacketed handgun bullets offered by more than a dozen bullet makers. Speer, Hornady, Sierra, Nosler, Barnes and others all offered a wide range of .38/.357, .44 and .45 caliber bullets designed, for the most part, to expand and transfer energy at velocities not all that different from velocities produced by .45, .50 and .54 caliber muzzleloading hunting rifles. In 1985, Ramsey established Muzzleload Magnum Products and began marketing small plastic sabots that allowed black powder shooters to load and shoot these bullets from muzzleloading rifles. His concept has done as

Del Ramsey, owner of Muzzleload Magnum Products, is the mastermind behind the use of saboted bullets in muzzleloading big game rifles. He's shown here with an outstanding Arkansas buck taken with a saboted bullet.

much as the modern in-line percussion rifle in revolutionizing the sport of muzzleloading.

Today's saboted handgun bullets offer muzzleloading hunters the most versatile projectile system available. Del Ramsey's plastic sabots allow hunters to load a .50 or .54 caliber big game rifle with several hundred different bullet brands, weights and designs. The selection runs from lightweight bullets of 180 grains to heavy powerhouses of more than 600 grains. This variety allows hunters to tailor their loads according to the game being hunted. A small southern whitetail obviously doesn't require the same punch needed to down an Alaskan brown bear. One way to look at the plastic sabot is to think of it as similar to a modern patch. Its role is basically the same. The sabot, made of an extremely tough plastic, holds the undersized

projectile and transfers the spin of the rifling to the bullet. The fit of the bullet in the sabot—and the fit of the sabot in the bore—are critical for optimum accuracy and performance. Ramsey's company and a number of other makers now offer a variety of plastic sabots that enable shooters to experiment with different sabot and bullet combinations in an effort to find the load that performs best with a particular rifle.

Unlike the patched round ball, saboted bullets turn in their best performance when fired from rifles with a fast one-turn-in-20 to 38 inches. The modern handgun bullets are still cylindrical projectiles, requiring more spin for proper stabilization in flight. When loaded into the bore of a muzzleloader, the petals, or sleeves, of a one-piece sabot compress, gripping the bullet tightly,

Thompson/Center's three-piece Break-O-Way sabot is shown loaded with a 275 grain Hornady XTP jacketed hollow-point.

while at the same time compressing slightly into the grooves of the rifling. The fit of a bullet and sabot in the bore needs to be snug, but not too tight. Bullet/sabot combinations that fit properly are usually pushed into the bore with a slight pressure on the bullet nose with the palm of the hand. Once started, the saboted bullet slides down the bore with only a reasonable amount of pressure on the ramrod. The one-piece plastic sabots from Del Ramsey's company and a few others feature a deeply cupped base, similar to the hollow base of a Minie bullet from the Civil War era. When the powder charge fires, pressure from the burning gasses expand the plastic base into the rifling grooves. Rifling deeper than .006" often allows some pressure to escape around the outside of the sabot, causing accuracy to suffer.

Thompson/Center Arms has taken a slightly different approach with its three-piece "Break-O-Way" sabot. It involves two plastic sabot sleeves locked together at the base with a doughnut-shaped wool felt ring or wad. In its assembly, the two plastic halves are placed around a .44 caliber (.429" or .430" diameter) pistol bullet. The felt

ring is then slipped over an extension at the base of each half, whereupon the assembled sabot and bullet enter the bore together. As the sabot and bullet leave the muzzle, pressure exerted by the burning powder charge causes the plastic sleeves to disengage from the heavier bullet. The sabot then breaks away from the projectile within inches of the muzzle. When a one-piece sabot and bullet leave the muzzle, the pliable plastic petals peel back and away from the bullet, allowing it to continue on to the target. Separation of sabot from bullet takes place within inches of the muzzle.

Several makers of one-piece plastic sabots offer a variety of sabots for the same caliber. Muzzleload Magnum Products packages a blue sabot for loading .38/.357 bullets in a .45 caliber. It also offers a tan sabot for loading slightly larger 10mm or .40 caliber handgun bullets in the same caliber muzzleloader. For the .50 caliber, a green sabot (for .44 caliber bullets) and a black sabot (for loading and shooting .45 caliber bullets) are available. The company also offers white sabots for use with .44 bullets, red sabots for loading .45 bullets, and a purple sabot for loading a .50 caliber handgun bullet into a .54 caliber rifle.

Plastic sabots allow the black powder shooter to load and hunt with a wide range of modern bullet designs, including this 260 grain Speer jacketed .45 hollow-point.

The introduction of the plastic sabots during the mid-1980s did as much to revolutionize muzzleloading as the modern in-line rifle. The plastic sleeves enable the black powder hunter to load a wide variety of bullets.

Experienced saboted bullet shooters realize that more often than not their rifles will shoot more accurately when loaded with a bullet that's closer to the bore size of the rifle. In other words, a .45 rifle performs best with a .40 caliber bullet, a .50 caliber rifle shoots more accurately with a .45 caliber bullet, and a .54 turns in tighter groups when loaded with a saboted .50 caliber bullet. That's not always the case with a given rifle, but a growing number of saboted bullet shooters are making the switch to the larger diameter bullets and sabots because of the improved accuracy. As a rule, a .45 caliber bullet of .451" diameter in a black sabot made by Muzzleload Magnum Products doesn't load into a .50 caliber muzzleloader with any more difficulty than does a .44 bullet of .429" diameter in a green sabot. Sabot makers have sized the cup and petals that fit alongside the cylindrical bullets accordingly. Why does the larger diameter bullet tend to turn in the best accuracy? The answer lies in the thickness of the plastic between the bullet and bore. The thinner sleeves or petals of the black .50 caliber sabot are more pliable than the slightly heavier petals of the green sabot. The sabot simply peels away from the bullet quicker, with less time

to alter bullet flight once sabot and bullet both leave the muzzle.

The effect of a heavy sabot is even more evident with the .54 caliber. Tests with Del Ramsey's white sabots (.44 caliber bullets), red sabots (.45 caliber bullets) and purple sabots (.50 caliber bullets) reveal that optimum accuracy is achieved with larger diameter bullets and thinner plastic sleeves. In fact, recovered sabots also indicate that the heavier sabots tend to stay with the bullets longer. Most of the thin-sleeved purple sabots lay on the ground about five yards in front of the muzzle. The slightly heavier red sabots generally traveled another two to three yards, while the still heavier white sabots were found nearly ten yards from the muzzle.

The most popular among today's modern in-line rifle shooters is definitely the .50 caliber. The selection of .44 and .45 caliber handgun bullets that can be fired from a half-inch bore is truly amazing. These same bullets can, of course, be fired with a sabot from a .54 caliber rifle as well; but it takes a heavier sabot to use them, which adversely affects accuracy. When loaded with the same saboted bullet, today's hunter knows that going to a larger .54 caliber rifle offers no ballistic advantage. With identical powder charges behind the same saboted bullet, a .50 caliber rifle will deliver everything a .54 caliber can muster—and do it more accurately.

Not all handgun bullets are suited for big game hunting. Many bullets available to the reloader are for handgun calibers that never exceed 1,000 f.p.s. Bullets designed for calibers like the old .44 Smith & Wesson Special, .45 Automatic and even the .45 Long Colt are lightly constructed to allow expansion at 800 to 900 f.p.s. When these bullets are pushed from the muzzle of a frontloading rifle at twice those velocities, the bullets may tend to fragment or expand prematurely when driven into

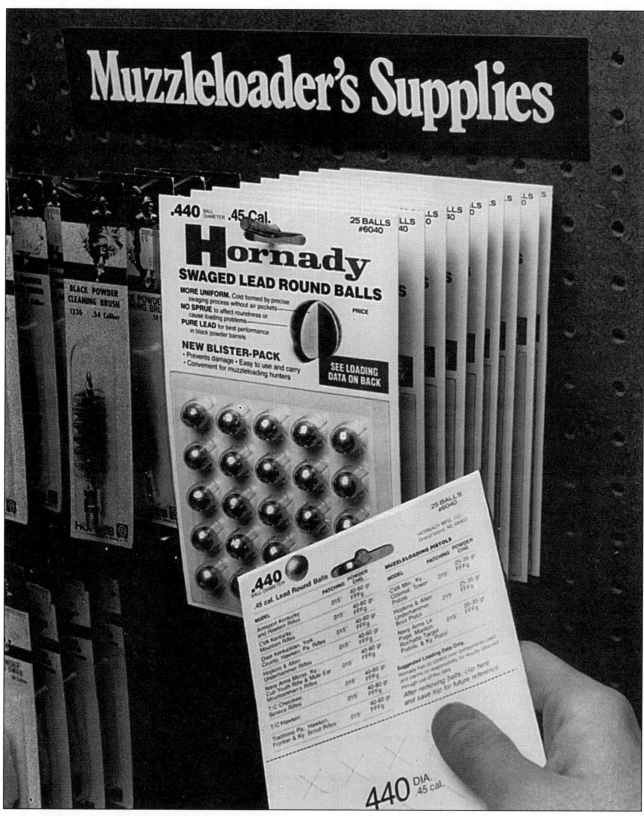

Hornady, Speer, and Buffalo Bullet Company all package precise swaged round balls in most popular diameters. The Hornady 20-pack includes loading data for many current reproduction guns.

The Barnes all-copper Expander-MZ bullet now offers performance-minded hunters a premium bullet that guarantees maximum expansion and transfer of energy.

a big game animal only 20 or 30 yards away. Once these bullets have slowed down at 75 or 100 yards, they usually perform satisfactorily on big game, but up close they might fail to penetrate deep enough to transfer killing energy to the vital organs. On the other hand, a few bullet designs are simply too tough for any expansion to occur at muzzleloader velocities. Some have been built to withstand the high velocities of a .44 Remington Magnum cartridge loaded for use in a carbine or rifle instead of a handgun. While these bullets may still shoot with extreme accuracy from a muzzleloading rifle, it's likely they'll pass right through a deer-sized game animal without ever expanding. In other words, the exit hole could be a mirror image of the entrance hole.

Modern Muzzleloading, Hornady Manufacturing, Thompson/Center Arms and a few others now pre-package sabots and jacketed bullets that are proven performers with muzzleloading rifles designed to shoot saboted, conical bullets. Modern Muzzleloading packages high-quality Speer jacketed bullets with a one-piece plastic sabot. For deer-sized game, it offers a choice of a 240 grain .44 jacketed hollow-point bullet or a

260 grain jacketed hollow-point .45 caliber bullet for both .50 and .54 caliber rifles. For larger game like elk, the company packages a 300 grain jacketed flat-nose bullet for both calibers. For the .54 caliber it offers Speer's big 325 grain jacketed hollow-point .50 caliber handgun bullet with a purple sabot. For those shooters who still prefer an all-lead bullet, Modern Muzzleloading produces saboted 260 and 310 grain bullets for .50 and .54 caliber rifles.

Hornady and Thompson/Center both rely on Hornady's well-designed jacketed XTP bullets for their packaged saboted loads. The Hornady line-up includes a 159 grain hollow-point .357 bullet for .45 caliber rifles, both a 240 grain and 300 grain hollow-point .44 bullet for the .50 caliber, a 265 grain flat-point and a 300 grain hollow-point .44 bullet (for the .54 bore), and a saboted 300 grain XTP hollow-point .45 (for a .58 caliber), all using a one-piece plastic sabot. Thompson/Center packages its three-piece "Break-O-Way" sabot with 240 grain, 275 grain and 300 grain .44 caliber XTP jacketed hollow-point bullets for .50 and .54 caliber muzzleloading big game rifles. The prepackaged sabots and bullets available from these suppliers will shoot well out of most rifles with a faster rate of rifling twist. The shooter who wants to develop the optimum load, in terms of both accuracy and down range performance on big game, should still consider buying sabots and bullets separately. After all, half the fun of hunting with a muzzleloader is taking game cleanly with a load that was custom-built for a specific rifle.

Barnes Bullets offers a saboted bullet that many big game hunters consider the most advanced projectile available: the all-copper Barnes Expander-MZ. The success of the Barnes X-Bullet for modern centerfire rifles convinced Barnes' designer and owner, Randy Brooks, that the same deep hollow-cavity principle and all-copper construction could be used to make an improved muzzleloading bullet for hunters. The Expander-MZ, a well-designed and engineered hunting projectile, features a deep hollow nose cavity that extends nearly one-third the length of the bullet. Upon impact, the nose peels back into six separate, razor-edged petals, turning the animals' internal organs to mush while transferring energy much more efficiently than a mushroomed lead or jacketed bullet. The all-copper construction and unique design of the Barnes product allows it to expand fully at velocities well under 1,000 f.p.s., yet holds together when pushed along at velocities greater than 2,000 f.p.s. Even after the deadly petals have fully opened, the solid copper base of this bullet keeps on pushing for outstanding penetration.

Barnes Bullets offers 250 and 300 grain .45 caliber bullets for .50 caliber muzzleloaders, along

It takes a fast rifling twist to stabilize this long saboted spitzer boat tail bullet from Buffalo Bullet Company.

with saboted 275 and 325 grain .50 caliber Expander-MZ bullets for the .54 caliber front-loaders. Modern Muzzleloading offers these same bullets under its "Red Hot Bullets" label, plus lighter 180, 200 and 220 grain bullets made for them exclusively. While shooting three 50 grain Pyrodex Pellets (150 grain charge) behind a saboted 180 grain all-copper bullets, Modern Muzzleloading has chronographed velocities of well over 2,200 f.p.s.

For black powder shooters who want to blend the modern technology of a sabot with the more traditional all-lead bullet, a great selection is available. Connecticut Valley Arms, Traditions, Lyman, Modern Muzzleloading, Buffalo Bullet Company and a few others all offer a variety of saboted lead bullets. A few years ago several states allowed muzzleloading hunters to shoot saboted bullets, but they outlawed the use of jacketed or all-copper projectiles. While most states have now relaxed regulations to allow the use of more effective bullet designs, saboted all-lead bullets still enjoy a great deal of popularity in many parts of the country.

Of the all-lead bullets designed for use with sabots, the boat-tailed spitzer hollow-point bullets made by Buffalo Bullet Company are the winners. This modern bullet design simply offers superior accuracy over the blunter, almost semi-wadcutter designs made by its competitors. It's also available in a wide range of bullet weights. For a .50 caliber bore, Buffalo Bullet markets this saboted bullet in weights of 225, 252, 302, 375, 435 and 450 grains. The .54 selection includes 225, 252, 302 and 435 grain bullets. The 435 grain bullet for each caliber is available in hollow-point or solid-point configuration. All are .45 caliber, which should translate into good accuracy from .50 caliber fast twist barrels. The length of a 450 grain boat-tailed spitzer bullet for the .50 caliber is three times greater than its diameter. It's doubtful that these bullets will perform all that well in bores with rifling that spins slower than one-turn-in-32 inches, and even that may be on the slow side. The Barnes Expander-MZ 300 grain .45 bullet (for the .50 caliber) is more than twice as long as its diameter. Getting these bullets to shoot accurately with a one-turn-in-32 inches rate of twist, as opposed to a slightly faster one-turn-in-28 twist barrel, is difficult. The same will doubtless prove true with the longer boat-tailed spitzers made by Buffalo Bullet.

As these bullets are pushed down the bore with a ramrod, the pronounced hollow-point nose of the Barnes Expander-MZ and the sharp point of the Buffalo Bullet Company spitzer can be damaged easily. One way to avoid flattening or distorting the fragile nose of these two bullets is to hollow out a loading tip that fits over the bullet nose and exerts loading pressure on the ogive, or curved portion of the bullet. Barnes' Aligner-MZ tip prevents damage to the bullet nose; it also comes in .50 or .54 caliber sizes, which ensures that the bullet will be perfectly straight in the bore as it's seated over the powder charge. With some extra work on the cupped cavity of the Aligner-MZ, this tip should prove equally effective with Buffalo Bullet Company's soft lead spitzer.

IT'S ALL A MATTER OF CHOICE

Since muzzleloading is now a hunting-driven sport, most of the newer bullets have been designed with the big game hunter in mind. Muzzleloading rifle manufacturers have nearly used up all avenues to make the rifles themselves more efficient, more sure-fire, more weatherproof, and more accurate. But as muzzleloading heads into the new millennium, bullet and powder manufacturers are certain to utilize new technology that can take muzzleloader performance to ever higher levels.

When buying a new muzzleloader, take time to determine which projectile you intend to shoot, then concentrate on those models with rifling designed to shoot that type of projectile. With a muzzleloader designed to shoot a patched round ball and with rifling that spins at a slow rate of twist, all the experimenting in the world won't make it shoot a conical bullet accurately. By the same token, when looking for top accuracy with a patched round ball ahead of heavy hunting charges, stay away from rifles that have a fast rate of rifling twist. *Buy a rifle that's been designed to shoot the projectile you want to shoot and hunt with. You'll not only enjoy better accuracy, you'll be rewarded with better performance—and that means bringing home more game.*

WORKING UP LOADS

The black powder shooter who wants to use the same rifle for both competitive shooting and hunting is faced with a dilemma. Very often the load that tends to turn in the best accuracy for serious target shooting won't produce enough energy for bringing down a big game animal. Likewise, a load that generates enough knockdown power for a clean kill on deer and other big game is usually built around a projectile that's not allowed during sanctioned matches, or which may shoot accurately enough for hunting but isn't quite good enough to walk away with top honors during competition. Fortunately, some rifles are versatile enough to be completely re-sighted with two entirely different loads.

In this book we've discussed so far the types of rifling required to get the best accuracy from either a patched round ball, a more powerful conical bullet, or from a saboted bullet. As you'll recall, the patched round ball generally shoots most accurately from a bore that's rifled with .008" to .010" grooves, spiraling at a slow one-turn-in-60 to 72 inches (for

.50 caliber and larger bores). The bore that produces the best accuracy with a heavier, longer and more powerful conical hunting bullet will usually feature shallow grooves of around .005" depth and which spin at a much faster rate of one-turn-in-20 to 38 inches.

All the experimenting in the world with different conical bullets, bore-sized or saboted, plus varying powder charges, most often will not make a slow twist "round ball" barrel shoot an elongated bullet with enough accuracy for either hunting or target use. Many shooters who have switched to one of the fast-twist modern in-line percussion rifles, or one of the traditionally styled "hybrids" featuring a fast-twist barrel for better accuracy with saboted bullets, have discovered that reduced powder charges result in great accuracy with a patched round ball. Many modern in-line percussion rifles, such as the Knight MK-85, Remington 700ML, Thompson/Center FireHawk and Connecticut Valley Arms Apollo shoot saboted 240 to 300 grain bullets with authority

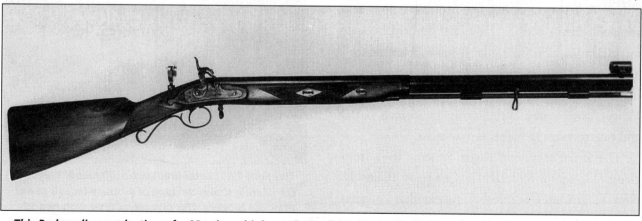

This Pedersoli reproduction of a Mortimer high-grade English target rifle features a fast twist. It shoots well with both elongated conical bullets and some saboted bullets.

Instruction manuals accompanying most new rifles give shooters suggested starting loads. Only time spent at the shooting bench will reward the shooter with the most accurate load for his rifle.

when stuffed with 90 to 110 grains of FFg black powder or Pyrodex "RS/Select." With a lighter 30 or 40 grains of powder (often FFFg or Pyrodex "P"), the same fast twist rifles will shoot a patched round ball with unbelievable accuracy.

Unfortunately, many matches sanctioned by the National Muzzle Loading Rifle Association will not permit the use of a modern in-line percussion ignition system. Those traditionally styled side-hammer rifles featuring fast-twist conical barrels can live a dual life, however, as big game hunting rifles loaded with conical bullets and heavy powder charges, or as accurate target rifles loaded with lighter powder charges and patched round balls. Two excellent examples of a "traditional-modern hybrid" muzzleloading rifle are the Lyman "Deerstalker," built with a 21-inch barrel and a fast one-turn-in-24 inches rate of rifling twist, and the Connecticut Valley Arms' "Grey Wolf," with its 26-inch barrel and one-turn-in-32 inches rate of twist.

The Interchangeable Barrel System (IBS) from Green Mountain Rifle Barrel Company (Conway, New Hampshire) is a handy system that converts half-stock rifles like the Thompson/Center Hawken into one of the most versatile muzzleloaders the

black powder shooter can own. The IBS barrels permit the switch from a true slow-twist, round ball barrel to a much faster rate of twist with a conical bullet barrel in a matter of seconds. With the Hawken's hooked breech system, the factory barrel can be removed simply by tapping out the wedge that holds the barrel to the stock assembly, then lifting the barrel from the recessed tang at the rear of the barrel channel. A Green Mountain IBS barrel can then be dropped back in place just as quickly. This system allows owners of reproduction Hawken rifles to install custom-quality barrels on their muzzleloaders for a fraction of the cost involved in buying a true custom barrel. Green Mountain round ball barrels, which are used by top competitors, feature relatively deep .008" grooves. The company recently offered the IBS round ball barrels in a choice of .32, .50 and .54 caliber. Two larger bores come with a slow one-turn-in-70 inches rate of rifling twist, while the smaller bore .32 has a one-turn-in-48 inches rate of twist.

The most accurate target loads developed for these guns often require shooting a round ball that's .005" smaller than actual bore size, and patching that

This tight 1¼" cluster fired with a .50 caliber Knight D.I.S.C. rifle shows the type of accuracy today's newer rifles can produce. This group was fired with two 50 grain Pyrodex Pellets, a saboted 260 grain Speer jacketed hollow point, and shotgun primer ignition.

The one-turn-in-48 inches rate of twist in the barrel of this custom .45 caliber Thompson/Center Hawken shoots well with a conical, but not a round ball. The Interchangeable Barrel System from Green Mountain Rifle Barrel Company allows the Hawken rifle shooter to switch to appropriate barrels for patched round balls or modern saboted bullets.

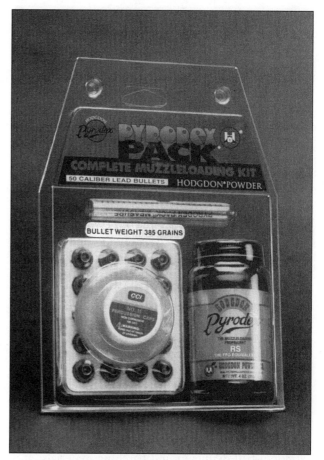

This starter kit from Hodgdon Powder Company includes all the loading components a beginner needs to start shooting a new rifle.

ball with .010" to .015" thick patching. Formal target competition often provides the shooter with a loading bench, with plenty of room for laying out a wide variety of loading accessories. Nylon starters enable competitors to force an extremely tight patch and ball through the muzzle with a hammer. And super-strong stainless steel loading rods allow serious target shooters to load very tight ball and patch combinations, something that's impossible to do when loading from a pouch, or while hunting in the deer woods.

To tweak optimum accuracy from any top quality round ball barrel often requires a considerable amount of experimentation. Two identical barrels of

the same caliber, made of the same steel and produced on the same rifling machine may end up shooting their best with slightly different loads. One .50 caliber Green Mountain IBS round ball barrel might produce the best target accuracy when loaded with a saliva dampened .020" pillow ticking patch and a .490" round ball, while the next barrel might prefer a .015" patch lubed with mineral oil (or Wonder Lube) and a slightly larger .495" diameter ball. Likewise, one barrel may turn in the best target accuracy with a 40 grain charge of powder, while another does better with 60 grains. By the same token, one barrel may perform best with black powder and another with Pyrodex, or one may do better with FFFg while another likes FFg powder. It all boils down to the fact that no one can prescribe

When loading and shooting a patched round ball, a good patch lube helps keep fouling soft. During extensive shooting tests with Natural Lube, Thompson/ Center shooters fired this New Englander more than 1,000 rounds without having to stop and wipe the bore free of fouling.

the best round ball target load for a particular barrel simply by knowing the caliber, rate of twist, or depth of groove. Every bore is different; only by shooting a variety of ball diameters and patching materials, and by experimenting with powder charges, can target shooters discover the most accurate load for their particular barrel.

For serious big game hunters who entertain the idea of doing some target shooting, the Green Mountain IBS "Long Range Hunter" barrels are ideal. They feature a fast one-turn-in-28 inches rate of rifling twist and are designed to deliver exceptional hunting accuracy with hefty powder charges behind saboted bullets. As with the fast twist hybrid rifles mentioned earlier, though, these barrels can also produce exceptional target accuracy with a patched round ball when loaded with lighter powder charges and the proper diameter round ball and patch combination. The grooves found in an IBS Long Range Hunter barrel measure only about .004" deep and are designed primarily for optimum fit with a plastic sabot. When loading a round ball into a .50

caliber Long Range Hunter barrel, shooters can load with a .490" ball and .015" patching or a .495" ball and thinner .010" patching. Either combination tends to load a little tight—but not so tight that it's impossible to shove it down the bore with a ramrod. Thanks to the fast twist of these Green Mountain barrels, light 40 to 50 grain powder charges normally produce the best accuracy. Even so, when determining the best round ball target load for any fast twist barrel, some experimenting with charges is called for, whether it be black powder or Pyrodex.

These Long Range Hunter barrels excel when loaded with 90 to 110 grain charges of FFg or Pyrodex "RS/Select" behind a plastic saboted bullet. Actually, they're basically the same barrels found on the Knight in-line percussion rifles. Green Mountain uses the same steel and the same machinery; moreover, the same range of bullets that shoot so well from one of the Knight rifles also perform well in the Green Mountain barrel.

HUNTING LOADS

When developing target loads for muzzleloading rifles, the goal is to determine the absolute best shooting combination of powder and projectile that can deliver the highest degree of accuracy. When

Competition shooters fire hundreds of rounds to determine the most accurate ball diameter, patch thickness and powder charge for a quality target rifle.

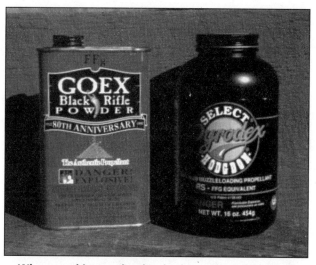

When working up loads, shooters should try both black powder and Pyrodex.

competing in longer 100-yard matches, more powder is required than when shooting a 25-yard match. Most shooters tend to shoot the same load for 25-, 50- and 100-yard competition, compensating for drop by holding different sight pictures at different yardages. Loads used for hunting big game, however, must deliver projectiles with enough energy to ensure a clean kill while maintaining a high degree of accuracy. In order for that energy to be effective, the projectile must be placed where it can do the most damage to vital organs.

As we've seen, black powder hunters can choose from three different projectiles: the patched round ball, the bore-sized heavy lead conical bullets, or the modern plastic saboted bullets. The following is a look at the advantages and disadvantages of each type and the loads required to produce enough energy for clean kills on larger game animals. Of the three, the patched round ball is by far the least effective. More than a few round ball advocates will argue with that statement, but knowledgeable muzzleloading hunters who use a patched round ball have come to accept the limitations of the round ball and hunt accordingly. In addition, the soft lead round ball, being a perfect sphere, sheds velocity and much-needed energy quickly as it heads down range. At the

muzzle, the patched round ball produces some impressive energy levels; but once it gets out past 50 yards these levels take a nosedive. In fact, a .50 caliber Thompson/Center Hawken rifle loaded with an 80 grain charge of FFg black powder and .015" patched .490" round ball (as recommended by the rifle manufacturer for best accuracy and performance) is good for a velocity of 1,838 f.p.s. and slightly over 1,300 ft. lbs. of energy at the muzzle. But by the time the 178 grain sphere reaches 100 yards, the energy level drops off to 450 lbs. That's hardly a potent whitetail killer.

Most .50 and .54 caliber muzzleloading hunting rifles can be stoked up to push a patched round ball from the muzzle at velocities exceeding 2,000 f.p.s. without creating dangerous pressure levels. Thompson/Center lists 110 grains of FFg as a maximum load for shooting a patched round ball out of the 28-inch barrel of a .50 caliber Hawken rifle, pushing the .490" ball out of the muzzle at 2,135 f.p.s. with 1,772 ft. lbs. of energy. At 100 yards, the ball will hit a whitetail buck with about 575 ft. lbs. of energy.

As the size of the bore increases, so does the diameter and weight of the appropriate round ball for the larger caliber frontloaders. For a .54 caliber

When it comes to down range energy, the round ball is the worst projectile the muzzleloading hunter can shoot. On close 30- to 60-yard targets, however, the soft lead spheres flatten quickly and transfer energy effectively for a kill.

A 128 grain .440" round ball (left) is compared to a 224 grain .530" ball. The heavier ball will hit with a lot more authority, but requires a much heavier powder charge.

Thompson/Center Hawken to exceed 2,000 f.p.s. with a patched 230 grain .530" round ball, more than the 120 grain maximum charge of FFg (as recommended by the company) is required. Even that load would push the heavier ball from a .54 caliber bore at 1,983 f.p.s., generating 2,009 ft. lbs. of muzzle energy. Down range at 100 yards, the .530" ball is still effective with 700 ft. lbs. of knockdown energy.

Unfortunately, as bores get bigger the more powder is needed to tap into the energy potential of heavier and larger diameter balls. Several years ago, Lyman Products did some extensive testing of different powder charges and projectiles in every caliber available. The highest velocity they could get from a 32-inch .58 caliber barrel with a patched 279 grain .570" diameter round ball was about 1,730 f.p.s.—and that was with 180 grains of FFg black powder. The load was good for about 1,740 ft. lbs. of energy at the muzzle, which dwindled to about 650 ft. lbs. at 100 yards.

Pacific Rifle Company (Newberg, Oregon) has built a beautiful reproduction of an underhammer percussion rifle (c. 1840) that duplicates a style of percussion rifle once popular with shooters in every regard except for its bore size. Pacific Rifle's "Zephyr" comes with a huge .62 caliber bore rifled with an extremely slow one-turn-in-144 inches rate of twist. This closely duplicates the shallow-grooved, slow twist rifling of the big-bore Forsythe rifles of the early to mid-1800s. They were designed for shooting spheres the size of bowling balls with voluminous quantities of black powder. For the Zephyr, Pacific Rifle recommends light loads of 175 grains of FFg black powder fired behind a heavily patched .600" round ball, a powder charge that pushes the huge 325 grain sphere from the muzzle of this rifle's 32-inch barrel at 1,700 f.p.s. with 2,200 ft. lbs. of muzzle energy. Still, the ball slows quickly to less than 1,350 f.p.s. at 50 yards and 1,100 f.p.s. at 100 yards. Thanks to the weight of the heavy lead ball, however, the residual energy left over at 100 yards is about 900 ft. lbs. The maximum powder charge recommended for this $7^{3}/_{4}$ pound frontloader is 200 grains of FFg black powder.

In summation, too many self-proclaimed black powder authorities are tied romantically to the past, constantly touting the effectiveness of the patched round ball as a big game hunting projectile. If that's so, why were they abandoned so quickly during the heyday of muzzleloading sporting rifles? The answer is simple: the patched round ball doesn't maintain energy sufficiently to be considered an effective hunting projectile, even when fired with heavy

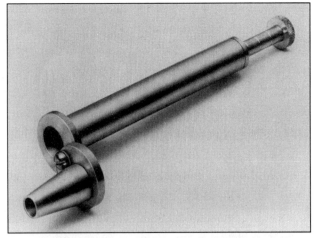

A good adjustable powder measure plays an important role in working up loads for any muzzleloading rifle.

hunting charges. Those who feel compelled to hunt deer or other big game with muzzleloaders loaded with a patched ball should think twice about taking shots out to (or beyond) 100 yards.

THE CONICAL BULLET: A COMPARISON

Bore-sized lead conical bullets have been around in one form or another since the 1830s. As such, they are just as "traditional" as many of the original percussion rifle designs, especially the American underhammer rifles. Pacific Rifle Company would find a better market for its muzzleloader if it built the rifle with a more acceptable bore size and a much faster rate of rifling twist, such as those usually found on many original underhammer rifles produced by the likes of Norman Brockway and William Billinghurst. Some of the original underhammer rifles featured rates of twist as fast as one-turn-in-20 inches, and even faster. These guns were clearly designed and built to shoot elongated conical bullets, not a patched round ball. Another believer in long, heavy conical bullets was Sir Joseph Whitworth, whose hexagonal bore was time-consuming to load and expensive to make. His rifles proved to be the most accurate long range muzzleloaders of the time, though, as reported by the British War Office. Their tests in 1957 revealed that the fast one-turn-in-20 inches rate of twist in a Whitworth bore could keep the big 530 grain .45 caliber bullets inside a 12-inch circle at 500 yards.

Bore-sized lead conical bullets—along with the rifles built to shoot them—quickly became the choice of serious big game hunters worldwide. Not only were the fast twist barrels and longer bullets more accurate than the patched round ball at longer distances, but the heavier bullets developed and maintained energy better than the lighter spheres of lead. Today's black powder hunters have a wide range of conical bullets at their disposal. Fortunately, a growing number of fast twist muzzleloading rifles

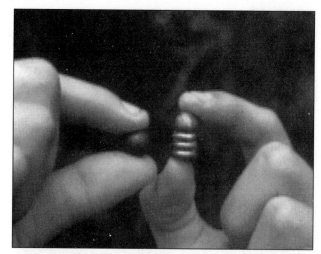

It takes an entirely different rate of rifling twist to get the best accuracy from either a round ball or elongated lead conical. There is no such thing as a rate of twist that shoots either one equally well.

can fire these bullets with such accuracy that even veteran black powder burners are amazed. For some unknown reason, a few manufacturers have retained the one-turn-in-48 inches rate of twist which was popularized during the early 1970s. A few makers offering this rate of twist still claim it delivers equal accuracy with either ball or bullet. At best, the one-turn-in-48 rate of twist won't deliver exceptional accuracy with either projectile when loaded with hefty hunting charges. As we've seen, a round ball prefers slow twist rifling, while the long conical bullet requires a much faster rate of twist.

Most modern in-line percussion hunting rifles on the market, plus a few traditional size-hammer models now offered, come with fast one-in-20 to one-in-38 inches rates of rifling twist. These bores generally produce the best accuracy with longer conical bullets. The faster the rate of twist, the longer the bullet it will stabilize. That doesn't mean a one-in-48 inches twist barrel won't shoot a conical (like the Thompson/Center Maxi-Ball) with enough accuracy to warrant its use for white-tails, elk or any other big game animal; but that a faster rate of twist is more likely to shoot it with greater accuracy.

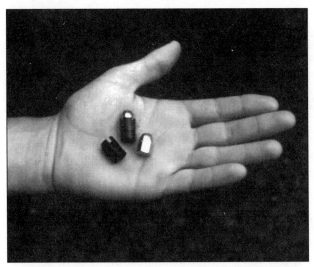

Saboted handgun bullets, like this .45 caliber Speer jacketed hollow point, are now used by more black powder big game hunters than any other style of projectile.

The added weight of a bore-sized lead conical is both a blessing and something of a curse. The big heavy bullets do slam home with authority once they've hit the chest cavity of a big game animal; but being so much heavier than a patched round ball often requires more powder to get them rolling at acceptable velocities. The added weight can also mean a healthier recoil and a bigger drop to contend with out past 100 yards. Loaded with a 100 grain charge of FFg black powder or the volume equivalent of Pyrodex "RS/Select" and a 370 grain Maxi-Ball, a 28-inch .50 caliber IBS Long Range Hunter barrel produces a muzzle velocity of about 1,525 f.p.s. and a muzzle energy of 1,900 ft. lbs. The superior aerodynamics and great mass of the conical bullet allow it to maintain velocity and energy better down range than the patched round ball. At 100 yards, it will still hit home with close to 1,300 ft. lbs. of energy and more than 1,000 ft. lbs. of energy at 150 yards. Barrel length can play a major role in the ballistics of a heavy bore-sized conical bullet. When this same load is fired from one of the shorter 24-inch Green Mountain IBS barrels, velocity drops nearly 100 f.p.s., bringing the muzzle energy down to around 1,675 ft. lbs. Even so, the 370

grain Maxi will hammer a whitetail at 100 yards with about 1,100 ft. lbs. of energy.

Buffalo Bullet Company, Hornady, Big Bore Express and a few other bullet makers have dealt with the age-old problem of poor expansion with elongated conical bullets by producing designs that include a hollow point nose. Loading requires more care but when a hollow nose hits its intended target, it will produce better expansion and transfer of energy. Some bullet designs are somewhat more responsive, while others are more finicky when too much propellant is used to push the hollow points down the barrel. If accuracy is less than desired, try loading with more (or less) powder. If the rifle won't shoot with one design, try another.

THE PLASTIC SABOTED BULLET

Anyone who is interested in buying a muzzleloader specifically for hunting big game and who demands the best performance available from a muzzleloading hunting rifle should forget the patched round ball and the heavy lead bore-sized conical bullets. For greater versatility, better accuracy, less recoil and superior knockdown power, take a good look instead at the various modern in-line percussion rifles designed to shoot the modern plastic saboted bullet. In the span of a single decade, plastic saboted bullets overcame the criticism of most veteran black powder shooters and the muzzleloading industry in general to become the most widely used hunting projectile. First introduced during the mid-1980s, plastic sabots and jacketed handgun bullets quickly became outlawed in more than a dozen states and were shunned by longtime traditional muzzleloading hunters. In their eyes, this new projectile system made the old sport too modern. In addition, several manufacturers of muzzleloading rifles stated in their owners' manuals that using plastic sabots would void their warranties. Most claimed that the small plastic sleeves created dangerous residue in the bore that could hamper loading and prevent shooters from seating the projectile over the powder properly. Still, most hunters liked the way saboted bullets shot; equally important, they liked the way an improved jacketed hollow-point pistol bullet downed deer more cleanly than with a simple hunk of lead, whether round or conical in shape.

Credit for bringing the sabot system to market belongs to Muzzleload Magnum Products (Harrison, Arkansas), which now markets a wide range of sabots for several diameter pistol bullets in all popular muzzleloading rifle bore sizes, including .36, .45, .50, .54 and .58 caliber rifles. The company also produces plastic sabots for several other makers of muzzleloader bullets and rifles who offer pre-packaged saboted bullets. The role of the plastic sabot is much like that of the cloth patch used for loading and shooting a round ball. The cup-shaped sabot fills the void between the undersized projectile and the larger bore of the rifle. It also grips the rifling and transfers the spin of the bore to the projectile. When the bullet and sabot exit the muzzle, the plastic sleeve peels away and a well-designed modern projectile speeds on its way to the target, whether it's paper or muscle and hair.

One benefit in shooting and hunting with saboted bullets is the opportunity to tailor the load for whatever game is hunted. Modern Muzzleloading,

Thompson/Center, Buffalo Bullet Company and several other companies offer good selections of different weight bullets already packaged with the appropriate sabot for .50 and .54 caliber rifles. These selections usually include a lighter 200 to 260 grain bullet for whitetails and other game of that size, and bullets of 300 to 325 grains for elk and other larger game. The shooter who is eager to find the best shooting and top performing bullet for a fast-twist muzzleloader can purchase sabots made by Muzzleload Magnum Products, then select from several hundred different handgun bullets that are compatible with his particular rifle. Speer, Sierra, Nosler, Hornady, Accuracy Unlimited, Barnes and other bullet makers offer a large variety of .44 and .45 caliber handgun bullets, all of which can be loaded with a plastic sabot into .50 and .54 caliber muzzleloading rifles. The selection ranges from light-weight bullets of around 180 grains to heavy weights of more than 600 grains, enabling the muzzleloading hunter to load and shoot a bullet of appropriate size for the game being hunted. A pronghorn antelope, after all, doesn't require the same knockdown energy it takes to down a bull moose!

For both .50 and .54 caliber rifles, Muzzleload Magnum Products offers several different sabots. For the .50 caliber bore, the company makes a green sabot for shooting .44 (.429") bullets and a black sabot for shooting .45 (.451") bullets. For the .54

Markesbery Muzzleloaders' line of semi-traditional in-line rifles are now offered with a choice of No. 11 percussion cap or small rifle primer ignition. The "Black Bear" shown was designed to shoot hot 150 grain Pyrodex Pellet powder charges.

caliber, they offer white sabots for loading .44 pistol bullets and red sabots for shooting .45 bullets, plus a purple sabot for using one of the big .50 caliber jacketed handgun bullets in a .54 caliber rifle. When looking for top accuracy, concentrate on those combinations of sabot and bullet which utilize a projectile closest to the actual bore size of the rifle. In most cases, this means a saboted .45 caliber bullet will shoot more accurately out of a .50 caliber rifle, and a .50 caliber bullet and sabot will deliver top accuracy from a .54 caliber rifle. Then why do so many bullet makers package saboted .44 caliber bullets for both the .50 and .54 caliber rifles? A good question, for which there is no logical answer.

Over the years, I have fired more than 12,000 plastic sabots and bullets through dozens of different fast-twist barrels. I discovered early on that most rifles work best with the largest diameter projectile and sabot combination that can be loaded into a frontloader. Recovered sabots, we learned, tell the story. When shooting .44s with green sabots from a .50 caliber bore, the small plastic cups were found lying on the ground two to three yards farther from the muzzle than the black sabots we used to shoot

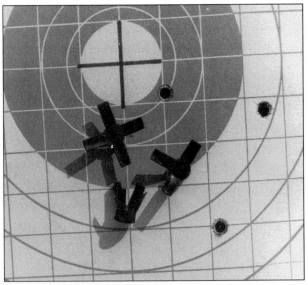

Recovered sabots reveal why a rifle isn't producing good accuracy. Frayed edges around the base or sleeves that are torn off can affect accuracy.

.45 bullets from the same rifle. Because of the slightly heavier plastic around the bullet, the green sabots had a tendency to stay with the bullet a little longer, which in turn affected bullet flight to a small degree. Assume that a rifle loaded with a Speer .44 caliber 240 grain jacketed hollow point produces a group measuring less than two inches at 100 yards. Simply by switching to the 260 grain .45 caliber version of the same bullet and an appropriate black sabot, the group usually shrinks to $1^1/_2$ inches. This problem becomes more pronounced when .44s are fired from a .54 caliber hunting rifle. Even the red sabots used to load and shoot .45 caliber bullets are extremely thick, often making it difficult to attain a high degree of accuracy. Generally speaking, a .50 caliber handgun bullet loaded with a purple Muzzleload Magnum Products sabot seems to produce the best accuracy with most .54 caliber fast-twist barrel muzzleloaders. Unfortunately, there aren't too many different bullets to choose from.

The wider range of saboted bullets available that shoot accurately with a .50 caliber rifle has made frontloaders with a half-inch bore the top choice among muzzleloading hunters. When loading and shooting saboted bullets, there is no advantage, ballistically speaking, to hunting with a .54 caliber rifle. Indeed, a .50 caliber rifle loaded with a modern pistol bullet and sabot can do anything the .54 caliber bore can do—and usually with more accuracy. Interest is growing, by the way, in the use of ultra-modern, all-copper bullets with sabots for big game hunting. New designs like the Barnes Expander-MZ feature a pronounced hollow point nose cavity that guarantees exceptional expansion even at slower long range velocities, while the all-copper construction ensures that the bullet holds together when firing into a big bull elk a few yards distant. One drawback to these big game bullets, unfortunately, is their high price tag. A shooter can purchase a 100-count box of Speer .45 caliber 260 grain jacketed hollow point

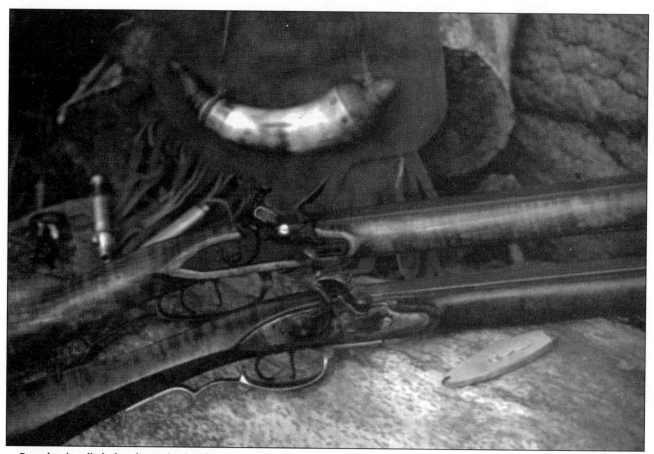

Pyrodex is a little harder to ignite than black powder, so the flash of powder in a pan may not set off a charge in the barrel. A percussion rifle with a good ignition system will generally give good ignition using either powder.

bullets and two 50-count bags of Muzzleload Magnum Products sabots for about one-fourth the cost of shooting 100 Barnes saboted 250 grain Expander-MZ bullets. If the all-copper bullets are ever to catch on, manufacturers will have to get the price down.

Another drawback to loading and shooting saboted bullets is the total absence of lubrication. As a result, when fired with black powder charges fouling builds quickly; after one or two shots, it's next to impossible to ramrod a sabot and bullet down a dirty bore. Charges comprised of Pyrodex "RS" or "Select" burn cleaner, true, but after two or three shots with un-lubed plastic sabots, fouling begins to cake slightly, spoiling accuracy. The best groups are always achieved when time is taken to run a damp patch down the bore between each shot. But

most hunters, eager to get off a follow-up shot, won't take the time. When it comes to reloading saboted bullets in the field, Pyrodex is more forgiving than black powder.

In a sense, saboted bullets offer today's hunter the advantages of both the patched round ball and the heavier bore-sized lead conical. Lighter 200 to 260 grain bullets fired ahead of 90 to 110 grain powder charges result in the lighter recoil and faster velocities of a patched round ball, while the true conical shape maintains higher energy levels down range. Many of the .44 and .45 "Magnum" handgun slugs have been constructed to expand and transfer energy at velocities of 1,300 to 1,400 f.p.s., which is exactly the speed they're traveling at 50 to 100 yards when fired from a .50 or .54 caliber muzzleloader with 90 or 100 grains of powder.

CONICAL BULLET BALLISTICS

BULLET	POWDER CHARGE	MUZZLE VELOCITY	MUZZLE ENERGY
.45 Caliber – *(Avg. 24 to 28-Inch Barrel)*			
285 gr. Buffalo Bullet Hollow-Base Hollow-Point	90 gr. FFg	1,487 f.p.s.	1,340 ft. lbs.*
240 gr. Thompson/Center Maxi-Ball	90 gr. FFg 100 gr. FFg	1,672 f.p.s.** 1,735 f.p.s.**	1,583 ft. lbs.** 1,705 ft. lbs.**
.50 Caliber – *(Avg. 24 to 28-Inch Barrel)*			
385 gr. Buffalo Bullet Hollow-Base Hollow-Point	90 gr. FFg	1,496 f.p.s.*	1,914 ft. lbs.
370 gr. Thompson/Center Maxi-Ball	90 gr. FFg 100 gr. FFg	1,465 f.p.s.** 1,525 f.p.s.**	1,764 ft. lbs.** 1,911 ft. lbs.**
.54 Caliber – *(Avg. 24 to 28-Inch Barrel)*			
425 gr. Buffalo Bullet Hollow-Base Hollow-Point	100 gr. FFg	1,432 f.p.s.*	1,936 ft. lbs.*
430 gr. Thompson/Center Maxi-Ball	100 gr. FFg 110 gr. FFg 120 gr. FFg	1,345 f.p.s.** 1,428 f.p.s.** 1,499 f.p.s.**	1,748 ft. lbs.** 1,970 ft. lbs.** 2,171 ft. lbs.*

*Buffalo Bullet Company Ballistics **Thompson/Center Arms Ballistics*

SABOTED BULLET BALLISTICS

BULLET	POWDER CHARGE	MUZZLE VELOCITY	MUZZLE ENERGY
.50 Caliber – *(Avg. 22 to 26-Inch Barrel)*			
180 gr. Knight (.45) Red-Hot Bullet	100 gr. Pyrodex Select	1,784 f.p.s.*	Not Available
	100 gr. Pyrodex Pellets	1,953 f.p.s.*	Not Available
	150 gr. Pyrodex Pellets	2,269 f.p.s.*	Not Available
250 gr. Knight (.45) Red-Hot Bullet	100 gr. Pyrodex Select	1,687 f.p.s.*	1,570 ft. lbs.
	150 gr. Pyrodex Pellets	2,013 f.p.s.*	Not Available
300 gr. Knight (.45) Red-Hot Bullet	100 gr. Pyrodex Select	1,621 f.p.s.*	1,750 ft. lbs.*
	100 gr. Pyrodex Pellets	1,687 f.p.s.*	Not Available
	150 gr. Pyrodex Pellets	1,904 f.p.s.*	2,365 ft. lbs.
260 gr. Speer (.45) JHP Muzzleload Mag.Prod.Sabot	100 gr. Pyrodex Select	1,620 f.p.s.	1,550 ft. lbs.
200 gr. Hornady .44 XTP/ T/C Break-O-Way Sabot	100 gr. Pyrodex Select	1,730 f.p.s.**	1,329 ft. lbs.**
240 gr. Hornady .44 XTP/ T/C Break-O-Way Sabot	100 gr. Pyrodex Select	1,640 f.p.s.**	1,434 ft. lbs.**
300 gr. Speer (.45)/ Muzzleload Mag. Prod. Sabot	100 gr. Pyrodex Select	1,525 f.p.s.	1,575 ft. lbs.
.54 Caliber – *(Avg. 22 to 26-Inch Barrel)*			
200 gr. Hornady .44 XTP/ T/C Break-O-Way Sabot	100 gr. Pyrodex Select	1,709 f.p.s.**	1,297 ft. lbs.**
	120 gr. Pyrodex Select	1,871 f.p.s.**	1,555 ft. lbs.**
240 gr. Hornady .44 XTP/ T/C Break-O-Way Sabot	100 gr. Pyrodex Select	1,662 f.p.s.**	1,472 ft. lbs.**
	110 gr. Pyrodex Select	1,728 f.p.s.**	1,592 ft. lbs.**
260 gr. Speer (.45)/ Muzzleload Mag. Prod. Sabot	100 gr. Pyrodex Select	1,607 f.p.s	1,490 ft. lbs.
300 gr. Speer (.45)/ Muzzleload Mag. Prod. Sabot	100 gr. Pyrodex Select	1,530 f.p.s.	1,576 ft. lbs.

*Data Source: *Knight Rifles ballistics **Thompson/Center Arms ballistics*

ROUND BALL BALLISTICS

POWDER CHARGE	MUZZLE VELOCITY	MUZZLE ENERGY
.45 Caliber Thompson/Center Hawken (28-Inch Barrel) – .440" RB (128 gr.) – .015" Lubricated Patch		
50 gr. FFg	1,605 f.p.s.	727 ft. lbs.
60 gr. FFg	1,720 f.p.s.	825 ft. lbs
70 gr. FFg	1,825 f.p.s.	940 ft. lbs.
80 gr. FFg	1,929 f.p.s.	1,050 ft. lbs.
90 gr. FFg	2,003 f.p.s.	1,132 ft. lbs.
100 gr. FFg	2,081 f.p.s.	1,222 ft. lbs.
110 gr. FFg*	2,158 f.p.s.	1,314 ft. lbs.
.45 Caliber Thompson/Center Hawken (28-Inch Barrel) – .490" RB (177 gr.) – .015" Lubricated Patch		
50 gr. FFg	1,357 f.p.s.	716 ft. lbs.
60 gr. FFg	1,434 f.p.s.	799 ft. lbs.
70 gr. FFg	1,643 f.p.s.	1,050 ft. lbs.
80 gr. FFg	1,838 f.p.s.	1,313 ft. lbs.
90 gr. FFg	1,950 f.p.s.	1,478 ft. lbs.
100 gr. FFg	2,052 f.p.s.	1,537 ft. lbs.
110 gr. FFg	2,135 f.p.s.	1,772 ft. lbs.

POWDER CHARGE	MUZZLE VELOCITY	MUZZLE ENERGY
.54 Caliber Thompson/Center Hawken (28-Inch Barrel) – .530" RB (224 gr.) – .015" Lubricated Patch		
60 gr. FFg	1,253 f.p.s.	815 ft. lbs.
70 gr. FFg	1,469 f.p.s.	1,102 ft. lbs.
80 gr. FFg	1,654 f.p.s.	1,397 ft. lbs.
90 gr. FFg	1,761 f.p.s.	1,584 ft. lbs.
100 gr. FFg	1,855 f.p.s.	1,758 ft. lbs
110 gr. FFg	1,931 f.p.s.	1,905 ft. lbs.
120 gr. FFg*	1,983 f.p.s.	2,009 ft. lbs.

*Maximum recommended powder charge
All round ball ballistics are from Thompson/Center Arms

SIGHTING IN AND COPING WITH MUZZLELOADER TRAJECTORY

Compared to a modern centerfire rifle, even the best-shooting loads fired from a muzzleloading rifle produce a rainbow trajectory. Whether a rifle is sighted in to hit dead on at 50, 75, or 100 yards, a shooter must learn to compensate for higher or lower impacts, especially when shooting at paper targets. To win any formal target competition requires pinpoint placement of shots on the target, which means they must be placed as close to dead center as possible. On the other hand, a hunter's shot can hit a deer an inch or two above or below point of aim and still go home with a freezer full of venison.

When loading and shooting conical bullets, the heavier the projectile, the faster it returns to earth—or so it seems. Actually, time of flight for most conical projectiles is about the same. From the moment a projectile leaves a perfectly horizontal barrel until it hits the ground, time of flight is about the same for a 300, 400, or 500 grain slug. By the time it leaves the muzzle, any one of these slugs has reached its maximum forward velocity, whereupon the effects of gravity begin to pull it down. Lighter bullets tend to develop higher velocities, allowing them to fly farther from the muzzle before its descent to the ground. But the time that a lighter bullet spends in the air isn't that much greater, if at all, than what one would expect from a heavier bullet. The slower the velocity, the less distance a heavier bullet travels before gravity pulls it down.

A muzzleloading rifle is only as accurate as its sighting system. If regulations require the use of open sights, a rifle should be equipped with high-quality rear and front sights.

Open sights are fine for close range hunting, but a heavy front sight, blade or bead often covers the entire front shoulder of a deer at 100 yards, making it difficult for most shooters to place a shot accurately.

Knowing the trajectory of his load and rifle allowed black powder hunter Tom Fegely to take this mule deer buck at nearly 150 yards.

These Knight in-line rifles have been fitted with good variable scopes making them excellent close and long range hunting rifles.

Such factors as the shape of the bullet nose, and the extent to which the base of a soft lead bullet flares as it's pushed from the muzzle, all have an effect on velocity and the distance a bullet flies before it drops out of the sky. How long the projectile is actually in flight, however, is another matter. Tests conducted by ballistics experts have shown that if a bullet is dropped at the same exact moment an identical bullet is fired from a perfectly horizontal barrel placed at the same height, both bullets will hit the ground at basically the same instant. It doesn't matter if the bullet is pushed by 60, 80, or 100 grains of powder. Gravity rules!

So the determining factor in how far a projectile flies before it drops is clearly *velocity*. A bullet that is aerodynamically designed will commonly exhibit less drop at practical hunting ranges than a blunt or inferior projectile of the same weight, or even

lighter. A patched round ball pushed from the muzzle of a .50 or .54 caliber hunting rifle by 90 or 100 grains of FFg black powder or Pyrodex "RS/Select" develops an impressive muzzle velocity, often topping 1,900 f.p.s. Being a perfect sphere, and therefore aerodynamically inferior to almost any conical design, the round bullet sheds velocity quickly. By the time it reaches 100 yards, the same load that produced 1,900 f.p.s. at the muzzle has only 1,000 f.p.s. left. From the muzzle to 100 yards, that ball can drop anywhere from seven to eight inches.

Pushed from the muzzle of an in-line percussion rifle with a 24-inch barrel by two 50 grain Pyrodex Pellets, a saboted 180 grain .44 caliber Hornady XTP jacketed hollow point is good for 1,900 f.p.s. Down range at 100 yards, this modern bullet design is still moving along at more than 1,500 f.p.s. From the muzzle to 100 yards, it drops only about

$1^1/_2$ inches. Even though it weighs practically the same as a .495" round ball fired from a .50 caliber muzzleloader at basically the same muzzle velocity, it experiences only about 20 percent as much drop from the muzzle out to 100 yards, thanks to superior aerodynamics and velocity retention. From 100 to 150 yards, a load that utilizes a 180 grain Hornady bullet will drop another four inches, whereas a .50 caliber rifle loaded with 100 grains of Pyrodex "Select" and a patched 183 grain .495" round ball drops another 13 inches. In other words, the saboted 180 grain conical drops around five inches from muzzle to 150 yards, while the 183 grain soft lead ball drops around 20 inches. At that distance, the modern jacketed hollow point is good for almost 1,000 ft. lbs. of energy, while the round ball hits with only 320 ft. lbs.

Heavy lead conical bullets do retain energy well at extended ranges, but their slower velocities cause these big bullets to begin dropping out at 150 yards. Once a 400 grain conical bullet starts rolling, it tends to maintain velocity at longer ranges. The problem lies in getting it to leave the muzzle with enough velocity to reach down range before gravity starts pulling it down. Even with a 100 grain charge of FFg or Pyrodex "Select," it's hard to get much more than 1,500 f.p.s. muzzle velocity with a .50 caliber bullet of 400 grains or so. At 100 yards, a load like that is good for about 1,000 f.p.s., with some 6 inches of drop. At 150 yards, that same bullet impacts at 15 inches below target.

SIGHTING IN WITH A GOOD SCOPE

Whether shooting and hunting with a patched round ball, heavy lead conical or modern saboted bullet, each muzzleloader can be sighted to make the most of the trajectory produced by one's favored load. As noted, target loads need to be sighted dead on to put each shot as close to the bullseye center as possible. With a target rifle capable of printing tight groups, accuracy is wasted if it's above or below point of aim—somewhere in the "six" or "seven" ring. While some rifles will print "dead on" at different ranges with lighter or heavier powder charges, don't count on it. A change in the amount of powder that's loaded behind a projectile can also produce shots slightly to the right or left, so the rifle must then be resighted to print dead center. Some competition shooters learn to hold slightly higher or lower on targets at different ranges to compensate for trajectory, while serious target competitors often have different rifles sighted for each match they enter.

The muzzleloading big game rifle is a lot more forgiving. The "kill zone" on whitetails and other big game usually measures nearly a foot square, encompassing that portion of the chest cavity which contains the heart, lungs and liver. A solid hit with any projectile that has enough energy and penetration to pass through this area will usually do the job. My own favorite whitetail load has long been 100 grains of Pyrodex "Select" and a saboted 260 grain Speer .45 caliber jacketed hollow point. Shot from a 24-inch barreled .50 caliber

The scope on this Thompson/Center Scout doesn't make it shoot farther, but it does enable the hunter to place a more accurate shot.

Lyman Products offers its popular No. 57 SML receiver sight to fit many of the more popular in-line percussion rifles, such as this Knight MK-85.

Knight MK-85, this load generates up to 1,640 f.p.s. at the muzzle. At 100 yards, the bullet is still traveling at more than 1,400 f.p.s. and the drop at that point is just 1¹/₂ inches low. At 150 yards, the 260 jacketed hollow point is still moving at nearly 1,300 f.p.s., hitting less than six inches low. At the muzzle, that same load generates more than 1,500 ft. lbs. of energy and retains more than 1,100 ft. lbs. at 100 yards and nearly 1,000 ft. lbs. at 150 yards.

To take full advantage of these ballistics, I've sighted my scoped rifle to print two inches high at 100 yards. So sighted, the rifle prints approximately 3¹/₂ inches high at 50 to 75 yards and less than four inches low at 150 yards. This rifle and load have accounted for several dozen good whitetails taken at ranges from 35 all the way out to nearly 150 yards. Not once did I compensate for trajectory. By holding "dead on," this rifle put every shot squarely into the vitals of each deer, and none required a follow-up shot. When faced with a 150-yard shot on a whitetail, some shooters sight similar loads to print dead on at 100 yards. Even if most of the shots are taken at 50 yards with the rifle sighted dead on at 100 yards, most loads will impact only an inch or two high at closer ranges. The slightly

higher impact on a deer at 25, 50, or 75 yards won't make much difference. For shooters who have taken the time to practice shooting at 150 yards, a slight adjustment at that distance should put the projectile straight into the kill zone.

More state now allow the use of a scope during special muzzleloader seasons than states which do not. Twenty years ago, only a half-dozen or so had the foresight to permit the use of optics on a muzzleloading hunting rifle. Today, more than half, plus most of the Canadian provinces, allow their use. Those states still clinging to old-fashioned regulations prohibiting scopes simply don't recognize the desires of the hunters they serve. When scoping a muzzleloading big game rifle, hunters should choose a scope that provides the preferred magnification and style of reticle. Any so-called "centerfire" rifle scope will work equally well on a frontloading rifle. An important feature to look for is good eye relief. Black powder and Pyrodex loads take most of the barrel before they're completely burned, resulting in longer recoil. Scopes with only 2 to 2¹/₂ inches of eye relief may not position the eye far enough behind the rear

Trajectory tables and charts provided by muzzleloading rifle and powder manufacturers are helpful, but they should never take the place of shooting a muzzleloader at all possible hunting ranges.

Where muzzleloading hunting regulations prevent the use of telescopic sights, shooters often turn to a "peep" sight for improved long range accuracy.

objective to prevent shooters from being hit by their scopes at full recoil. To avoid going home with a nasty cut over the eye, concentrate instead on models with $3^1/_2$ to 4 inches of eye relief.

As for power, many shooters prefer a simple, straight 4x scope, which for most hunting situations is all that's required. My personal favorite is a variable, generally a 3-9x with a good light-gathering 40mm front objective lens. Because I hunt in a variety of terrain, some mornings find me sitting in a treestand overlooking a well-used trail 30 or 40 yards away. In that situation, the 3x setting of a variable offers all the magnification needed, with a wide field of view making it easier to find a deer at close range than it would at a higher power. The next day, though, I may be hunting the edges of an open pasture or cornfield, where shots must reach out to 150 or even 175 yards. The added magnification of a 9x setting makes good shot placement easier.

Where regulations disallow the use of a scope, many hunters faced with long-range shooting now turn to a receiver or "peep" sight. Such sights are more precise than a simple open rear sight mounted on the barrel. Their tiny apertures, however, can

make it difficult to locate game in early morning and late evening. Those who plan to hunt with a receiver sight may opt for a slightly larger "peep" than what comes standard on most target sights. Some shooters drill out the size of the aperture, or they replace interchangeable apertures with one that has a larger opening. For shots under 50 yards, the aperture can be unthreaded from the sight, using the hole through the sight itself as the aperture. In the hands of an experienced shooter, an accurate rifle fitted with a quality receiver sight can produce groups that are almost as impressive as those shot with a scope. More than one arms expert has claimed that the best quality barrel in the world is only as accurate as the sighting system installed. Shooters should never consider the cost of a scope, mount or receiver sight as an expense, rather they should consider it the price of an investment in better shooting. Take the time to work up an accurate load, then shoot enough times to know where the shots impact at all reasonable hunting ranges. *Only then is a hunter truly ready to go after big game, confident that the lethal pill can be placed exactly where it's needed.*

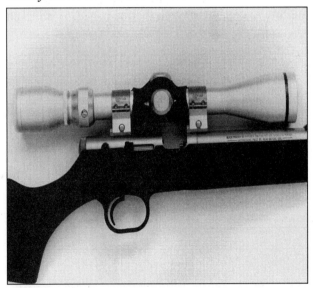

A quality scope can enhance the accuracy of any top-quality, in-line muzzleloader such as this Thompson/Center model with a scope protector.

TIPS ON HOW TO IMPROVE ACCURACY WITH A MUZZLELOADING RIFLE

Since the introduction of the first hand cannon sometime during the 14th century, shooters have strived for better accuracy and performance with frontloading guns. The subsequent development of the matchlock, wheellock, snaphaunce, miquelet, flintlock and percussion ignition systems during the 500 years that followed was driven by one desire: the ability to place shots more accurately on the intended targets. Even the popularity of modern in-line percussion rifles is directly attributed to shooters who've demanded a more accurate hunting rifle. Fast lock time, the distance that fire from an exploding percussion cap must travel to reach the powder charge, the added confidence among shooters in general, all contribute to improved muzzleloader performance. Taking this performance to an even

The refined in-line percussion ignition of this Thompson/Center Thunder Hawk is the end product of more than 600 years of muzzleloader evolution.

greater level, many shooters have forsaken the old percussion cap and have turned to hotter, more efficient rifle and shotshell primers.

Fast, positive ignition does indeed play a vital role in better accuracy from a muzzleloading rifle, but a number of other factors can and do affect how accurately these guns will perform. Of no less importance is the overall quality of the gun itself, whether or not it's loaded with the proper components, the shooter's ability to determine how and why accuracy is affected, and how to remedy these problems. The following tips represent a helpful guide to more enjoyable, more rewarding black powder shooting.

1. BUY THE BEST QUALITY MUZZLELOADING RIFLE YOU CAN AFFORD

The old adage—"You get what you pay for"—is never more true than when buying a muzzleloading rifle. True, some "good buys" will always be discovered on the market, but there's no such thing as a bargain when buying a frontloading rifle, one that the shooter expects to perform as well as more costly models. Unfortunately, price is usually a direct reflection of the kind of quality employed by a manufacturer of muzzleloaders in general. It stands to reason that a $200 muzzleloader won't have the same quality barrel, lock, trigger or other components as a rifle costing twice as much. During the late 1970s, several

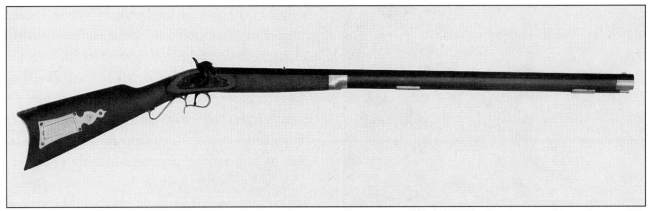

During the late 1960s and early 1970s, the market was filled with dangerous and cheaply made muzzleloading guns.

fly-by-night importers tried to flood the market with cheap, shoddy and often dangerous muzzle-loading guns retailing for less than half the price of other imported muzzleloaders with superior quality. The barrels on some of the cheap guns, for example, were made from soft steel tubing. The rifling was rough and crude, making any degree of accuracy impossible. Even more serious, however, was the poor quality of steel that was never meant to contain the pressures of burning powder charges. The only saving grace that prevented shooters from injury were the poorly designed and constructed locks, triggers and other components of these rifles, making it next to impossible to fire them at all.

When buying a muzzleloader for the first time, shooters should pay special attention to the quality of the barrel, ignition system, and trigger—the three components considered the most important in achieving good accuracy. Buying a better-known brand is a step in the right direction, but even then buyers should seek the advice of an experienced muzzleloading shooter, especially when buying a used gun. It's impossible to determine the quality or condition of a barrel simply by looking at the gun's outside surfaces. Some of the newer in-line models feature a removable breech plug that allows buyers to look through the bore. The trouble is, most inexperienced shooters won't know what they're

The bottom nipple on this "Zephyr" underhammer delivers spontaneous ignition.

Two or three percussion caps should be used on any percussion rifle to clear the ignition system before loading.

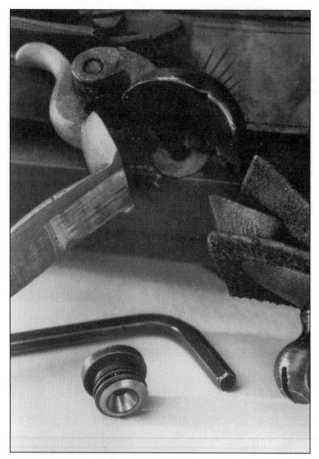

Uncle Mike's removable flintlock vent is countersunk from the bore side, reducing the distance that flash from the pan must travel to ignite the powder charge.

looking for anyway. The bore, for example, should be bright and shiny, devoid of dark spots and tooling marks. A good way to get a "feel" for the quality of an internal barrel surface is to run a tightly patched cleaning jag down the bore. By pushing a ramrod or cleaning rod down slowly, it's possible to feel any rough spots that could ruin accuracy.

The hammer of a percussion gun should drop squarely on the nipple. Don't dry-fire the gun, because it might flatten and damage the nipple. Instead, lower the hammer gently and check the alignment. If the hammer makes contact at an angle or is severely off to one side or the other, that means something is out of alignment and could eventually lead to a misfire. Potential buyers of a flintlock rifle should ask the shop (or current gun owner) to install

a flint in the jaws of the hammer. The sharpened edge of the flint should strike the hardened surface of the frizzen near the top, scraping its full length as the hammer travels downward. The result should be a shower of white hot sparks falling directly into the pan. A truly cooperative dealer or owner may even let potential buyers snap a few caps on a percussion gun, or flash a pan of priming powder in a flintlock. This will definitely indicate how well the ignition system functions. Also, when working the lock, feel for any roughness or binding of internal parts. Poor alignments can be revealed with the plunger-style hammer of a modern in-line percussion gun. Slowly draw the hammer back until it locks up with the trigger sear, then slowly lower it while the trigger is pulled. Any binding that might soften the hammer fall or slow down lock time should be detectable.

The trigger also plays an important role in enhancing accuracy. A muzzleloader built with a trigger requiring eight or nine pounds of pull will probably never reward a shooter with tight groups. Many modern in-line percussion rifles feature the excellent Timney adjustable trigger (or a close copy of one). Shooters with comparatively little gunsmithing knowledge can easily adjust the pull weight on these triggers. Some more traditionally

The burned spot on this patch indicates that plenty of fire is getting through the ignition system.

The so-called "mule ear" or "side slapper" percussion ignition systems of the early to mid-1800s positioned the nipple directly into the side of the barrel, allowing fire from a cap to reach the powder charge without having to travel around corners.

styled side-hammer muzzleloaders, especially the various "Hawken" rifles, come with a "double-set" trigger. This mechanism allows shooters to fire a rifle by pulling the front trigger alone, usually with five or six pounds of pull. The rear trigger can also be pulled back first into the "set" position, converting the front trigger into a much lighter trigger of two to three pounds.

All these components—barrel, lock or ignition system, and trigger—are important factors in achieving accuracy with a muzzleloading rifle. If any of these elements are of inferior quality, accuracy will suffer. Still other features—the sights or the feel and fit of the stock—can also have serious effects on how well a particular muzzleloader will shoot. When shopping for a muzzleloading rifle, it's important to set high standards and continue searching for the quality and features desired.

2. CHOOSE THE RIGHT RIFLING

Accuracy with a top-quality muzzleloading barrel requires shooters to load the type of projectile for which the barrel was rifled. It takes an entirely different rate of rifling twist to produce optimum accuracy with a patched round ball or conical bullet. With the proper projectile rammed down the muzzle and seated over the powder charge, the accuracy produced by some of today's barrels is absolutely amazing. But when a shooter insists on loading and shooting the wrong projectile, all other efforts become a waste of time, powder and lead. True round ball rifling features deep .007" to .010" grooves, which spin with slow one-turn-in-60 to 70 inches rate of twist. Those deep grooves allow the use of a heavy .018" to .020" thick patch filling the grooves and transferring the spin of the rifling to the undersized soft lead ball. A patched round ball loaded into a bore with shallow groove rifling, or one that spins with a much faster rate of twist, resists a proper spin by the spiraling grooves. The faster velocities produced by hefty hunting charges exaggerate this problem.

Longer conical bullets perform best with much faster rates of rifling twist. Long bullets like the Thompson/Center Maxi-Ball or the heavier Buffalo Bullet Company conicals require rifling twists ranging from one-turn-in-20" to 38" for proper

The rate of twist will determine which projectile is best suited for a particular rifle. The 1-turn-in-32" twist of this barrel means it will shoot best with either a long conical or saboted bullet.

stabilization. The length of these big slugs is easily more than twice their diameter. Slower rates of rifling twist simply won't impart enough spin on the elongated bullets to keep them spinning on their axis. These soft lead bullets must often be engraved by the rifling during loading, and all require obturation (or flattening) of the bullet in the bore at the moment of ignition for a precise fit with the rifling. Such bullets perform out of shallow rifling with grooves of only about .004" or .005" deep. While most plastic-saboted bullets are much shorter than bore-sized conical bullets, they are still conical bullets requiring faster twists for best accuracy.

Before buying any muzzleloading rifle, especially one meant for hunting big game, shooters must first determine which projectile best fits their needs, then buy a rifle designed to shoot that type of projectile. Round ball barrels with their slower twist were never rifled to shoot a longer conical bullet. Some faster twist barrels, though, can be loaded with a light powder charge and a tightly patched round ball to produce decent target or plinking accuracy. In general, greater satisfaction is always the result when shooting the projectile for which the rifle was designed. But what if your rifle simply won't shoot the type of projectile recommended by the manufacturer? Most reproduction guns now on the market feature barrels that have been button rifled, a process that compresses the grooves into the bore with a slightly over-sized hardened "button" pulled hydraulically through a polished, smooth bore. This process often results in a microscopic wire edge on the lands, which can affect accuracy. On the other hand, higher quality cut-rifled barrels found on a few top-of-the-line production muzzleloaders (and many custom-built guns) feature rifling with knife-sharp edges on the lands which can also affect accuracy adversely.

Lots of shooting will often take care of either problem. When a muzzleloader is fired over and

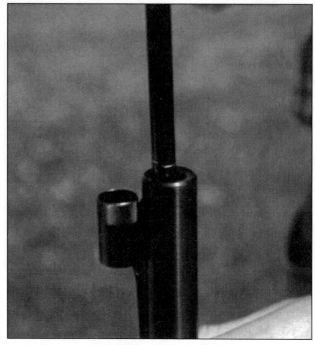

A reference mark on the ramrod tells the shooter at a glance if the right amount of powder has been loaded.

over, then cleaned with a series of cleaning patches, the wire edge of a button rifled barrel is smoothed and the knife edge of a cut rifled bore dulled. These problems are more easily diagnosed when shooting a patched round ball than with a bore-sized conical or saboted bullet. Patches that are recovered five or more yards from the muzzle quickly indicate if the material has been cut by the rifling. Slits in the cloth mean that the rifling is either cutting or ripping the patch, or that the patch material is simply too thin. Recovered sabots whose sides or plastic cups have been shredded indicate that the rifling is likely too rough or too sharp. Not many shooters will put up with poor or barely acceptable accuracy for as many as 200 to 500 rounds. One way to speed up the breaking-in period is to lap the rifling lightly. Not the sophisticated process gunsmiths use to lap the barrel of a long range centerfire match rifle. Rather, take the time to run several hundred patches through the bore, coating them with a light application of polish or abrasive. Or use a damp patch that's been sprinkled with a household scouring powder, such as Comet or Ajax.

The idea is to clean up the edges of the rifling, not put wear on the bore. Start by running the patch the full length of the bore about 200 times, applying more polish or abrasive to the patch after each 50 passes. Then clean the bore thoroughly and head back to the shooting bench. If the condition persists, run another 50 strokes to the bore and test again. If accuracy doesn't improve after the second or third attempt, something other than rough or sharp rifling must be affecting accuracy. Rough spots in the bore could also be the result of corrosion or rust. Light spots can usually be lapped out using the method just prescribed; but heavy corrosion could easily pit the inner surface of the barrel, ruining all hope of achieving accuracy. Shooters should be especially attentive to the condition of the bore when buying a used muzzleloading rifle. Poor cleaning practices by the previous owner may have rendered the bore a total loss.

3. THE IMPORTANCE OF REMOVING OIL AND SOLVENTS BEFORE LOADING

The leading cause of misfires or hangfires with a percussion muzzleloading gun is probably oil or cleaning solvent in the ignition system. It takes only a small amount to keep the fire from reaching the powder charge in the barrel. Even when the fire is hot enough to burn the solution, the result is often a much slower ignition time, or a hangfire. The lag time between the moment the percussion cap fires and when the powder charge ignites can seem like an eternity. In reality, most hangfires last less than a second, but that's long enough for most shooters to pull off target, or to pull off on a big buck at 100 yards.

Of the different ignition problems confronting the percussion rifle shooter, oil and solvents are

When using a saboted, jacketed hollow-point bullet, care should be taken not to damage the fragile bullet nose.

actually the easiest to remedy and eliminate. Before loading a percussion gun, always take time to run a dry patch down the bore to wipe excess oil from inside the barrel, then snap two or three percussion caps on the nipple before pouring in a powder charge. Experienced shooters will run a patch down the bore with the cleaning jag on the ramrod; then they pull the patch back out, turn it over, and run the dry side back down the bore. Leaving the ramrod, jag and patch sitting at the face of the breech plug, they snap several caps. Instead of throwing oil out of the ignition system and into the bore, the solution is thrown onto the cleaning patch. One or two caps are usually enough to clear the flash channel, while the third cap burns any oil or solvent that remains in the system. When a good fire is getting into the barrel, a dark burned spot on the patch will be observable as the ramrod is pulled out.

It only takes a minute or so to run a patch or two down the barrel, then snap several caps on the nipple to ensure positive ignition with a percussion

Compressed Pyrodex Pellets not only speed up the loading process, they produce consistent powder charges from shot to shot.

4. KNOW YOUR POWDER

When it comes to the type of powder one should load and fire in a muzzleloader, shooters have several choices. First, there's black powder, that odorous mixture of sulfur, potassium nitrate and charcoal that's been around since before the invention of the gun. Then there are the modern black powder substitutes, the most successful being Pyrodex, made by Hodgdon Powder Company (Shawnee Mission, Kansas). The main disadvantage of black powder is that it burns so dirty. One or two shots often leave so much fouling in the bore that it's almost impossible to load the next projectile. Loads containing a plastic saboted bullet are the most affected. The patched round ball and most bore-sized conical bullets utilize some type of patch or bullet lubricant to help keep this fouling soft. Saboted bullets, with no lube whatsoever, generally result in fouling, which turns to a dry crust, making it difficult to load a "dry" plastic sabot. The fouling itself can destroy accuracy by producing inconsistent pressures behind the sabot and bullet, while ramrod pressure on the nose of a bullet that refuses to be

The tiny vent holes near the top of these "Hot Shot" nipples reduce compression by a fired cap, allowing more fire to enter the barrel for better ignition.

muzzleloader. Any oil or solvent in the ignition system will be burned with the first shot of the day. But if time is not taken to clear the ignition system, it might not fire at all. Even if it does, a resulting hangfire could cause enough movement to miss the target completely. That's no big deal if the target is simply a piece of paper; but if the target is a whitetail, elk or other game animal, there's a good chance the hunter will go home empty-handed. Always take time to clear a percussion ignition system before loading. Even experienced flintlock shooters insist on running a vent pick through the opening in the side of the barrel. The idea is to make sure that nothing keeps the flash in the pan from reaching the powder charge in the barrel.

pushed down a dirty bore often results in damage to the projectile, affecting accuracy as well.

Black powder does have some advantages over its modern substitutes, however, the most significant being ease of ignition. This age-old propellant is more heat-sensitive than the modern powders, more easily ignited by some ignition systems. Flintlock shooters have shunned substitute powders because of ignition problems. Also, some percussion ignition systems utilize a "drum and nipple" arrangement, which threads into the side of the barrel. With this method, fire from a percussion cap must travel a lengthy channel before reaching the powder charge. The weak flame that results will often ignite a charge of black powder easier than it will Pyrodex or other modern substitutes. Black powder may also perform better than a charge of Pyrodex when loaded behind a bore-sized conical bullet. Hodgdon Powder Company recommends that Pyrodex charges be lightly compacted for best ignition and complete burn. Bore-sized conical bullets don't grip the bore sufficiently to keep a charge of Pyrodex compacted. Variations in how tight the bullet keeps the powder compressed can result in slight differences in pressures, which affects how well the load shoots.

One of several big advantages Pyrodex offers over more traditional black powder is that it burns so much cleaner. Whatever fouling it produces is much lighter than that left by a charge of black powder. Also, the fouling doesn't tend to build up as fast as with the older propellant. The burn of the second shot seems to consume the fouling left from the first, then the third shot does the same, and so on. Eventually, this fouling does begin to build, but not nearly as fast as with black powder. Some of the more advanced lubricants will allow round ball and bore-sized conical bullet shooters to continue loading and firing with Pyrodex loads for as many as ten shots without having to wipe the bore. The lighter fouling also affects saboted bullets less. In a field situation, black powder hunters who use Pyrodex and sabot can load and fire three or four times before fouling adversely affects accuracy. Accuracy won't be as good as when shooting at the bench, where the bore can be wiped between every shot, but it does mean hunters can place follow-up shots with enough accuracy to put in a finishing shot on big game.

The loading data found in the instruction manual accompanying all new muzzleloading guns should indicate the recommended type and granulation of powder. Black powder has traditionally been offered in four granulations, the finest being designated FFFFg. This is a super-fine, almost dust-like powder used for priming the pan of a flintlock. It's too fine for use as a main powder charge and could result in dangerous barrel pressures in many reproduction muzzleloaders. Most guns are loaded with either FFFg or FFg black powder, the former being commonly used in smallbore rifles and pistols of .32 to .45 caliber. Some patched round

Carefully measured powder charges are a must for consistent accuracy. Care should be taken so that every grain goes into the muzzle.

ball shooters will use FFFg in rifles all the way up to .54 caliber. The best accuracy in most larger bore .50, .54 and .58 caliber frontloaders is achieved with FFg black powder, especially behind heavy, bore-sized conical bullets and some saboted bullet loads. Coarse Fg black powder is occasionally used in big .69 and .75 caliber smoothbores but is generally considered cannon-grade powder.

Hodgdon produces Pyrodex in several grades or granulations as well. The finest granulation is "P" grade, which is the equivalent of FFFg black powder and is designed for use in smallbore rifles and pistols. Pyrodex "RS" and "Select" are the most widely used granulations, duplicating FFg. The velocities and pressure generated by both "RS" and "Select" are practically the same. When small amounts of each are sprinkled onto a sheet of white paper, the granules of the "Select" grade are much more uniform, which translates into more consistent pressures when fired and better groups down range. Hodgdon also offers a still coarser grade of Pyrodex—"CTG"—for use with black powder cartridge rifles. Shooters should always load with the type and granulation of powder recommended by the rifle manufacturer. Black powder shooters are notorious for experimenting, and often this practice does lead to a more accurate load. But when too much of a finer power is loaded into a muzzle-loading rifle, barrel pressures can reach dangerous levels. When determined to load and shoot finer grades, shooters should at least cut the weight or volume of the charge by 10 or 20 percent. An 80 grain charge of FFFg usually results in velocities comparable to what 100 grains of FFg produces behind the same projectile.

Pyrodex should always be loaded on a volume-to-volume basis with black powder. Pyrodex is bulkier than black powder, and by actual weight it's lighter as well. A 100 grain volume equivalent charge of Pyrodex "RS" will actually weigh just 80

Pyrodex has been formulated for cleaner burning, but the powder still leaves behind a small amount of fouling. For best accuracy, bore-sized conicals and patching for the round ball should be well lubricated.

grains; but since Pyrodex has been designed to perform on a volume-to-volume basis with black powder, a one-pound can produces about 20 percent more shots. Also available in pellet form, eliminating the need for measuring out precise loads for some rifles. Since compressed Pyrodex pellet charges are more difficult to ignite than loose Pyrodex, Hodgdon recommends that they be loaded and fired only in modern rifles with an efficient in-line percussion ignition system. The breech plug in most cases will still measure an inch or two in length. When the Pyrodex pellets are dropped down the muzzle, the compressed charges stop at the face of the breech plug sitting an inch or two from the base of the nipple. For better ignition, one end of each pellet has a light coating of a more sensitive igniter. Ignition may not be sufficiently spontaneous, though, to warrant their use in some traditional side-hammer rifles. Some of these guns can be fitted with a replacement nipple or ignition arrangement utilizing a hotter rifle or shotshell primer for better ignition.

Black powder and Pyrodex are both moisture sensitive. Powders that have been subjected to damp conditions, or even high humidity levels, start to break down. Rarely will they fail to fire, but they can deteriorate to the point where velocities are much slower than those fired with fresh powder. Shooters who burn only a pound or two a year should at least start the hunting season with a fresh can. Several new substitute powders are now on the market that bear inspection, but shooters should do so well ahead of the hunting season.

5. LOAD WITH A RELIABLE POWDER MEASURE

Consistency has its rewards, and with a muzzle-loading rifle the reward is usually better accuracy. The trick is to load each and every shot with the exact same amount of powder. The accuracy of larger .50 and .54 caliber hunting rifles won't be greatly affected by powder charges that vary two to three grains from shot to shot. In fact, 90 to 100 grain volume measured charges will often vary that much. Even when the side of the measure is tapped as it's filled with powder, the result will vary by a grain or more. The market today is filled with powder measures of varying quality. Most are adjustable, allowing shooters to work with different charges while working up a load. They can also be used for measuring the loads for several different muzzleloading guns. When setting a measure, make sure it's exactly at the index mark for a given powder charge. When a measure is locked in place a fraction of an inch too far it could add a few more grains to the variation in powder charge. Five or six grains could make a significant difference in how a muzzleloading rifle with a larger bore will print down range. It's equally important to use the same

exact powder measure for each shot. A recent study of different powder measures revealed up to a 20 percent variation in the charges measured. So if five different measures are used to load 100 grain charges for a five-shot group, the powder charges could vary by as much as 20 grains.

To learn how close a volumetric measure is to the weights indicated, a precision balance beam scale can be useful. A setting that's off one or two percent isn't too significant; but one that's off five or ten percent means that you're not loading with the charge you thought you were. By itself, this shouldn't hurt accuracy so long as the same amount is used from the same measure each time. It does mean, however, that you're not getting the desired velocities and energy levels. Meticulous shooters often rely on weighed charges exclusively. The exact charges are generally carried to the range or field in small plastic tubes, or "speed loaders," which also contain the projectile. This ensures that you're loading with the same exact charge of powder for each shot. When measuring Pyrodex, remember to compensate for the fact that it's lighter than black powder. A weighed 100 grain charge of Pyrodex is actually equivalent to more than 120 grains of black powder.

Accuracy with a round ball requires the proper patch thickness and lube.

Conical bullets such as these cold swaged pure lead projectiles from Buckskin Bullet Company require a fast rate of rifling twist for best down range accuracy, whether fired with or without a sabot in the bore.

6. LOAD WITH THE PROPER PROJECTILE

A powder charge and projectile that shoot well from one muzzleloading rifle may not shoot accurately from another, even though it's the same model. Finding a projectile that performs most effectively often requires a great deal of experimentation. Earlier, we covered the types of rifling required for shooting the different muzzleloader projectiles. Here, we'll look at variations in projectiles which influence the accuracy of a frontloading rifle.

A few years ago, I measured the bores of more than a dozen different .50 caliber muzzleloading rifles. Surprisingly, the land-to-land measurements of the bores ran from .498" on the tight side to .504" on the loose side. Even though all rifles were marked ".50 Caliber" on the side of each barrel, there was clearly a .006" variation in the bore size of the rifles tested. Even if all had the same rate of rifling twist, it would be impossible to achieve the same degree of accuracy with the same projectile. A

round ball shooter can adjust to a "tight" or "loose" bore more easily than one who loads with bore-sized conical or saboted bullets. The easiest approach would be to switch to a thicker patch for a loose bore, or a thinner patch for a tight bore. A ball that is severely undersized means it's time to move up to the next commercially available diameter. For example, a .490" ball may load much too easily into a slightly overbored .50 caliber rifle, even with a thick .020" patch. Instead of loading with still heavier patching, the shooter should go with a .495" diameter ball for improved accuracy.

Bore-sized conical bullets and saboted bullets load and shoot fairly well in bores with a variation of several thousandths of an inch. When the bore is much too loose, though, proper bullet-to-bore fit, which is necessary for good accuracy, becomes more difficult to achieve. Likewise, when a bullet or saboted bullet fits too tight into the bore, the bullet's fragile nose can be easily damaged when started into the bore. Once again, accuracy suffers. Ideally, a projectile should fit the bore reasonably snug, with only a minimal amount of pressure at the start, and offer reasonable resistance as it is pushed down the bore with a ramrod. It shouldn't be necessary to wrestle the projectile down the barrel; if it is, a different ball or bullet should be used.

Plastic sabots come in several different sizes for some calibers, providing the shooter a wider range of bullet and sabot combinations when tailoring a load for a rifle. Several sabot producers offer a choice of shooting either .44 or .45 bullets for a .50 caliber rifle. Each requires the use of a different sabot, i.e., a .45 bullet that is placed in a sabot for a .44 bullet is unlikely ever to get through the muzzle, unless it's pounded in with a hammer. On the other hand, a .44 bullet placed in a sabot for a .45 bullet could produce such a loose fit that the bullet will actually slide out of the muzzle with the rifle carried muzzle down. Either way, accuracy is impossible to achieve.

The same amount of pressure should be used each time on the ramrod when seating a muzzleloader projectile over the powder charge.

Shooters must make sure the sabots they're loading are meant specifically for the diameter or caliber of the bullet they are shooting.

7. SEAT THE PROJECTILE PROPERLY

The amount of pressure used to seat a projectile over the powder charge can influence how well a rifle shoots. Unknowingly, most muzzleloader shooters apply between 30 and 50 pounds of pressure on the ramrod when seating a projectile. How much pressure is ideal? Ask a dozen experienced black powder shooters that question

and you'll probably receive at lease a half-dozen different responses. So long as the same amount of pressure is used for each load, and enough pressure is applied on the ramrod to ensure the projectile is solidly seated, it probably doesn't matter all that much.

Shooters who are at the shooting bench with their favorite rifle, and who are shooting a load they know shoots accurately, should try this experiment: Load one round with about 10 pounds of seating pressure, another load with 20 pounds, another with 30, another with 40, and one more with 50. Then note what kind of groups result down range. Next, load five rounds with the amount of pressure normally used and compare the groups. The one with the consistent seating pressure is the tightest.

When pushing a projectile down the bore, do so in one continuous stroke with the ramrod. Don't jab at the projectile as you push it down the bore. And once the projectile makes contact with the powder

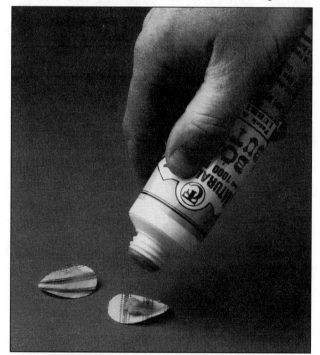

A well-lubed patch keeps the fouling in the bore of a round ball rifle soft, allowing the muzzleloading hunter to load follow-up shots without having to wipe the bore.

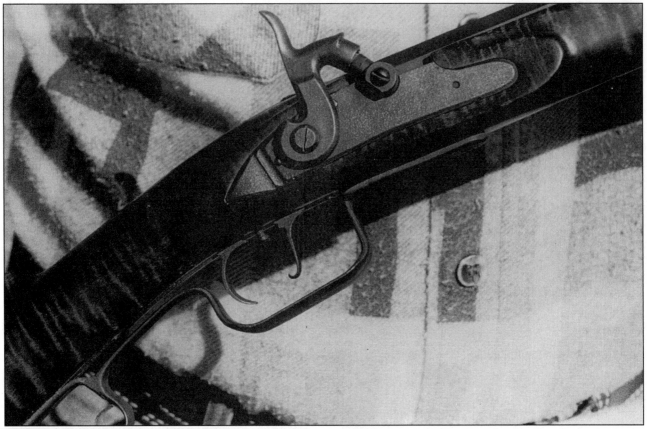

The "drum and nipple" arrangement of this traditionally styled percussion southern mountain rifle allows cleaning solvent or oil to accumulate, which could cause a misfire. For positive ignition, the flash channel must be cleared before the rifle is loaded.

charge, apply enough pressure so that it's properly seated. Old-timers once claimed you should "bounce" the ramrod on the projectile to make sure it's seated all the way. Don't! It will only damage the leading face of a ball or the nose of a bullet.

8. WIPE THE BORE BETWEEN SHOTS

One of the leading causes of poor muzzleloader accuracy is burned powder fouling left in the bore. Black powder produces more fouling than Pyrodex, but both powders can leave enough residue behind to cause shots to wander after a few rounds. Lubricated patched round balls and bore-sized conicals are less affected than non-lubricated plastic saboted bullets, but accuracy from a dirty bore with any projectile is never as good as from a clean bore.

Top competition shooters have always realized this and often painstakingly run several cleaning patches through the bore after each and every shot. One easy solution is to run at least one damp patch down the bore after each shot is fired. Don't soak the patch with cleaning solvent, however; it will add moisture in the bore, which could contaminate the next powder charge. Many shooters simply place a patch on their tongue and lightly dampen it with saliva. If a cleaning solvent is used, squeeze out as much of the liquid as possible. The idea is not to scrub the bore spotless, but to dampen the patch enough to get rid of as much fouling as possible.

The patch and cleaning jag should fit the bore snugly before the patch is pushed slowly down the bore. When nearing the breech end of the barrel, use short up and down strokes. That will prevent the fouling from caking around the patch, causing it to stick in the barrel. A patch that's not damp enough will simply scrape the fouling from the bore, increasing the likelihood of a patch getting stuck. Once the bottom of the bore has been reached, pull the patch out of the muzzle. Some shooters will turn the patch over and run it down the barrel again in an effort to wipe still more fouling from the bore. Avoid using long up-and-down scrubbing strokes, though; this will only throw damp fouling and powder residue into the ignition system, causing a hangfire or a misfire.

The first shot from a spotless bore may impact somewhat differently than will following shots, even if the bore has been wiped. Many target shooters, therefore, fire off a fouling round before shooting for the record. Should the first shot impact a lot differently than the follow-up shots, sight in for wherever that round impacts. When hunting, of course, the first shot is often the only one the shooter gets. If it hits where the rifle is aimed, it could be the only shot required.

9. GET OUT AND SHOOT MORE OFTEN

There's no substitute for experience when it comes to loading and shooting a muzzleloading rifle with confidence. The more time shooters spend at the bench with a frontloader, the more accustomed they'll become with what might have seemed difficult and confusing. Good accuracy and down range performance are rarely accidental. Tight groups on the target more likely represent the shooter's search for the optimum load. The best performing loads are often the result of considerable experimentation with various powder charge and bullet combinations. It's not uncommon for a muzzleloading rifle manufacturer to insist that shooters load and fire only their brand of projectiles with one of their rifles. Truth is, finding the best shooting bullet for almost any modern muzzleloader requires shooting something other than those bullets packaged by the riflemaker.

Every time powder and projectile are loaded into a muzzleloading rifle, the load should be thought of as a "custom reload." In essence, that's exactly what it is. Finding the ideal powder charge, determining the best ball diameter or type of bullet, and gaining enough loading expertise to achieve high accuracy from a muzzleloading rifle requires lots of hard work and attention to details. Tailoring a load that converts a frontloading rifle into a tack driver is the real fun and challenge of shooting muzzleloading guns.

New black powder shooters should buy the best quality black powder gun they can afford, such as the Thompson/Center New Englander.

SMALL BORE MUZZLELOADERS FOR SMALL GAME

The number of squirrel hunters in this country has definitely been on the decline in recent years. Before the explosion of the whitetail population, any hunter worth his salt hunted squirrels. Fall bushytails are a true test of a hunter's ability to slip undetected beneath a towering hickory or oak and tumble out a squirrel or two. But today, when muzzleloading hunters find time from their busy schedules to hunt, they usually go after more glamorous game, such as the white-tailed deer. Because of this obsession, there now exists a tremendous selection of top-quality muzzleloading big game rifles. Unfortunately, since fewer hunters

find time to chase squirrels and other small game, the selection of small-bore, small game rifles has dwindled. No longer in current production, for example, are such small-bore muzzleloaders as the .36 caliber Thompson/ Center Seneca or Cherokee. Also gone is the Hatfield "Squirrel Rifle" and the Navy Arms' "Mule Ear," both of which were available in .32 or .36 caliber. Hopkins & Allen's low-priced underhammer "Buggy Rifle" in .36 caliber is also no longer in production. Some were produced in relatively large quantities, so black powder hunters who frequent gun shows may run across one of these rifles in good to excellent

There is no better way to hone shooting skills than hunting small game. Late season hunting for cottontails can extend the muzzleloading hunter's time afield.

This .32 caliber Tennessee Mountain Rifle is well made and deadly accurate.

condition. Since few early reproduction muzzleloaders have yet to reach collector status, some of these used guns can be purchased at friendly prices.

For those who can't locate these models, a reasonably good selection of small bores is still available. Among the more popular ones are the long-barreled, full-stock Tennessee Mountain Rifles in .32 caliber (Dixie Gun Works, Union City, Tennessee). Connecticut Valley Arms also offers several models in .32 and .36 caliber, and Traditions (Deep River, Connecticut) builds a short .32 caliber half-stock small game rifle. Fans of the Thompson/Center Hawken can quickly turn this big-bore, big game model into a superb small game rifle simply by dropping one of the .32 caliber IBS

(Interchangeable Barrel System) barrels made by the Green Mountain Rifle Barrel Company into the stock assembly. Fans of the modern in-line percussion ignition system can purchase an optional .32 caliber barrel for the Thompson/Center Arms "System 1" interchangeable barrel muzzleloading system. And Knight Rifles offers a "special order" .36 caliber lightweight LK-93 Wolverine.

It's apparent that a good selection exists for the small game hunter who seeks a muzzleloading rifle with an appropriate bore size. For it's the size of the bore more than anything else that distinguishes a true small game muzzleloading rifle. Many of the early reproduction muzzleloaders were offered in .44 or .45 caliber, which manufacturers and importers often touted as ideal for hunting large or small game. With light 20 to 30 grain powder charges behind a .440" or .445" patched round ball, they claimed, their rifles were loaded adequately for squirrels, cottontails and other small game. With heftier 70, 80 or 90 grain charges of powder behind the same diameter round ball, these rifles could down deer-sized game. In truth, the .45 caliber bore is not ideally suited for either large or small game. Even with light charges, it's much too destructive for smaller game; moreover, it fails to produce enough energy with a round ball for downing deer and other large game cleanly.

Even the .40 caliber bore of the original "Squirrel Rifle," which Dixie Gun Works introduced in 1956,

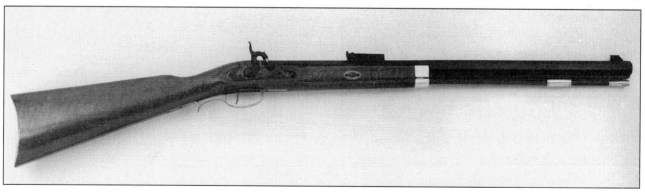

Connecticut Valley Arms' .32 caliber "Varmint Rifle" is ideal for squirrels, rabbits and other small game.

The .32 caliber Hopkins & Allen underhammer rifles were popular with muzzleloading small game hunters during the 1960s and 1970s. Used rifles can still be found at gun shows and in gun shops at affordable prices.

The ideal squirrel rifle should be small enough to perform with light loads that closely duplicate the ballistics of a .22 long rifle cartridge.

was too large to become a serious small game muzzleloader. The idea of potting a few squirrels or rabbits is to provide meat for the table, and even with relatively light powder charges the .40 caliber bore destroyed targets as small as bushytails or cottontails. Hunters who are seriously considering a small bore frontloader for hunting small game should concentrate on .32 or .36 caliber rifles.

FINDING THE RIGHT COMBINATION FOR SMALL GAME HUNTING

With most small bore muzzleloaders, the smaller the bore the faster it fouls, so small game hunters intent on maintaining pinpoint accuracy should run a damp patch down the bore between each shot. A bore that's been fouled by just one shot will produce slightly different pressures than when the same load is fired from a spotless bore. Depending on caliber when shooting light round ball projectiles of 45 to 70 grains, even the slightest variation in pressure or resistance in the bore will adversely effect the impact of the projectile on the target. When shooting larger bore .50 and .54 caliber muzzleloading rifles, powder charges varying as much as one or two grains from shot to shot generally have little effect on how the rifle groups down range. But it doesn't take much variation from charge to charge to open up groups with a small bore frontloader. With powder charges that are measured by volume, as little as half a grain variation can cause a light sphere to hit one-half to an inch high or low at 25 yards. That's enough variation to result in a clean miss on a feeding bushytail.

Black powder hunter Gary Clancy worked up an accurate varmint load for his Knight MK-85 to take this prime northern coyote.

A smallbore .32 or .36 caliber rifle will take wood-chucks cleanly, but it requires pinpoint placement of the shot to down a mature chuck.

It's safe to say that the .36 caliber rifles are less finicky to load and shoot than smaller bore .32 caliber rifles. But what about the destructive nature of a slightly larger bore and projectile? The discontinued .36 caliber Thompson/Center Seneca was rifled with a one-turn-in-48 inches rate of rifling twist. To shoot this rifle well with a patched round ball required a powder charge of at least 30 grains of FFFg or Pyrodex "P" grade powder. This combination pushed a patched 65 grain .350" ball from the muzzle of a 27-inch barrel at slightly over 1,700 f.p.s., developing close to 500 ft. lbs. of energy at the muzzle. That's about 1 1/2 times the energy produced by the .22 Winchester Magnum Rimfire, which is far too destructive for hunting small game. Even if this rifle shot a lighter 20 or 25 grain charge of powder accurately, the .350" ball would still cause considerable meat loss.

The .32 caliber Thompson/Center Cherokee, which hit the market during the mid-1980s, was one of the finest small game muzzleloading rifles ever made. This light half-stock rifle featured a short, fast-handling 24-inch barrel with a fast one-turn-in-30 inches rate of rifling twist. A 30 grain charge of FFFg or Pyrodex "P" pushed a light 45 grain .310" diameter patched ball from the muzzle at less than 1,700 f.p.s. Thanks to the lighter weight of the smaller diameter ball, this load generated only about 300 ft. lbs. of energy at the muzzle; but it was still close to twice as much energy as that developed by most high-velocity .22 long rifle ammo, making it still more destructive than desirable for small game. With the faster rate of rifling twist, many Cherokee shooters discovered that this rifle performed accurately with powder charges as light as 15 grains, bringing its ballistics in line with most standard velocity .22 long rifle cartridges. Unfortunately, Thompson/Center had to discontinue this great small game rifle a few years ago.

With small bore muzzleloaders, a longer barrel length can create higher velocities. When Dixie's long 41-inch barreled Tennessee Mountain Rifle in .32 caliber is loaded with a 30 grain charge of FFFg or Pyrodex "P" and patched .310" ball, as fired from the Cherokee, the pea-sized 45 grain ball leaves the muzzle at nearly 1,800 f.p.s. The energy level is pushed to about 350 ft. lbs. of muzzle energy. A still lighter 20 grain charge of FFFg would drop the velocity to a little over 1,500 f.p.s., with muzzle energy decreasing to about 200 ft. lbs. If accuracy could be maintained with this light load, it would be the best choice, ballistically, for small game hunting with the Tennessee Mountain Rifle. However, the Dixie rifle features a slow one-turn-in-56 inches rate of rifling twist; some rifles might not shoot well with such a light charge.

With the same loads fired from Dixie's .32 caliber longrifle, Thompson/Center's .32 caliber System 1 26-inch barrel produces lower velocities and lower energy levels. According to Thompson/Center ballistics, a 30 grain charge of FFFg black powder behind a patched 47 grain .315" diameter round ball is good for 1,714 f.p.s. at the muzzle and generates 307 ft. lbs. of energy. Compared to the 30 grain charge shot from Dixie's longer barrel, the .315" ball fired from the shorter 26-inch barrel leaves the muzzle with nearly 100 f.p.s. less velocity and approximately 50 lbs. less energy. Thompson/Center rifles this barrel with a one-turn-in-48 inches rate of twist.

Black powder arms manufacturers have competed so hard to produce higher velocities and energy levels, they've forgotten the credo for small game: less is best. Bigger, harder-hitting powder charges and projectiles may produce better kills on big game, but small game hunters are in the market for guns and

It takes good shooting and an accurate small caliber muzzleloading rifle to pot a few late season bushytails.

loads that can duplicate the ballistics of a .22 long rifle, not a .22 Winchester Magnum Rimfire. Shooters can choose between the less finicky but harder-hitting .36 caliber rifles, or the smaller .32 caliber frontloaders, which are harder to load but cause less meat destruction. While the current crop of small bore muzzleloaders may not seem the optimum choice for hunting squirrels and other small critters, most .32 and .36 rifles are acceptable for a variety of hunting situations, provided the shooter is prepared to cope with the limitations of his choice.

The frail wooden ramrods that are now available for many small bore muzzleloaders have one useful purpose: to slip back into the rifle when it's hung on the wall or placed in the gun rack for display. Black powder hunters of small game should replace these rods with one of the tougher synthetic kind, such as the "Super Rod" made by Mountain State Muzzleloading Supplies. Those tiny diameter wooden rods simply won't stand up to the use and abuse of repeated loading and wiping of the bore. After all, a few mornings in the squirrel woods can produce more action than an entire season pursuing whitetails. It's not unusual to ease in under a nut tree and discover four or five squirrels feeding in the limbs above. To take full advantage of these opportunities, it pays to be organized. Since small bore frontloaders are so sensitive to powder charges, hunters would be smart to carry pre-weighed charges in small plastic tubes. Another good idea is to carry several pre-patched round balls in a handy loading block, ready to be loaded simply by aligning the patch and ball with the bore and pushing one on through the block with a short starter and into the muzzle. A supply of pre-dampened cleaning patches carried in a small moisture-proof pouch or plastic bag will speed up the process of wiping fouling from the bore.

An experienced bushytail hunter will slip up behind the cover of an adjacent tree, take a solid rest and place his shots more accurately, rather than trying off-hand shots. The tree trunk can also provide concealment from other bushytails as the hunter reloads his muzzleloader. By the time the barrel has been wiped, a powder charge poured carefully down the bore, and a patched ball seated over the powder charge, squirrels that might have scampered to the safety of leafy cover at the sound of the first shot may have resumed feeding. The patient hunter can often pick off two or three critters before moving on.

In most states in the east, south and Midwest, squirrel seasons open in late August, September or early October. Throughout the West, meanwhile, cottontail rabbit seasons have already opened well ahead of most big game seasons. Sharpshooting cottontails or bushytails is an excellent way to introduce a young hunter to the sport of muzzle-loader hunting. Not only does it teach the importance of good, consistent loading practices, it also emphasizes the need for proper shot placement and the ability to slip quietly into position for a shot. Besides, there isn't a more challenging or enjoyable way to hunt small game than to rely on a small caliber muzzleloading rifle with an effective range of

25 or 30 yards. Aside from being ideal for taking small game, the tiny bores of a .32 or .36 caliber frontloader also make them the most economical muzzleloaders available. Consider that a pound of powder weighs exactly 7,000 grains. If you were to load a 25 grain powder charge, you would get exactly 280 shots from a can of FFFg black powder. Since Pyrodex "P" is approximately 20 percent bulkier, and assuming it's loaded on a volume equivalent basis with black powder, that comes close to 50 additional shots. Likewise, the small diameter soft lead balls loaded into and fired from these rifles cost less. A 45 grain .310" diameter ball costs proportionately more per grain than a 178 grain .490" ball for a .50 caliber rifle, but a box of 100 will usually retail for about 30 percent less than the larger diameter ball. By casting your own projectiles, the lighter lead spheres will definitely stretch your supply of pure soft lead.

Small bore rifles, which many hunters consider the ".22s of muzzleloading" are fun to shoot. Light powder charges and light projectiles result in zero

A 50 grain powder charge and a 93 grain .395" patched round ball produced more than enough knockdown to take this big dog coyote with a .40 caliber Dixie "Cub."

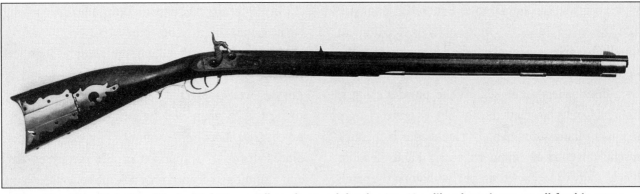

The .40 caliber Dixie Gun Works "Cub" is a well-made muzzleloader. Its .40 caliber bore is too small for big game, however, and too large for small game, making it ideal for varmints.

recoil, making them a great way to introduce youngsters to the sport of muzzleloading. The soft report is easy on the ears and not nearly as frightening as the roar of a big-bore hunting rifle. Many target shooters rely on the tightest patch and ball combination they can get through the muzzle and down the bore. It's not uncommon for a serious competitor to load a .36 caliber rifle with a .350" ball and heavy .015" patching, or even a .32 caliber rifle with a ball as large as .315" with .015" patching. Such combinations may perform exceptionally well on the range, but they could prove too difficult to load in the field for use on small game. It stands to reason that a tiny .32 or .36 caliber bore won't have rifling grooves as deep as those found in a .50 or .54 caliber round ball barrel (and the patching has to go somewhere, too). For most hunting situations, a .350" ball with .010" patching works fine in most .36 caliber rifles, while a .310" ball and .010" patching loads easily into a .32 caliber rifle, enough to produce the accuracy needed for shooting a squirrel in the head at 25 or 30 yards.

GOING AFTER VARMINTS WITH A MUZZLELOADER

There was a time—from the mid-1800s until the waning days of the muzzleloader era— when the vast majority of "sporting" muzzleloaders built in this country wouldn't have qualified as suitable for small game or for big game either. Back then, bore sizes weren't large enough to develop the wallop needed to ensure a clean kill on deer or other larger game; but at the same time they were so large that they completely destroyed all edible portions of a cottontail or bushytail

Target shooting was America's favorite pastime in those days. Every Sunday afternoon, large numbers of local marksmen would gather at a nearby range or meadow to display their expertise with a rifle. Those big .50 or .54 caliber rifles ate up too much lead and powder, yet these marksmen demanded a caliber that bucked cross winds better than the smaller squirrel calibers. Also, because they loaded directly from pouches hanging at their sides, these shooters wanted rifles that were less affected by slight variations in powder charges. What developed was a real love affair for the "mid" calibers, creating a demand from about 1840 until the early 1880s that accounted for more rifles with bores between .38 and .42 caliber than all other caliber rifles combined.

As popular as those mid-range calibers were back then, today's selection is pretty slim. Dixie Gun Works has offered a fullstock .40 caliber rifle with a 28-inch barrel, known as the Deluxe Cub Rifle, available in flint or percussion ignition. This bore size still enjoys a certain popularity among target shooters. During the 1960s and early 1970s, more reproduction guns were produced in .45 caliber than any other. As target shooting matured into big game hunting, shooters demanded something with a little more knockdown power; thus the .50 caliber bore quickly became the number one seller.

Going after varmints with a muzzleloading rifle is a challenging way to go after foxes, coyotes, woodchucks, or raccoons—and that's where the mid-range caliber muzzleloaders excel. Loaded with 40, 50 or 60 grains of FFFg black powder or Pyrodex "P" and a patched round ball, any accurate .40 or .45 caliber frontloader will deliver more than enough punch to down even the toughest coyote. For furbearing animals, such as foxes, bobcats or raccoons, damage to valuable pelts can be kept to a minimum with these combinations. Other varmints, including the woodchuck and groundhog are favorites among many muzzleloading hunters for sharpening their shooting skills for big game. Throughout the Midwest and New England, these pesky critters go on feeding binges every fall to put on body fat for the oncoming winter. Slipping within muzzleloader range of a wise old woodchuck is often a real test of a hunter's ability. Getting within 100 yards of a groundhog who is out feeding in an open hay field can be tough. Making a good hit with a frontloader calls for an accurate rifle, a good load, and a honed shooting eye.

With older groundhogs not destined for the table, most hunters like to shoot the same rifle and load they would on deer, elk or other big game. But hunters who are after big game animals for their valuable fur pelts should opt for a load that won't blow a huge hole in their prey. For foxes, bobcats and even coyotes, one of the mid-range caliber rifles with a moderate load, or one of the so-called "squirrel rifle" calibers with a hefty load, should keep damage to a minimum. When hunting with a .50 or .54 caliber muzzleloader, shooters may want to try shooting only 40 or 50 grains of powder behind a patched ball. If the results are acceptable, a light load can prevent heavy damage to the hide.

The fast twist bores of modern in-line percussion rifles perform relatively well with reduced loads. A 50 grain charge behind a saboted 200 to 250 grain jacketed bullet usually produces excellent accuracy out to 100 yards. The slower velocity produced by a reduced load will prevent most of these bullets from too rapid expansion—or no expansion at all. The result is often an exit hole not much larger than the entrance wound—and a pelt that is still intact! Those who prefer shooting full 90, 100 or 110 grain hunting charges can load their rifles with a saboted full-metal jacket bullet, such as the Speer 230 grain TMJ (Total Metal Jacket) for the old .45 auto handgun round. *Even at velocities exceeding 1,600 f.p.s., these bullets will not expand far enough as to rip a huge hole in a pelt.*

The short length, light weight and gentle recoil of the .40 caliber Dixie "Cub" makes it perfect for young shooters.

STOKING THE MUZZLELOADING SHOTGUN

When small game hunters first decided to use a muzzleloading smoothbore, logic likely played an important role. Since the first hand-held muzzleloaders were basically scaled-down versions of earlier cannon, some of the first loads fired from these guns were probably scaled-down loads for smaller bores. Even as early a the 14th Century, cannons were often loaded with a kind of wooden "over-powder" wad, then stuffed with a healthy load of large one-to-two-inch diameter iron, brass, or stone balls, then fired into the ranks of an oncoming army. This huge shotgun-like cannon and its load could mow down an entire front line with only a few shots.

Past historians failed to duly record the first use of a hand-held or shoulder-mounted smoothbore and a load of shot with which to hunt small game. Whether the shot was fired from one of the earliest hand cannon, or from a later matchlock or wheel-lock muzzleloader, the shooter must have surmised that if far heavier powder charges and larger diameter shot could reduce enemy ranks during battle, lighter powder charges and smaller diameter shot would work equally well for small game meant for table fare. With the development of the true flintlock ignition system came the widespread use of smoothbored "fowlers" for hunting waterfowl and upland game. By the middle of the 1600s, the shotgun had been born, destined to become the hunter's gun worldwide—a role that modern autoloaders and pump guns still enjoy.

Rifles with spiraling grooves in their bores didn't enjoy large-scale use until after the turn of the 19th

century. Hundreds of thousands of large caliber, smoothbored flintlock muskets were used for nearly 200 years by such major military powers as England and France. Despite the popular notion that the American Revolution was won because of the unparalleled accuracy of the early American longrifle, most of the battles were actually fought with smoothbored muskets. The two most commonly used long guns of the Revolutionary War were the .75 caliber British Brown Bess and the .69

Some of the finest sporting shotguns ever produced, including this stylish William Moore side-by-side percussion model, came from England during the mid-1800s.

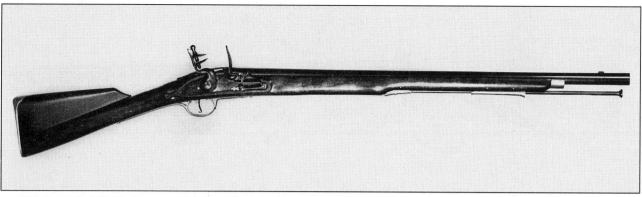

Military-styled flintlock smoothbore muskets, such as this shortened .75 caliber Brown Bess from Dixie Gun Works, double nicely as a fowler.

caliber French Charleville. Truth is, most of these long barreled smoothbores probably saw more action after the war as flintlock fowlers loaded with a charge of shot than they did as military muskets loaded with large patched round balls.

By the 1840s, muzzleloading shotguns had reached their peak of development. The late percussion smoothbores produced by noted gun makers of their day still rank among the finest examples of high-quality armsmaking. Some had such innovative features as sliding hammer-lock safeties on the lock plate, or grip safeties that prevented the hammer from accidentally falling (the grip safety found on several existing original percussion muzzleloading shotguns operates in basically the same manner as the grip safety found on the Colt .45 Auto handguns). A few high-quality muzzleloading shotguns exist in good shootable condition, but demand among collectors

has pushed the price beyond the budgets of most black powder shooters. Even English- and Belgium-made doubles of average quality can bring upwards of a thousand dollars. Fortunately, the current crop of modern-made reproduction smoothbores are more reasonably priced. They are, moreover, built of much stronger steels than were available 150 to 200 years ago. Also, shotguns, being working tools for the hunter, are subjected to repeated use, hence are bound to need servicing sooner or later. Parts for this service are readily available for any modern-made reproduction.

Navy Arms, Dixie Gun Works, Cabela's and a number of other companies currently import from Italy a line of extremely high-quality muzzleloading shotguns. The name of the importer is usually stamped onto the barrels of these smoothbores, and in most cases owners will find a second stamped into the steel: Davide Pedersoli & Co. When it comes to

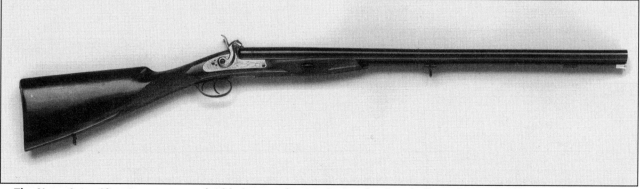

The Navy Arms 10 gauge magnum double is one of several reproductions built to shoot steel shot waterfowl loads.

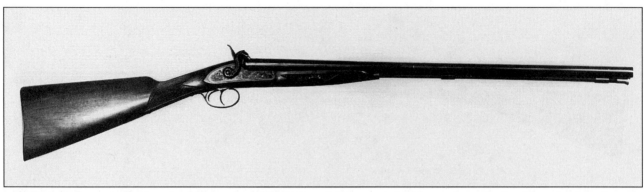

Italian-made reproduction doubles, such as this Pedersoli 20 gauge double, are excellent copies of originals.

muzzleloading shotguns, no other manufacturer comes close to matching the production of this gun maker from Brescia, Italy. In fact, no other reproduction manufacturer anywhere can offer the broad spectrum of newly-made muzzleloaders as Pedersoli, whose line includes more than 60 different models from the past, several of which are offered in three or four different variations. For muzzleloading shotgunners, side-by-side percussion doubles, as well as flintlock and percussion single-barrel fowlers, are available. (The only full-line distributor of the Pedersoli line in the U.S., by the way, is Flintlocks, Etc., P.O. Box 181, Richmond, MA 01254.)

The most popular muzzleloading shotgun in the Pedersoli line—a classic copy of a percussion English side-by-side—is imported by both Dixie Gun Works and Navy Arms. Light in weight (6 3/4 lbs.), Dixie's 20 gauge model comes with 27 1/2-inch barrels, choked cylinder bore and improved cylinder. A 12 gauge version weighs only 7 pounds and has a 28 1/2-inch barrel choked cylinder bore and modified. The big "Ten Bore" model, which weighs 7 1/2 lbs., features a 30-inch barrel choked cylinder bore and modified. All three versions have chrome-lined barrels for shooting lead or steel shot. Navy Arms' lineup also includes several different versions of the Pedersoli doubles, including 10 and 12 gauge side-by-sides built with twin 28-inch cylinder bore barrels. Navy Arms also catalogs a 10 gauge Magnum model built with chrome-lined 28-inch cylinder bore barrels designed for shooting steel shot waterfowl loads. For turkey hunters and muzzle-loading trap shooters, a T&T model (turkey & trap) features twin full choke 28-inch barrels.

Navy Arms and Dixie Gun Works also offer an outstanding Pedersoli reproduction of a high-quality Mortimer flintlock fowler. This 12 gauge

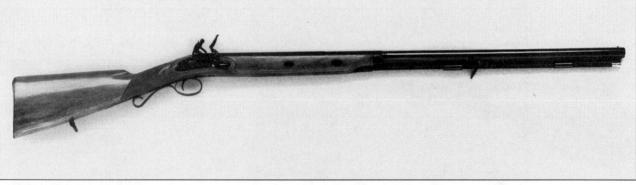

This Pedersoli reproduction of a high-quality Mortimer flintlock shotgun is far more serviceable than a 200-year-old original of the same design.

single-barrel shotgun is built with a long 36-inch cylinder bore barrel. Pedersoli's smoothbore features a top-quality lock and an internal mechanism built with close tolerance for smooth, trouble-free functioning. An original English flintlock fowler of this quality in shootable condition demands upwards of $3,000 to $4,000.

Cabela's (Sidney, Nebraska) offers another version of the Pedersoli-built percussion doubles for hunters looking for improved patterns. The 28½-inch barreled 12 gauge and 30-inch barreled 10 gauge models offer a screw-in choke system. Each comes with an extra-full, modified and improved cylinder choke tube, plus optional full and cylinder bore choke tubes as well. With careful loading, these doubles can perform on a par with modern breechloading shotguns having the same choke constriction at the muzzle. Cabela's also offers a lightweight 20 gauge version equipped with side-by-side improved cylinder and modified barrels. Another reproduction muzzleloading shotgun currently available is a side-by-side percussion 12 gauge imported from Spain by Connecticut Valley Arms. Its 28-inch barrels are both choked modified and come with chrome-lined bores for shooting steel shot waterfowl loads. The gun, which weighs in at nine pounds, is designed to handle heavy magnum waterfowl loads. Another top-quality traditionally styled percussion shotgun is a 12 gauge single-barrel with a removable improved cylinder screw-in choke tube. The company offers accessory modified and full choke tubes as well.

Those who seek a flintlock military smoothbored musket—one that doubles as a flintlock fowler—will be amazed at the variety of other authentic reproductions now available. Both Dixie Gun Works and Navy Arms offer faithful copies of the .75 caliber Brown Bess muskets along with new Pedersoli-made versions of the .69 caliber French Charleville musket and excellent reproductions of

More than 100 years after it was built, this Belgian percussion double still produces game-getting performance.

the .69 caliber U.S. Model 1816 flintlock musket. All three, with the proper combination of powder, wads and shot, double nicely for potting small game. Thompson/Center Arms, Knight Rifles and Traditions all include modern in-line percussion muzzleloaders in their lineups. These smooth-bores—all built with screw-in choke systems—make these shotguns mighty versatile. Their stocks, having been fashioned after rifle stocks, make it somewhat difficult to wing shoot. But with a tight choke tube threaded into the muzzle and a hefty load, these guns are ideally suited for wild turkeys.

With so many different guns to choose from, hunters and shooters may find it difficult to choose the model that's best suited for their needs. The rest of this chapter explains how these guns are loaded, how they are turned into effective game getters, and the performance expected from the different gauges and choke constrictions.

CHOKE CONSTRICTIONS AT THE MUZZLE

Muzzleloading shotgun makers of the mid-1800s and earlier did not fully understand the principles of choke constrictions at the muzzle. Choked shotgun

Shotgun powder and shot measures, such as this volumetric measure from Connecticut Valley Arms, make it easy to stoke the muzzleloading shotgun with equal volumes of powder and shot for best patterns.

Traditional open-choked shotguns usually perform best when loaded with the proper combination of wads (left to right): a heavy over-powder card wad, a fiber cushion wad, and a thin over-shot card wad.

barrels for the most part did not begin to show up until after the Civil War, and while a few gun makers in England and Europe continued to build muzzleloading shotguns into the late 1800s, most original muzzleloading shotguns were made with a cylinder bore barrel. Not having a choke constriction of any sort at the muzzle makes loading a frontloading smoothbore much easier. But without a slight tightening of the bore at the muzzle, it's difficult to produce the game-taking patterns that modern shotgun shooters have come to expect. With the proper ratio of powder and shot, along with the right combination of wads, even an open-bored muzzleloading shotgun can be tamed to throw even patterns that can take upland game or waterfowl at relatively close range.

The cylinder-bored 12 gauge barrels of the Navy Arms "Fowler" double are probably more like the barrels used on original English doubles than the tubes one finds on most other modern reproduction muzzleloading shotguns. The bores of these barrels measure exactly the same at the muzzle as at the breech end, making them true cylinder bore barrels. To get this shotgun—or any other with a cylinder bore barrel—to perform successfully requires the

shooter to load with equal (or near equal) volumes of powder and shot; and the easiest way to accomplish that is to use the exact same measure for both. Connecticut Valley Arms markets a brass volummetric shotgun measure that's adjustable for measuring out 1, $1^{1}/_{8}$ and $1^{1}/_{4}$ ounce shot charges. The measure works well for loading heavy charges in a 20 gauge smoothbore, or light and medium charges in a 12 gauge like the Navy Arms side-by-side. Set at one ounce, it measures approximately 75 grains of FFg black powder, about 80 grains at 11/8 ounces, and just under 90 grains at $1^{1}/_{4}$ ounces.

When using shot sizes No. 6 and smaller, any adjustable powder measure is effective for measuring shot charges as well. The chambers of most small diameter measures usually are not very accurate when measuring larger shot sizes, especially pellets larger than No. 5. When bird hunting with No. $7^{1}/_{2}$ shot, and with the measure set at 90 grains, simply measure out a $3^{1}/_{4}$ dram charge of powder and $1^{1}/_{4}$ ounces of shot. But when larger No. 4s are poured into the measure, then weighed on a balance beam scale, the shot charge will be closer to $1^{1}/_{8}$ ounces; and with No. 2s it could weigh even closer to one ounce. The smaller the diameter of the powder measure chamber, the more it tends to cheat with larger-sized shot.

The clear plastic U-View powder measure made by Thompson/Center has sufficient internal diameter to measure out equal volummes of powder and shot, whether the load is No. 7½ or No. 4 shot. As one of the larger volume measure on the market, the U-View can measure powder charges all the way up to 125 grains. For some waterfowl and wild turkey hunting, hefty 4 dram (109 grains) and 4½ dram (123 grains) powder charges behind 1½ to 2 ounces of shot may be needed. (Note: For waterfowl, even black powder shotgunners are now required to use either non-toxic steel or Bismuth shot, which doesn't weigh as much as lead for the same volume of shot loaded.) Another advantage of the U-View is its ability to detect bridges caused by larger shot sizes. A few taps on the side of the measure usually eliminates that problem.

Experienced black powder shotgunners, shy away from most one-piece plastic shotgun wads. Many, having been sized to fit inside a shotshell hull, will fit the bore of a muzzleloading shotgun so loosely that pressure from a burning powder charge will escape around the wad.

The loads that perform best in many muzzleloading shotguns are made of several different card and fiber cushion wads. A common practice is to load a heavy .125" card "over powder" wad directly over the powder charge, followed by one or two fiber (or felt) wads to form a ³⁄₈" to ½" cushion for the shot charge. Once the shot charge has been poured through the muzzle, the entire load is topped with a thin .030" "over shot" card wad. Some experimenting with slightly different thicknesses or wads punched from different materials may be necessary to come up with the best shooting combination for a particular shotgun. The load most likely to produce the best patterns from a muzzleloading smoothbore probably won't vary all that much from the sequence described above.

Although the one-piece plastic wad units often fail to produce quality patterns from many muzzleloading shotguns, using the shot cup itself can help tighten patterns, or at least retain more shot toward the center where it's most needed. Many shotgunners simply trim the cupped obturator base from the one-piece wads and load the shot cup directly over the cushion wads. Those who find this

This 20-yard pattern produced by a cylinder bore reproduction 12 gauge is still relatively even, thanks to equal volumes of powder and shot plus the proper combination of card and fiber wads.

When loaded ahead of a felt cushion wad, plastic shot cups can tighten the patterns produced by cylinder bore reproduction and original muzzle-loading shotguns.

Despite its big double 10 gauge bores, this classic percussion shotgun from Dixie Gun Works is an excellent upland bird gun.

procedure works well can eliminate the extra step of cutting off the base simply by purchasing the shot cups alone. One of the best 12 gauge cups currently available is the BP12 (Ballistic Products, Inc., Corcoran, Minnesota). Designed for use with a separate gas seal out of magnum shotshells, it also loads easily into a frontloading smoothbore ahead of fiber or felt cushion wads. The raised ridges that run the full length of the BP12 result in approximately 50% actual contact with the bore, making it possible for the cup to be loaded through modified and even full choked muzzles. When loaded direct from the package, the cup and shot load will punch a huge hole in pattern paper at 20 yards, much like a shotgun slug. Four evenly spaced slits about a

half-inch long can be cut in the cup to create a foil, causing the cup to fall back shortly after leaving the muzzle, producing tighter patterns at 30 yards. For wider, even patterns, the slits can be cut back a full inch, whereupon the cup will peel away from the shot charge even faster.

Mountain State Muzzleloading Supplies (Williamstown, West Virginia) and Dixie Gun Works (Union City, Tennessee) both offer large selections of card and fiber wads for muzzleloading shotgun shooters. These wads are offered in true gauges, which means that when ordering 12 gauge wads the buyer gets wads that fit the bore of a 12 gauge muzzleloader. Every wad that is pushed down a bore should offer some resistance. When inserting over-powder and over-shot card wads, it's easier to start them sideways through the muzzle. The tip of the ramrod should include a jag or button that's close to bore size. Then, as the card wads are pushed down the bore, they'll turn to fit the bore and the large diameter jag or button prevents them from turning back sideways. Cushion wads, however, must be started straight into the bore. Fortunately, their fibrous or felt materials compress enough to allow the wads, which run $3/8$" to $1/2$" in thickness, to be pushed straight down the bore with minimal resistance. Wads that have been lightly lubed with a black powder grease-type lubricant, or simply a light coating of a shortening-beeswax mixture, will load easier than when loaded dry.

Most card wads can be loaded through even a full choke constriction without becoming so distorted they won't perform the job they were designed for. Fiber cushion wads, on the other hand, can be totally destroyed when pushed through modified or full chokes (guns fitted with removable screw-in choke tubes can make loading easier). It takes time, however, to remove chokes, then load and replace them afterwards. An easier approach is to use thinner felt cushion wads available from Thompson/

One-piece plastic wad units, like the Remington Power Piston, seldom perform well out of a cylinder bore muzzleloading shotgun barrel. When the shot cup is trimmed from the base and used with a card over-powder and fiber cushion wad, patterns generally improve.

Center Arms, Ox-Yoke Originals and a few others. These measure only about $^{1}/_{4}$" in thickness and are quite flexible, enabling them to be pushed one at a time through even an extra-full choke and still fit the bore tight enough to provide the seal needed for top performance.

It's Performance That Counts

Light or heavy loads often fail to produce the best patterns from a cylinder bore. Powder and shot charges considered medium loads tend to turn in the most uniform patterns. With the popular 12 gauge bores, this usually equates to a $1^{1}/_{8}$ or $1^{1}/_{4}$ ounce shot charge ahead of a $3^{1}/_{4}$ dram (89 grains) or $3^{1}/_{2}$ dram (96 grains) load of FFg black powder, or the volume equivalent of Pyrodex RS or Select. Smaller 20 gauge bores commonly prefer 7/8 or one ounce shot charges and $2^{3}/_{4}$ dram (75 grains) or 3 dram (82 grains) powder charges. For more knockdown power with a bigger 10 gauge bore, shooters often opt for loads of $3^{3}/_{4}$ drams (102 grains) or $4^{1}/_{2}$ drams (123 grains) of FFg or Pyrodex RS/Select behind $1^{1}/_{2}$ to $2^{1}/_{2}$ ounces of shot. These loads shot from a cylinder bore barrel generally produce patterns of about 50% at 30 yards, i.e., half of the pellets in a given shot charge should group inside a 30-inch circle at that distance. (Note: a one-ounce charge of No. 4 shot contains 132 pellets; No. 5 equals 168 pellets; No. 6 has 218 pellets; and No. $7^{1}/_{2}$ contains 388 pellets.) With an improved cylinder, patterns should tighten somewhat to nearly 60% of the pellets in the circle, around 70% with a modified choke constriction, and close to 80% with barrels featuring a full choke. When a frontloading shotgun isn't producing patterns of this quality, the fault probably lies with how the smoothbore is loaded. The wads may have to be modified, or a plastic shot cup introduced.

Shooters who are seriously considering purchase of a muzzleloading shotgun for hunting and who demand tighter, more uniform patterns should concentrate on models that feature built-in choke

The Thompson/Center 12 gauge New Englander, which is available with removable screw-in chokes, performs well with a variety of loads.

Shotgun competitors rely on modern frontloading smoothbores and proven loads.

WATERFOWLING WITH A MUZZLELOADING SHOTGUN

Many of the finest original muzzleloading shotguns of the past were built specifically for hunting ducks, geese and swans. More than a few of these top-quality side-by-sides and single barrel smoothbores featured huge 6, 7, and 8 gauge bores for throwing three or four ounces of shot. During the mid-1800s, it was considered more sporting to take waterfowl on the wing, but hunters then also knew that their "average" was upped considerably by flock-shooting ducks, geese and swans on the water or in the field. The more shot they could put into the air, the better their chances of potting a half-dozen or so birds with one or two shots. Since much of the waterfowl taken in this manner was intended for sale on the market, economics dictated that when the smoke cleared, several birds should be laying on the ground or in the water, a feat made easier by shooting something big at something that was not flying.

Most waterfowl guns of the early 1800s were built with more civilized bore sizes, primarily 10, 11, 12 and 14 gauges. Not only was recoil easier to handle, but the scaled-down dimensions of these guns made them better suited for swinging on flying waterfowl. Since the aerial target was commonly a single duck, goose or swan, there really wasn't much need for a four-ounce shot load. Waterfowl hunters learned to rely on the heaviest charge of powder and load their guns could handle and still produce clean kills. Hefty 4 or 4 1/2 dram loads (110 to 125 grains) of powder were often fired behind upwards of 2 to 2 1/2 ounces of shot. Hunters quickly learned that larger targets—ducks, geese and especially swans—were brought down more effectively with larger diameter shot. In fact, large shot nearly the equivalent of today's "buckshot" became known as "swan shot."

constrictions or a removable screw-in choke system. No matter how hard one works at developing loads, getting a cylinder bore barrel to produce full-choke patterns will never happen. By the same token, you'll never find a full choke barrel that loads as easily as a cylinder bore muzzleloading shotgun. But if muzzleloading shotguns were as easy to tame as a modern breechloading shotgun, what would be the challenge of hunting with them? The reward is in custom-tailoring a load for one of these smoothbores. True satisfaction comes from taking upland game and waterfowl up close and personal with an old-fashioned smoothbore design dating from the late 1700s or early 1800s.

Until the mandatory transition from lead to steel shot during the late 1970s and early 1980s, modern-day waterfowlers commonly relied on No. 2 and slightly larger BB-sized shot for most goose hunting. No. 4 or 5 shot was used for hunting larger ducks, such as mallards. Steel has less density than lead, so to maintain nearly the same killing energy at 30, 40 and 50 yards, waterfowlers were forced to move up to larger shot sizes. The current standards for geese are BBB and T-shot sizes. By comparison, old No. 2 lead shot commonly measured .150" in diameter, while that for the new BBB steel measures .190". For the goose hunter who needs more knockdown at longer range, there are still the TT steel shot measuring .210" and shot size F, which measure .220". To maintain killing power with steel shot, most duck hunters now rely on No. 1, 2 and 3 sizes. Steel shot can be rough on the bores of modern shotgun barrels, so as a result most of today's waterfowl shotshells incorporate a special tough plastic wad that keeps the hard steel pellets from making contact with the mirror-smooth surface of a quality bore. Even so, many waterfowlers have put away family heirlooms like granddad's old Winchester Model 12 to save them from being "shot out" by steel shot loads, opting instead for a newer gun with interchangeable screw-in chokes.

To those who've been tempted to hunt waterfowl with a high-quality original muzzleloading shotgun the best advice is simple. DON'T! Extremely hard steel shot will quickly eat away at the softer Damascus steel used to form the barrels on most of these guns. It takes only a dozen or so shots to ruin one of these fine guns forever. If a waterfowler has a yen to down a big Canada goose or a few mallards with a slow-to-load muzzleloading smoothbore, he'll find that several of the new guns now available are probably better suited than even the finest original. The percussion 12 gauge double from Connecticut Valley Arms is ideally suited for hunting ducks and geese. Tipping the scales at nine pounds, this hefty gun will soften recoil from heavy powder charges much better than a lighter 7½ or 8-pound shotgun. It also features modified choke constrictions, which perform better with steel shot than a full choke. Another good choice is the 10 or 12 gauge Pedersoli double (imported from Italy by Cabelas's) featuring a screw-in choke system. For waterfowl hunting, both tubes should have a modified tube screwed in place. With steel shot being so much harder than lead, it doesn't deform as easily, which usually means tighter patterns. One of Cabela's doubles with a hefty load of powder and steel shot can produce almost as tight a pattern with the modified tube in place as it does when loaded with the same powder charge and volume of lead shot fired through the full choke tube.

To maintain enough energy for downing ducks and geese, today's muzzleloading waterfowler should move up slightly in shot size. When loading steel shot into a modern-made muzzleloading smoothbore, it's a good idea to rely on a tough, protective plastic shot cup. Powder and shot should be loaded on a volume to volume basis. Steel is much lighter than lead, so a shot cup holding 1½ ounces of lead shot will hold about an ounce of steel

Non-toxic Bismuth shot nearly duplicates the performance of lead for duck and goose hunters.

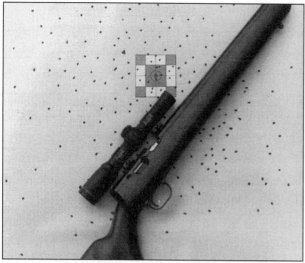

A 2 oz. load of No. 4 Bismuth shot produced this even pattern from a Thompson/Center System 1 12 gauge barrel with full choke tube.

shot by actual weight. When the same size shot is used, though, the volume and number of pellets remains the same.

Bismuth shot is a new, non-toxic alternative to both lead and steel. This special alloy is about 92% as dense as lead and does a much better job of maintaining killing energy at longer ranges than the lighter steel shot. Waterfowlers can thus shoot Bismuth shot loads made of pellet sizes that are more in line with the old lead shot loads. Bismuth isn't as hard as steel, either, nor as abrasive on the bore. The softer non-toxic alloy shot can also be used in older, original guns with no ill effect. Shooters who are concerned about possible wear and tear on the bore of an original in fine condition should load with a protective shot cup (assuming there's one available in the right size). The disadvantage of Bismuth is the cost. A 10-pound jar of Bismuth shot retails for at least five times the cost of a 10-pound container of steel shot!

Tests conducted with both steel and Bismuth shot loads reveal that both types of shot tend to produce better, more uniform patterns when loaded with a fine buffer compound. Patterns fired with a 12 gauge Thompson/Center System 1 shotgun

barrel with modified choke tube installed and a 12 gauge Knight MK-86 shotgun barrel with a modified Rem-Choke tube in place have proved impressive with steel shot loads. All loads were built with 100 grains of FFg black powder, a heavy .125" over-powder card wad, two Ox Yoke Original felt Wonder Wads, a Ballistics Products BP12 shot cup, an ounce of No. 4 steel shot, and two 1/8"-thick styrofoam over-shot wads. Patterns produced at 30 yards without any buffer compound usually placed 80% of the pellets inside a 30-inch circle. When buffer compound was mixed with the steel pellets, the same load grouped close to 85% of its pellets inside the same circle. More pellets also hit nearer the center of the pattern, producing less of a donut effect. The most uniform patterns were fired from both guns when the shot cup was slit with four evenly spaced cuts running back about half the length of the cup.

With modified choke tubes still installed, and with 1½ ounces of No. 4 Bismuth shot instead of steel, the Thompson/Center System 1 shotgun repeatedly patterned 67% of the load inside the 30-inch circle at 30 yards without any buffer added, and around 71% with the buffer compound. When

A modern screw-in choke system can greatly improve the performance of a muzzleloading shotgun.

Thanks to Bismuth shot, this black powder shotgunner can spend an afternoon hunting both bushytails and wood ducks.

Thompson/Center's full-choke tube was installed, patterns with a buffered shot charge tightened considerably, with nearly 87% of the shot charge placed inside the magical 30-inch circle. The Knight MK-86 did slightly better. With a Remington modified choke tube at the end of the barrel, this 12 gauge muzzleloader produced 70% patterns without buffer, and nearly 75% patterns with buffer added to the $1^1/_2$-ounce Bismuth shot charge. A switch to a full-choke tube taken from a Remington Model 870 pump tightened the buffered load to almost 90%. And when a standard Hastings .665" extra-full tube was threaded back into the muzzle, this smoothbore put 97% of the buffered Bismuth shot charge in the circle at 30 yards. *(WARNING: Do Not Attempt To Shoot Steel Shot Loads Through Any Full or Extra-Full Choke Constriction!)*

The screw-in choke systems used in some of today's muzzleloading shotguns are usually one of two different systems: the Rem-Choke (Remington) or Winchoke (Winchester) designs. Serious waterfowlers should determine which system has been used for their muzzleloading shotguns. Special "steel shot"choke tubes are available which tend to produce better results than the standard lead shot tubes. Before shooting steel through any of today's muzzleloading shotguns, though, be sure to contact the maker about shooting such loads. *And to anyone considering the purchase of a muzzleloading shotgun for hunting ducks and geese, the best advice is to make a few phone calls before buying a gun that could prove unsafe for shooting steel shot loads.*

BLACK POWDER GOBBLERS

The greatest challenge a muzzleloading shotgunner can tackle is indisputably the wild turkey. A wise old gobbler's uncanny ability to give a hunter the slip makes him as worthy a trophy as any big game animal. In fact, many experienced hunters refer to this magnificent game animal as America's "big game" bird, treating the wild turkey with the same respect given to a trophy class whitetail buck or bull elk. One thing is for certain, the hunter who underestimates the survival instincts of this big bird is destined to go home empty-handed. It takes a hunter with woods savvy to be successful with wild turkey season after season, especially with a muzzleloading shotgun.

Success with a muzzleloading rifle on whitetails and other big game has encouraged many hunters to turn to these guns for other species as well. Across the country, wild turkey populations are on the rise.

Each spring, more and more muzzleloading hunters go after wild turkey with a frontloading shotgun.

A few decades ago, many states offered limited turkey hunting opportunities—and those few had to enter into a special lottery drawing for one of the 2,000 to 3,000 permits available. Today, in many of these same states, turkey hunters can purchase a permit across the counter. In some states the limit is now two or three turkeys, and a growing number of serious wild turkey hunters have turned to the challenge of hunting with a muzzleloading shotgun to harvest at least one of these birds. A gobbler that's close enough can be taken with almost any muzzleloading smoothbore and load. But a big one that comes strutting down a ridge toward you can look as big as a barn. Even at 30 or 40 yards, a wild turkey seems much too big a target to miss. But keep in mind that a big gobbler topping the 20-pound mark can be a tough target to put down. You're dealing with a kill zone that measures approximately two inches wide and ten inches long. It takes only two or three pellets into the neck or brain of a turkey to produce a clean kill.

Most traditionally styled flintlock or percussion ignition shotguns with cylinder bore barrels can be loaded to produce even patterns that ensure enough pellets will hit the kill zone. This generally requires loading near equal volummes of powder and shot, plus the right combination of card and cushion wads. Even so, these guns should be considered 20-yard maximum range turkey guns. After that, the patterns are usually too open to be trusted. Fortunately, a number of excellent frontloading shotguns have been newly designed, especially for the muzzleloading turkey hunter, capable of

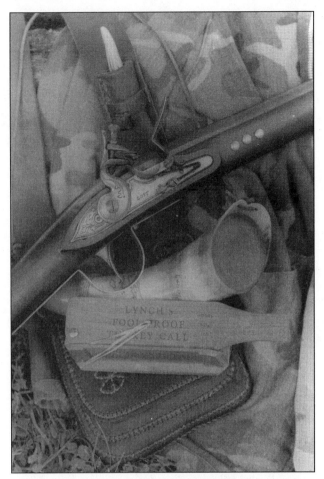

Taking a wary old gobbler with a flintlock smooth-bore represents one of the toughest challenges black powder hunters can tackle.

The muzzles of a Pedersoli percussion 12 gauge are threaded for screw-in chokes, making this reproduction double a great choice for wild turkey.

throwing tight patterns that rival the 30- and 40-yard performances of a modern 3-inch magnum breechloading shotgun.

The Knight MK-86 muzzleloading 12-bore shotgun, with its sure-fire in-line percussion ignition system, won immediate acceptance among turkey hunters. Its 24-inch 12 gauge barrel is threaded at the muzzle to accept Remington REM-CHOKE screw-in choke tubes (an extra-full choke tube is standard). Other features include the Knight double safety system, a receiver drilled and tapped for easy installation of scope bases or "peep" sight, and a removable breech plug. The entire barrel can be slipped from the receiver of the MK-86 and replaced with either a .50 or

.54 caliber rifle barrel, making this a true all-purpose muzzleloader.

Thompson/Center Arms also manufactures a muzzleloader of similar style, known as "System 1," along with .32, .50, .54 and .58 caliber rifle barrels for the modern in-line percussion muzzleloader, plus a 12 gauge barrel. While the line-up of rifle barrels may be of interest to black powder hunters who seek one gun with which to hunt everything, the smoothbored tube should catch the attention of serious turkey hunters. The shotgun barrel comes standard with a removeable full-choke tube; modified and improved-cylinder tubes are optional. Other features of the System 1 include an adjustable target-quality trigger, a receiver that's drilled and

The Thompson/Center System 1 shotgun barrel features a screw- in choke system. With the full choke tube installed, this muzzleloader makes a fine turkey gun.

the same barrel used in System 1, and threaded for interchangeable chokes. Several importers market the superb Pedersoli side-by-side percussion muzzleloading shotguns from Italy, available in 20, 12 and 10 gauge. Some of the larger 12 and 10 gauge models are available with interchangeable screw-in choke tubes, turning them into hard-hitting turkey shotguns. Navy Arms offers another 12 gauge version of this gun, which it calls the T&T, or "Turkey and Trap" model. This side-by-side 28-inch barrel is built with twin full-choked barrels (without removable choke tubes).

A tight constriction of the bore at the muzzle will indeed tighten and improve the performance of a muzzleloading shotgun, but it can also make loading a smoothbore more difficult. Traditionally, cylinder bored muzzleloading scatterguns were loaded with relatively tight fitting card and fiber cushion wads, which had to be slightly larger in diameter than the actual bore. If a thin over-shot card wad literally drops into a shotgun bore, or offers no resistance when pushed down with a ramrod, it's likely the shot charge will roll back out of the barrel when the shotgun is carried muzzle down. The tighter the choke, the more difficult it is to load with components that will still fit properly once they've been pushed through the constriction. Both the heavy over-powder and thin over-shot card wads often fit too loosely to be effective once

tapped, and a removable breech plug. Another modern in-line percussion shotgun that should appeal to turkey hunters is the 12 gauge Buckhunter Pro Shotgun made by Traditions (Deep River, CT). This 24-inch barreled muzzleloader also comes with a screw-in full choke tube and features a receiver that's been drilled and tapped, plus a removable breech plug for easy cleaning or unloading.

Shooters who prefer a shotgun with more traditional styling, but one that offers a good choke system, may opt for the Thompson/Center 12 gauge percussion New Englander, which is basically

The "Buckhunter Pro" in-line shotgun from Traditions features a screw-in full choke for tighter patterns.

The "Turkey Ranger" one-piece plastic wad from Ballistics Products tightens patterns produced by heavy turkey loads. The plastic cup must be slit (left) so the cup can separate from the shot charge.

they've been "sized." A fiber cushion wad can be literally destroyed once it's been forced through a full choke constriction. Trying to load with a one-piece wad can be next to impossible if it has to be punched through a choke.

Therein lies the beauty of a removable choke tube. Once the tube has been unthreaded from the muzzle, loading becomes as easy as loading a cylinder bore barrel. Card, fiber or even plastic wads can be pushed through the muzzle with just enough resistance to ensure their performance on the job. Some precautions should be taken, though, to prevent damaging the threads inside the barrel and on the tube itself. Otherwise, the choke will never fit back into the barrel. Even a few grains of powder caught in the threads can cause serious problems. To be safe, some shooters leave the choke in while pouring the powder charge, remove it during the rest of the loading process, then replace the choke before shooting. Without it, the pattern will be terrible and the threads could be ruined.

When cleaning these muzzleloaders, use a choke thread brush with stiff bristles until all fouling is removed from the threads. Because full and extra-full tubes must be removed when loading wads, the threads should be kept well-lubed with a special choke tube grease or a non-petroleum-based lube—the same as that used on the removable breech plugs of many modern in-line muzzleloaders. Should rust ever form in the barrel threads, removing and replacing the tube can become a major chore. When loading a new muzzleloading turkey shotgun featuring a modern removable choke, it's wise to forget about loading with card and fiber wads from the past. Most of these guns turn in exceptional patterns when time is taken to construct a load that utilizes a one-piece plastic wad.

Ballistic Products Inc. (Corcoran, Minnesota) offers an outstanding selection of reloading components for the modern shotgunner. The variety of wads found in their catalog covers shotgunners' needs from clay targets to waterfowling. For muzzleloading shotguns, there are several 12 gauge plastic wads for use with steel and lead shot loads. The Knight MK-86, performed well with several wads, but patterned best with the Turkey Ranger. This one-piece wad has a built-in gas seal

The "peep" sight mounted on the receiver of this Knight MK-86 provides positive aiming and also allows shooters to sight the center density of the pattern.

(or obturator) at the base, so the wad can be pushed down directly over the powder charge without first inserting a separate gas seal or cushion wad. The shot cup holds 1³/₄ ounces of lead shot. Their BP12, which holds a 1¹/₂-ounce load of lead shot, requires the use of a separate gas seal or cushion wad. Slits must be cut down the sides of the shot cup, forming petals that peel the wad away from the shot charge as it leaves the muzzle. If either the Turkey Ranger or BP12 are loaded without these slits, the plastic cup will stay with the shot charge for a long distance. This could create much tighter patterns at 40 and 50 yards, while at 20 yards or closer it will act much like a shotgun slug, leaving little left of a turkey to admire or eat. It only takes a few minutes to cut four evenly spaced slits with a sharp pocket knife or scissors.

The Knight MK-86, with its extra full choke tube, produces excellent patterns with the Turkey Ranger wad, whether it's slit back one-quarter or three-fourths of the way. The farther back the cuts, the quicker the wad will leave the shot charge and allow the pattern to open up slightly. Even with petals nearly three-fourths the length of the shot cup, patterns at 30 yards are tight with excellent center density. Loaded with 110 grains of Pyrodex Select behind a Turkey Ranger wad and a full two ounces of No. 5 shot, all topped with a single styrofoam over-shot wad, the Knight MK-86 will retain nearly 100 percent of the pattern inside a 30-inch circle at 30 yards. With that in mind, when the center of a target represents the silhouette of a turkey head and neck, upwards of 40 or more pellets should impact inside the kill zone.

The Thompson/Center System 1 muzzleloading shotgun barrel shoots well with either the Turkey Ranger or BP12 plastic wads. When loading with the one-piece Turkey Ranger, the full choke tube must first be removed. This requires some poking before the flanged base of the gas seal can move past

the threads in the barrel. With a 100 grain charge of Pyrodex "Select" and 1³/₄ ounces of No. 5 shot loaded into one of the wads, and with the cup slit about one-third of the way down, the full choked tube will produce 90 percent-plus patterns at 30 yards. And when fired on a standard turkey head patterning target, the load will consistently place 20 to 25 pellets in the kill zone. Actually, the Thompson/Center shotgun turns in better patterns with the BP12 cup slightly over-filled with 1⁵/₈ ounces of No. 6 shot. With no slits in the cup, the wad, upon firing, hits the patterning board nearly every time, ripping huge holes in the paper. The pattern is tight, with some 96 percent of the shot load landing inside a 30-inch circle at 30 yards. When the shot cup has been cut with four evenly spaced slits about a quarter of the way down, the wad should land about half-way to the patterning board, with 93 percent or more within the 30-inch circle. The smaller No. 6 shot obviously adds pellets into the shot load, resulting in a denser pattern, consistently putting 30-35 No. 6 pellets into the kill zone of a turkey head target at 30 yards.

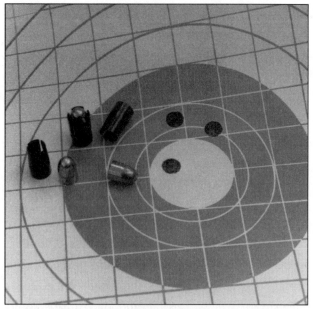

Saboted full metal jacketed bullets like the 230 grain Speer .45, when loaded with light powder charges, produce excellent accuracy out to 100 yards.

Most modern in-line muzzleloading shotguns share a common fault: they are fitted with stocks much better suited for a rifle. The combs are often too low for snap shots at a rising ringneck rooster, speeding bobwhite, or darting cottontail. The shooter must carefully position his cheek on the stock and sight down the barrel, as he would with a rifle. The more the turkey hunter treats a wild turkey like big game, the more successful he'll be—and that includes taking deliberate aim on a relatively small kill zone.

SCOPING THE GOBBLER

A large aperture peep sight or a low magnification scope can be easily mounted on most of these guns, giving hunters an even more precise sighting system. It's not uncommon for a shotgun barrel to pattern low, high, right or left when a standard bead is all there is for aiming. A peep sight or scope allows the impact of a shot load to be adjusted, the same as with a rifle. Several seasons back, I installed a "Pro Diamond" shotgun scope made by Simmons aboard a Knight MK-86. The center reticle of this scope forms a diamond just large enough for a turkey's head to fit into at 12 to 15 yards. Thanks also to the low 2x magnification, this combination accounted for nearly a dozen spring and fall gobblers over the course of several seasons. I've since replaced that scope with a Williams' standard "peep" sight. Here the front bead of the Knight shotgun is mounted on a short ramp, elevating it slightly up and off of the barrel. When hunting in low light conditions, I remove the tiny aperture by unthreading it from the rear of the sight. With a much larger aperture now, it's much easier to sight in on a gobbler that comes in to my calls minutes after flying down from its roost. While not quite as precise as aiming through the smaller aperture, it still provides positive aiming during the dim light of early morning.

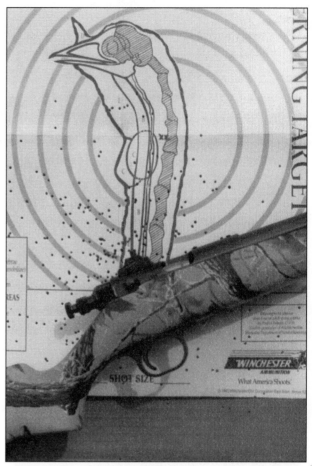

This pattern is too low for effective turkey hunting.

The Thompson/Center System 1 muzzleloader is equally suitable for use with either a scope or receiver sight. When mounting one of the excellent Pentax Zero-X Lightseeker scopes on the shotgun, and using a set of Weaver-styled bases and rings, the job took only five minutes. This scope offers absolutely no magnification, making it easier to locate an oncoming gobbler, put his head in the circle, and ease back on the trigger.

While a growing number of states now conduct a fall season for turkeys, spring is considered the only true turkey-hunting season by connoisseurs of the sport. Fall tactics often require glassing and stalking to get within range, much like hunting big game. Once you've hunted the wild turkey gobbler in spring at the height of his mating showmanship, though, you'll understand why serious turkey hunters look down their noses at fall hunting.

CALLS, BAD WEATHER AND BIG GAME RIFLES

One of the keys to luring a gobbler within muzzleloading shotgun range is good calling. With the variety of box calls, push-button calls, slate calls, tube calls, and mouth-blown diaphragm calls now on the market, anyone who really wants to hunt turkeys can find a call that duplicates the sounds made by a wild turkey hen. These are the same sounds that can drive an old gobbler crazy come spring. The hen turkey makes a wide range of sounds, a combination that often works better than others when luring a gobbler in close. But if you can learn only one call, make yourself the best damned yelper in the woods. More gobblers have been brought to gun with a simple yelp than all other sounds combined. And having mastered the yelp, work on the cluck, the purr, the cut and the cackle. Soon you'll sound like the real thing.

Spring turkey seasons unfortunately coincide with some of the wettest weather of the year, which makes a turkey hunter's life nothing short of miserable. When faced with damp weather or the chances of a sudden downpour, a few precautions can help ensure a hunter's old smokepole will, when it come time to pull the trigger, belch forth fire, smoke and a hard-hitting charge of shot. Easily the number one cause of misfires during rainy weather is a wet percussion cap. Indeed, the tiny metallic cap which provides the fire needed for ignition with most modern or traditionally styled muzzleloading shotguns is the most vulnerable part of the entire load. The main powder charge can be protected from dampness by slipping a latex rubber "muzzle mitt" over the muzzle, or sealing it off with some strips of electrician's tape. In fact, a load can be fired right through this covering without any danger

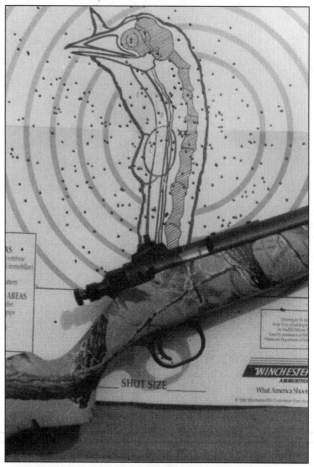

A slight adjustment of the "peep" sight brings the pattern up to print dead on at 25 yards.

or ill effect on a pattern. For loads requiring an over-powder card wad and a fiber cushion wad, adding a healthy squirt of lube between the two will form a moisture proof seal for the powder charge.

A percussion cap on the nipple of a traditionally styled side-hammer, cap-lock shotgun can be sealed from damp weather with just a little beeswax. Before sliding the cap onto the nipple, coat the cone of the nipple lightly with beeswax, or the bowstring wax used by archers. To make sure that none of this wax gets down inside the flash channel, first push a small-diameter wire or vent pick into the hole. Once the cap has been pushed onto the nipple, the wax will form a moisture-proof seal around the flange of the thin copper cup. With the cap now in place, it may be smart to rub some more wax around the skirt of the cap for added precaution. The nipple on most modern in-line muzzleloading shotguns isn't quite as exposed, but it can still get wet. But being located down inside the receiver, it's nearly impossible to waterproof them with beeswax or bowstring wax. Thompson/Center Arms offers an in-line breech cover, however, that fits most modern in-line percussion guns. It's made of a tough, elastic material that fits over the capping port and around the stock for moisture-proof protection.

Only a small handful of states allow the turkey hunter to use a rifle, whether it's modern or muzzleloading. In those states where a rifle can be used to hunt turkeys, it doesn't take anything big to do the job. The calibers and loads used to hunt most other small game should fill the bill nicely for turkeys. A good .32 or .36 caliber muzzleloader stuffed with 25 to 40 grains of FFFg black powder behind a properly patched round ball should produce all the punch needed, while leaving most edible portions intact. What about shooting turkeys with the same rifle used to hunt big game? So long as a favorite front loading big game rifle shoots well with greatly reduced loads, why not use it to take a gobbler? Keep in mind, though, that even with light 40 and 50 grain charges of black powder or Pyrodex, a .50 or .54 caliber muzzleloader loaded with a patched round ball is likely to destroy most edible meat on a 20-pound wild turkey. The faster rates of rifling twist found in most modern in-line rifles usually make them very accurate with light 30 to 35 grain charges behind a round ball. That in turn, could make it better suited than a traditional long rifle with a slow rate of twist requiring at lest 50 or 60 grains for acceptable accuracy. Saboted loads consisting of light 30 to 40 grain powder charges and a full metal jacketed bullet, similar to those often fired from a .45 Automatic pistol, should keep damage

This 25-pound Missouri gobbler can take a heavy punch to put down—and keep down.

to edible portions at a minimum. The key is to put the bullet exactly where it needs to go—cleanly downing the bird without destroying a lot of great eating. Be sure, though, that your state allows the use of rifles for turkey hunting. Most states do not.

Muzzleloading for spring gobblers isn't for everyone, but it's a challenging way to take this great game bird. It requires a lot of effort, scouting and hard hunting to bring home a gobbler with consistency. Turkey hunters who take the time to work up a good load, learn the limitation of their muzzleloading shotgun, and hunt hard enough to be successful will surely discover the real satisfaction of hunting the wild turkey—up close and personal.

LOADING DATA

Knight MK-86 12-Gauge Shotgun/ Extra-Full Choke Tube Load	Muzzle Velocity	Muzzle Energy
110 gr. Pyrodex Select (4 DRAMS)/2 oz. No. 5 shot	1,075 f.p.s.	1,875 ft. lbs.
Loading components: Ballistic Products, Inc. 12 gauge Turkey Ranger wad Knight styrofoam over-shot wad		
Pattern inside 30" circle at 30 yards: 100%		

Thompson/Center System 1 12-Gauge Shotgun/ Full Choke Tube Load	Muzzle Velocity	Muzzle Energy
100 gr. Pyrodex Select (3 3/4 DRAMS)/1 5/8 oz. No. 6 shot	1,225 f.p.s.	1,825 ft. lbs.
Loading components: 2 Thompson/Center lubed 1/4" thick wool felt over-powder/cushion wads Ballistic Products, Inc. BP12 plastic wad Knight styrofoam over-shot wad		
Pattern inside 30" circle at 30 yards: 93% avg.		

PACKING BLACK POWDER REVOLVERS AND PISTOLS

S ince Navy Arms introduced its first reproduction of the Colt Model 1851 Navy percussion revolver during the late 1950s, millions of various percussion revolvers and single-shot muzzleloading pistols have flowed into the U.S. from manufacturers in Italy and Spain. Black powder revolver makers have easily doubled or quadrupled the total number of originals produced by Colt and Remington; in fact, during the late 1980s one Italian manufacturer alone claims to have exported some 900,000 percussion revolvers to the U.S. during the past decade.

While copies of all the various cap and ball revolvers with their steel and brass frames have been imported by a wide range of importers—including Navy Arms, Dixie Gun Works, Euroarms of America, Connecticut Valley Arms and a few others—most were actually made by only a few companies. During the late 1970s and early 1980s, Lyman imported from Italy a line of high-quality percussion revolvers, including fine reproductions of the .36 caliber Colt Model 1851 Navy and the .44 caliber Colt Model 1860 Army, plus .36 and .44 caliber copies of the closed-frame Remington revolvers from the Civil War era. The Lyman revolvers retailed for $10 to $20 more than most comparable models produced by other importers at the time. Lyman paid a premium price for these guns because it wanted a top quality finish, including a deeper blue on the barrel and improved color case-hardening of the Colt frames. Internally, the Lyman revolvers (and those offered

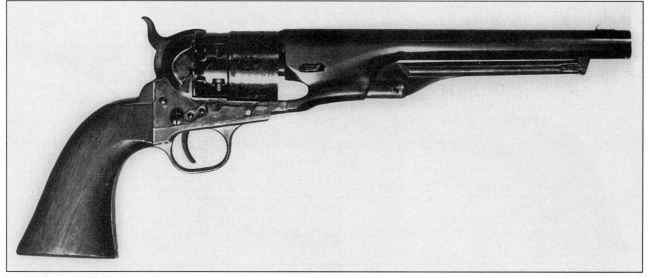

The Dixie Gun Works reproduction of the Colt Model 1860 Army is an authentic copy of the famous open-top frame Colt percussion revolver.

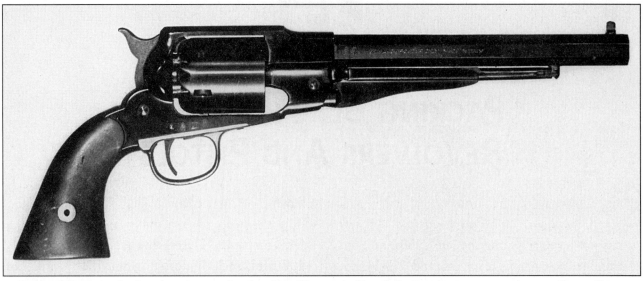

Serious black powder handgunners prefer the closed frame design of the Remington percussion revolvers. Shown is the .44 caliber Dixie reproduction of the Model 1858 Remington Army.

by several other importers) were basically the same. Externally, Lyman's were better duplications of the finish found on original Colt and Remington percussion revolvers. The company no longer markets percussion revolvers, but it does offer a single-shot muzzleloading pistol with nice styling, called the "Lyman Plains Pistol." Colt also offers reproductions of many of the early percussion models that gave the company its start, with many of its component parts coming from a highly reputable Italian manufacturer. The guns are finished and assembled in the U.S. and marked with the Colt name and address, as were the originals.

For the past quarter-century, Sturm, Ruger and Company has offered its well-built percussion .45 caliber "Old Army" model, which is basically a black powder version of the company's revered line of Blackhawk single-action cartridge revolvers. Had breechloading firearms not been developed, this percussion wheelgun would likely represent the end

Ruger's popular .45 caliber "Old Army" percussion six-gun features basically the same internal action as the famed Ruger "Blackhawk" cartridge revolvers.

When loading a percussion revolver, it's necessary to swage an over-sized ball into the chamber with a loading lever attached to the revolver.

product of percussion revolver evolution. Ruger's revolver has an internal working mechanism that is far superior to original percussion revolver designs from 1850 to 1860. Modern coil springs and refined engineering make the action of this revolver more reliable and dependable, while at the same time it is much smoother and more positive. Such quality has its price, of course, which is generally double that of most reproductions of comparable .44 caliber Colt and Remington design revolvers.

No matter whose name appears on a gun, or whether it's a copy of an original open-frame Colt or a closed-frame Remington design, all percussion revolvers basically load in the same manner. The process begins by making sure none of the chambers are already loaded. Because the chambers offer limited room for powder and ball, a projectile that's been seated in a chamber is easily observed at the mouth of the chamber. Simply place the revolver at half-cock and rotate the cylinder, visually checking each chamber to ensure that none contains a charge of powder and ball. Then, with the revolver still at half-cock, rotate the cylinder by hand, placing a percussion cap on each nipple.

Next, snap each cap to make certain the flash hole is clear of oil or debris. The revolver is now ready to be loaded. Most .36 or .44 caliber black powder revolver chambers can't accept a heavy powder charge. The most that can be poured into a .36 caliber Navy Model Colt and still have room for seating a ball is about 29 grains of FFFg. The slightly larger .44 Army models can be stoked up to about 37 grains of FFg, or the volume equivalent of Pyrodex "P". The best accuracy with most of these guns, though, is with powder charges that are 30 to 40 percent lighter.

A powder flask with a properly sized spout screwed in place is the easiest way to place a charge into a chamber. One simply places a finger over the open end of the spout, with the flask held upside down, and works the spring-powered lever with the thumb. When the spout is filled with powder, the lever is released. The flask is then turned upright, leaving the spout filled with one full charge of powder. Connecticut Valley Arms offers a revolver spout set containing 20, 30 and 40 grain spouts. Dixie also has spouts for measuring revolver charges from as little as 12 grains all the way up to 50 grains (for the big .44 Colt Walker), while several other suppliers sell a variety of spouts that can be threaded into most flasks currently available.

This Remington-style brass flask from Connecticut Valley Arms has a spout that measures out powder charges for percussion revolvers.

The Navy Arms "Hawken" single-shot pistol is fine as a back-up gun, but with a patched round ball its short barrel can't produce enough wallop to be used as a primary hunting gun.

Once the powder charge has been poured into the chamber, it's time to place the projectile into (or over) the mouth of the chamber. Black powder revolvers are usually loaded with a round ball, but some shooters prefer short conical bullets. Original Colt revolver bullet molds dating from the 1860s had two cavities, one for casting an appropriately sized round ball, the other for turning out a squat conical bullet for the same caliber revolver. To fit properly, whether a round ball or a conical bullet is used, the projectile has to be slightly larger in diameter than the chamber. With the projectile set at the front of the chamber, rotate it until it's in alignment with the rammer of the loading lever. Using the lever, force the projectile into the smaller diameter chamber. As it's pushed into the chamber, a thin ring of lead will peel away from the outside circumference of the ball or bullet, creating the tight fit necessary to keep the projectile in place until the gun is fired. The chambers of most .36 caliber percussion revolvers measure exactly .375" from wall to wall, while the chambers of most .44 cap and ball handguns are approximately .450". Traditionally, .36 caliber revolvers were loaded with

a .376" diameter ball, while .44 calibers were stuffed with a .451" ball. Many percussion revolver shooters feel that .001" is not enough to ensure a fit tight enough to guarantee that recoil from shooting adjacent chambers won't cause a ball to work forward. Should a projectile protrude far enough to catch on the rear of the barrel, it could prevent the cylinder from rotating. Many .36 caliber handgun shooters now rely on slightly larger .380" balls, and .44 black powder handgunners often load with .454" diameter balls. The manufacturer of Ruger's "Old Army," with chambers measuring .453", recommends loading with .457" diameter projectiles.

Once the projectile is seated over the powder charge, repeat the process with another chamber, then another and so on, until all are loaded. Some shooters charge all chambers of the cylinder first before seating each projectile. This could create several problems, the first being that, while it's virtually impossible to double-charge a chamber, it is possible to skip one and forget to pour in any powder at all. When more than one charge of powder is poured into a chamber, it will usually overfill; but when rotating the cylinder and pouring powder in all chambers before seating any of the projectiles, it's possible to rotate past a chamber, or to neglect pouring a charge into one before rotating to the next. If each chamber isn't inspected visually before the projectile is seated, you could end up with a ball (or bullet) seated all the way down the barrel with no powder under it. Also, when loading a really snug-fitting projectile, you may have to wrestle with the revolver somewhat, enough to force the ball or bullet into the chamber. This could jar a few grains of powder from one of the other chambers. Don't expect consistent accuracy from loads bearing assorted grains of powder behind the projectile.

After all chambers have been loaded with

powder and projectile, top each load with a generous dab of grease, black powder lube, or even good old Crisco. The grease will prevent fire in one chamber from finding its way around the projectile in another, causing it to fire simultaneously—but without a barrel in front of it! That's a condition known as a "chain fire." When a revolver is loaded with ill-fitting projectiles and without any lube, it's possible that every chamber could ignite simultaneously, ruining the revolver and certainly injuring the shooter. Another asset of grease is its tendency to soften any fouling at the face of the cylinder and in the barrel. Hard, crusted fouling can build to the point where cylinders can't rotate. Once it accumulates in the bore, accuracy will suffer. Ox-Yoke Originals packages dry-lubricated felt wads which, when loaded between the projectile and powder charge, do an excellent job of preventing several chambers from firing simultaneously. The dry lubrication used in these wads doesn't do much to help keep fouling soft, however. The combination of a single Ox-Yoke Revolver Wonder Wad under the projectile and a small dab of lube at the mouth of the chamber can double insurance against a chain fire, and at the same time keep the fouling soft and the revolver in operation.

The Buckhunter Pro pistols from Traditions exemplify the new muzzleloading handgun designs being introduced for big game hunters.

What kind of ballistics can these old fashioned five- and six-shooters produce? Not what you'd get from a "magnum" handgun, for certain. Firing a maximum 29 grain charge of FFFg black powder behind a 81 grain .376" ball, a .36 caliber Colt 1851 Navy with a 7 1/2" barrel produces a muzzle velocity of 1,100 f.p.s. That translates into 200 ft. lbs. or so of muzzle energy—about the same as a high velocity .22 long rifle. When shooting a conical bullet, the chamber's maximum powder capacity is reduced by the slightly longer projectile. In fact, behind most conical bullets, such as the 125 grain .36 caliber revolver bullet offered by Buffalo Bullet Company, maximum powder capacity of the .36 Navy chamber is less than 20 grains. With 18 grains of FFFg black powder, the heavier conical leaves the muzzle of the revolver at about 700 f.p.s. and around 150 ft. lbs. of energy. Because of the limited powder charge and much slower velocity, energy is actually lost by opting for the heavier conical bullet. Used with many revolvers, the conical bullets simply shoot more accurately.

Even the .44 caliber Army Model revolvers loaded with maximum powder charges fail as real powerhouses. The popular Colt 1860 Army with an 8" barrel and a chamber capacity of 37 grains of FFFg black powder and a 138 grain .451" soft lead ball is good for slightly over 1,000 f.p.s. and some 325 ft. lbs. of muzzle energy. With 27 grains of FFFg behind a longer 180 grain conical bullet made by the Buffalo Bullet Company, velocity drops back to a little more than 700 f.p.s., with muzzle energy reaching 200 ft. lbs.

The .45 caliber Ruger "Old Army" can consume up to 33 grains of FFFg behind the .457" diameter 190 grain Buffalo Bullet Company revolver conical. At the muzzle of a 7 1/2" barrel, this load has a velocity of about 775 f.p.s. and a muzzle energy of around 280 ft. lbs. Obviously, none of the .36 "Navy" or .44 "Army" percussion revolvers deliver

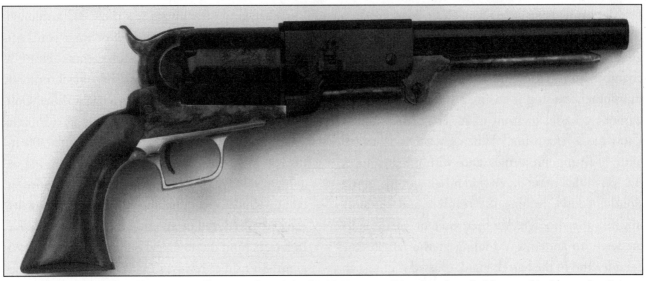

The five-pound .44 caliber Colt Walker was the original ".44 Magnum." Its chambers held more black powder than any other original percussion revolver. This Navy Arms reproduction is an excellent copy.

the knockdown power needed in a big game hunting sidearm. For that reason, most shooters with experience in percussion revolvers forget about developing maximum loads for these guns. They concentrate instead on working up reduced loads that turn in the best accuracy. A common problem shooters run into when firing $^1/_2$ or $^3/_4$ target charges in any of the guns mentioned is a tendency for the projectile to sit too far back in the chamber once it's been seated properly over the powder. This makes it difficult to place a lube seal over a loaded ball or bullet. It also allows the projectile to build up considerable velocity before it hits the barrel rifling, destroying accuracy. A remedy is to use filler of some kind between the powder and projectile, thereby keeping the ball or bullet at the mouth of the chamber. Many top percussion revolver competitors load with light 15 to 20 grain powder charges, then top the powder charge with a granulated buffer compound. To make certain the projectile sits in the same spot for each and every shot, the filler must be measured with the same care as the powder charge.

A shooter who's bound and determined to hunt big game species with a black powder revolver should concentrate on one of the big .44 caliber Colt Walker reproductions. The largest of all the Colt revolvers, this massive sidearm measures $14^1/_2$" in length and weighs just over $4^1/_2$ pounds. Its long chambers can contain as many as 50 grains of FFFg behind a tight-fitting .454" ball. This load pushes the 141 grain sphere from the muzzle of the Walker's 9" barrel at around 1,200 f.p.s. and generates approximately 450 ft. lbs. of energy. While many consider this revolver the original ".44 Magnum," it still doesn't produce energy levels high enough to warrant use on anything much larger than javelina, small deer or wild hogs at close range. And with its simple hammer-notch rear sight and squat blade front sight, it's doubtful that anyone will try shooting much of anything past 20 or 25 yards with Colt's big handgun.

SINGLE-SHOT MUZZLELOADING PISTOLS

Contrary to popular belief, the early American "longhunter" of the East and the hardy mountain men of the West rarely packed a sidearm. Often in the wilds for months on end, these rugged mountain men traveled light, often sleeping on the ground. They avoided packing anything that wasn't absolutely necessary for survival. While some probably wished they'd had access to a quick second shot, most simply put their trust in the long guns they packed. Before a practical frontloading revolver was introduced around 1840, most muzzleloading handguns were muzzleloading single-shot pistols. When an early frontiersman packed a sidearm at all, it was usually the same caliber as his rifle, utilizing the same patch and ball. Except for the amount of powder used in the shorter handgun, it was loaded in much the same manner. You begin by wiping the bore with a dry patch to remove any oil left from the last cleaning. If it's a percussion handgun, snap two or three caps on the nipple to clear the ignition system. To make sure all the oil has been removed from the flash channel and barrel, leave the cleaning jag and patch at the bottom of the barrel while snapping the caps. Instead of fouling up the barrel, any oil that remains will wind up on the dry patch.

For a flintlock pistol, first wipe the bore with a dry patch, then check the flash hole that runs from the pan into the rear of the bore. Push a small diameter wire or vent pick through the hole to ensure that nothing prevents the flash from reaching the powder charge in the barrel. Experienced flintlock shooters often leave a vent pick in the flash hole while loading. Once the handgun is loaded, the vent pick can then be removed, allowing the powder to lay loosely in the barrel against the bore side of the vent hole. Many shooters feel this practice contributes to sure-fire ignition with a flintlock.

Once the bore has been wiped and the ignition system cleared, the next step is to pour a measured powder charge through the muzzle before starting the projectile into the muzzle. Whereas a short starter is a handy accessory for loading a muzzleloading rifle, it's practically a necessity when loading a muzzleloading pistol. Ball and patch combinations that seem to load with relative ease into a rifle can be nearly impossible to push through the muzzle of a pistol. That's because a pistol is more likely to be loaded with its butt resting against the shooter's hip. When loading a rifle, the butt sits on the ground, providing more resistance as a tight patch and ball are pushed through the muzzle. Should a patch and ball be too tight when loading through the muzzle of a frontloading pistol, try a thinner patch material. Instead of loading with .015" patching, try .010" patching. A pistol with a shorter barrel won't use as much powder, of course,

The .50 caliber Great Plains Pistol makes an excellent side arm to accompany Lyman's Great Plains Rifle of the same caliber.

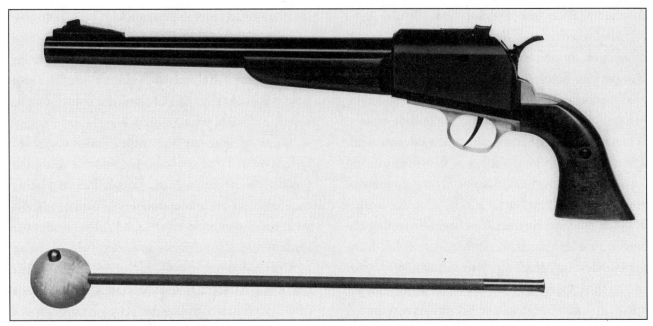

The Thompson/Center Scout Pistol features a fast-twist barrel for exceptional accuracy with saboted bullets, plus a reliable and fast in-line ignition.

so there shouldn't be as much pressure or velocity. Often a thinner patch will shoot just as well—and is a lot easier to load. Once the patch and ball are through the muzzle, seat them firmly over the powder charge with a ramrod.

Not many knowledgeable muzzleloading pistol shooters recommend loading and shooting "Maxi-style" lead conicals out of a single-shot front-loading handgun. Many of these guns have faster rates of rifling twist than are found in rifles, true, and they may shoot fairly well with a bore-sized lead conical. The problem is, these guns are usually carried with the muzzle pointing down and shoved into a belt or hanging from a special belt hook. A bore-sized lead conical that loaded relatively tight at the muzzle no longer enjoys the same tight fit. When a muzzleloading pistol is carried muzzle down, a loose-fitting conical starts working forward. By the time the shooter pulls the handgun and fires it, the projectile could be sitting just inches from the muzzle, posing the same danger as a barrel obstruction.

The .50 caliber Lyman "Great Plains Pistol" has a 9-inch barrel rifled with a one-turn-in-32 inches rate of rifling twist. Its recommended load is 30 grains of FFFg black powder behind a patched .490" round ball. The Connecticut Valley Arms .50 caliber Kentucky pistol features a 9³/₄-inch barrel with a one-turn-in-48 inches rate of rifling twist and has a recommended load of 30 grains of FFFg with a patched .490" round ball. The Navy Arms .45 caliber Kentucky pistol, with its 10¹/₄-inch barrel, has a one-turn-in-18 inches rate of rifling twist. The importer of handguns made by Pedersoli recommends loading with 25 grains of FFFg and a patched .440 ball. And finally, the Dixie Gun Works .45 caliber reproduction of a Charles Moore duelling pistol comes with a .44 caliber bore rifled with a one-turn-in-18 inches rate of twist. Its recommended load is still only 35 grains of FFFg and a patched .433 round ball. While all these guns and loads may produce fine target accuracy, and may be useful for shots at small game or for dispatching a wounded large game, none should ever be considered as a primary hunting muzzleloader. They simply don't produce enough energy to get the job done.

MUZZLELOADING PISTOLS FOR HUNTING BIG GAME

The reason why most game departments do not allow the use of muzzleloading handguns—especially percussion revolvers—for hunting deer and other big game is their inadequate energy levels. Most single-shot pistols stoked up with 40 or 50 grains of FFFg will not produce enough energy for downing even a small southern whitetail at relatively close range. However, several single-shot muzzleloading pistols are capable of taking some big game, but only when time is taken to work up the most accurate, hard-hitting load these handguns can handle. Three models in particular stand out as serious muzzleloading big game pistols: the Knight HK-94 Hawkeye, the Thompson/Center Scout, and the Kahnke Model 82. When loaded with maximum powder charges and modern plastic saboted jacketed handgun bullets, these in-line percussion handguns are capable of matching—even surpassing—the velocities and energies produced by many .44 Magnum cartridge revolver loads.

The Knight HK-94 Hawkeye is a handful of muzzleloading firepower. This .50 caliber single-shot frontloading handgun has many of the same features found on Knight's popular in-line rifles, including a unique double-safety system, removable breech plug for easy cleaning, adjustable trigger, and a receiver that's drilled and tapped for "no-gunsmithing" scope installation. But what makes this handgun better suited for hunting big game than the vast majority of others on the market is the 12-inch Green Mountain barrel. The pistol's fast one-turn-in-20 inches rate of rifling twist can handle a wide range of saboted handgun bullets accurately. Its added length also promises better utilization of heavy powder charges than even a slightly shorter 10-inch barrel might. This pistol is, in fact, fully capable of burning a 70 grain charge of FFFg or the volume equivalent of Pyrodex "P". When such charges are loaded behind a saboted 240 grain .44 or 260 grain .45 caliber Knight Big Game Bullet, the Hawkeye barks with authority. At the muzzle, these loads are good

The Knight HK-93 "Hawkeye" pistol is a serious hunting handgun that happens to load from the muzzle.

The Kahnke Model 82 is one of the hardest-shooting, most accurate muzzleloading big game pistols available, witness this 5-shot group fired from 50 yards with open sights.

for around 1,100 to 1,200 f.p.s. and energy levels topping 800 ft. lbs.

The Thompson/Center Scout, offered in .50 or .54 caliber, also comes with a 12-inch barrel, which allows complete utilization of 60 and 70 grain charges of FFFg or Pyrodex "P" behind saboted handgun bullets. Although available in both .50 or .54, most shooters find that the .50 caliber version produces the best accuracy without sacrificing power. Both pistols are commonly loaded with saboted bullets of the same diameter and weight, with bullet diameter and bore size being the only difference. Generally, the thinner the plastic sleeves of the sabot, the better accuracy is achieved. In that regard, the .50 caliber will usually outshoot the .54 while 70 grains of powder represent the maximum load for a Scout in either caliber. This much powder behind a Hornady 240 grain or a 275 grain .44 XTP jacketed hollow-point bullet loaded with a Thompson/Center "Break-O-Way" three-piece sabot should surpass the ballistics produced by factory .44 Magnum revolver loads.

As for the Kahnke Model 82, it is indisputably the "magnum" of today's single-shot muzzleloading big game pistols. In looks and design, it isn't much different than the Thompson/Center Scout Pistol. Both guns are built with a single-action revolver-styled grip and a barrel that's easily removed from the frame for cleaning. Their design places the rear of each barrel and the exposed nipple at the rear of the receiver, thus maintaining a good balance even with a long barrel length. Their designs also enable shooters to switch easily from one caliber barrel to another. The Kahnke Model 82 barrels are offered in .36, .45, .50 and .54 caliber, with each bore size available in lengths of 10½, 12 or 14 inches.

With a 70 grain charge of FFFg or Pyrodex "P", and a saboted 240 to 275 grain jacketed bullet, a 12-inch .50 caliber Kahnke barrel produces basically the same velocities and energy levels produced by similar loads in a Knight Hawkeye or Thompson/ Center Scout pistol. When one of the slightly longer 14-inch barrels is slipped into the receiver, the velocity and energy levels climb slightly. A saboted 240 grain .44 bullet is pushed from the muzzle of the 14-inch barrel by 70 grains of FFFg at almost 1,300 f.p.s, producing a muzzle energy of nearly 900 ft.lbs. Whether the 14-inch Kahnke barrel can fully consume 80 grains of FFFg, the heavier powder charge definitely pushes the 240 grain bullet out of the muzzle at slightly less than 1,400 f.p.s, which means energy levels are at an impressive 1,000 ft. lbs.

Such performance from single-shot muzzleloading handguns with their long barrels, maximum powder charges and hard-hitting saboted bullets have convinced game departments to take another look at these guns. In recent years, a number of game departments have, in fact, reversed regulations prohibiting the use of some front-loading pistols on deer-sized game. *To those who decide to give one a whirl, check first to make sure it's legal in the state where you plan to hunt, then take the time to work up as accurate a load as a legal handgun can muster.*

BLACK POWDER HANDGUN BALLISTICS

PERCUSSION REVOLVERS

POWDER CHARGE (FFFg)	PROJECTILE	MUZZLE VELOCITY (AVG.)	MUZZLE ENERGY (AVG.)
Colt Model 1851 Navy – .36 Caliber – 7 1/2" Barrel			
17 gr.*	81 gr./.376" RB	880 f.p.s.	140 ft. lbs.
20 gr.*	81 gr./.376" RB	965 f.p.s.	165 ft. lbs.
23 gr.	81 gr./.376" RB	1,015 f.p.s.	185 ft. lbs.
29 gr.**	81 gr./.376" RB	1,095 f.p.s.	215 ft. lbs.
Colt Model 1860 Army – .44 Caliber – 8" Barrel			
19 gr.*	138 gr./.451" RB	705 f.p.s.	150 ft. lbs.
25 gr.*	138 gr./.451" RB	805 f.p.s.	195 ft. lbs.
31 gr.	138 gr./.451" RB	935 f.p.s.	265 ft. lbs.
37 gr.**	138 gr./.451" RB	1,030 f.p.s.	325 ft. lbs.
Ruger "Old Army" – .45 Caliber – 7 1/2" Barrel			
30 gr.*	143 gr./.457" RB	850 f.p.s.	235 ft. lbs.
40 gr.	143 gr./.457" RB	925 f.p.s.	280 ft. lbs.
25 gr.*	190 gr./.457" BBC conical	710 f.p.s.	210 ft. lbs.
30 gr.	190 gr./.457" BBC conical	765 f.p.s.	250 ft. lbs.

SINGLE SHOT MUZZLELOADING PISTOLS

POWDER CHARGE (FFFg)	PROJECTILE	MUZZLE VELOCITY (AVG.)	MUZZLE ENERGY (AVG.)
In-Line Muzzleloading Pistol – 12" Barrel – .50 Caliber			
50 gr.	.44/240 gr. JHP	1,115 f.p.s.	660 ft. lbs.
60 gr.	.44/240 gr. JHP	1,200 f.p.s.	765 ft. lbs.
60 gr.	.45/260 gr. JHP	1,160 f.p.s.	775 ft. lbs.
70 gr.	.45/260 gr. JHP	1,200 f.p.s.	835 ft. lbs.
In-Line Muzzleloading Pistol – 14" Barrel – .50 Caliber			
70 gr.	.44/240 gr. JHP	1,280 f.p.s.	890 ft. lbs.
80 gr.	.44/240 gr. JHP	1,375 f.p.s.	1,010 ft. lbs

*Buffer required for best accuracy **Maximum chamber capacity load*

MUZZLELOADER SAFETY

Anytime a shooter picks up a muzzleloading rifle, pistol, shotgun, musket or frontloading cap and ball revolver, common sense dictates that he or she should handle it the same as any firearm. Always treat any gun as if it's loaded, keeping the muzzle pointed in a safe direction. While federal regulations may exempt frontloaders from many of the laws and restrictions now imposed on modern cartridge firearms, never lose sight of the fact that these are still indeed powerful weapons. When not handled properly, muzzleloading guns can cause serious injuries to shooters and bystanders alike. The way muzzleloaders are designed makes them even more dangerous to those who are inexperienced in the handling, loading, shooting and hunting with these guns. Powder loaded through the muzzle, external hammers, exposed ignition systems, an occasional misfire, all make loading and shooting a muzzleloader more of a "hands-on" experience than with a modern firearm. But that's part of the appeal. Those who are

Loading and shooting a muzzleloader is not difficult, even for this young shooter. It only requires the right combination of components, and a shooter who knows what he or she is doing.

new to muzzleloading will soon discover that shooting and hunting safety requires more than simply dropping a cartridge in the chamber, closing the action, slipping off the safety, taking aim and firing. The following section looks at the cause of most mishaps with frontloading guns and how to avoid these problems.

LOADING SAFETY

The first thing to do when picking up a front-loading gun is to check the ignition system to determine whether or not a percussion cap is in place on the nipple, or a charge of priming powder is in the pan of a flintlock. If so, there's a good chance a powder charge and projectile are down the barrel. Whether the ignition system is primed or not, however, always treat a gun as if it's loaded. When loading a muzzleloader, first remove the cap or priming powder from the ignition system. Next, to prevent double-loading a gun, make sure there isn't a load already in the barrel simply by dropping a ramrod down the bore. Since most ramrods are basically the same length as the barrel, they should lie flush with the muzzle. Occasionally, a rod may be slightly longer than the barrel, but no more than an inch or so. If three to four inches of rod extends from the muzzle, the gun is probably loaded.

If the loading components are not known, especially if the rifle has been loaded and handled by someone else, do not try shooting out the load. If the rifle has a removable breech plug, break the rifle down, then push the powder and projectile out of the barrel with a ramrod. If a rifle does not include a removable breech plug, a CO2 discharger is a handy accessory to own. It allows a shooter to blow the powder charge and bullet through the ignition system and out of the bore with a blast of compressed air. When using one of these dischargers, though, always keep the muzzle pointed in a safe direction. The projectile could be pushed from the

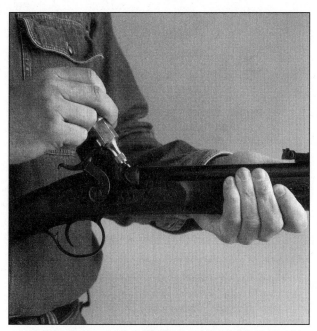

Compressed air bullet dischargers simplify removal of a projectile loaded without powder, or a load of uncertain components.

muzzle at considerable velocity, becoming almost as dangerous as when fired with a powder charge.

Once the rifle has been unloaded, it's safe to load. Start by making sure the ignition system is clear. Snapping several caps will usually do the job with a percussion gun. With a flintlock, push a small diameter vent pick through the vent hole to clear any fouling from the ignition system. Check a percussion gun by holding the muzzle next to a leaf or blade of grass as the cap is fired. If the system is clear, the leaf or grass will move as pressure from the cap travels the length of the barrel. Experienced percussion rifle shooters always wipe the bore with a dry patch to remove traces of oil. Then they push the cleaning jag and patch down to the breech plug and leave it there while snapping two or three caps to clear the ignition system. When the ramrod is pulled from the bore, a dark burned spot in the center of the patch will indicate a good fire is getting into the barrel.

When loading a muzzleloader at a bench, prop the gun so that the barrel is pointed away from the face and body. When loading in the field, hold

The open ignition system of this traditionally styled percussion rifle presents several safety concerns. This hunter should be wearing shooting glasses to keep cap particles and residue away from his face and eyes.

the muzzleloader between the knees—and never place the face directly over the muzzle when pouring powder or seating a projectile. And when dumping a charge of powder through the muzzle, always use a measure separate from the powder container. Don't adopt the dangerous practice of measuring directly from a flask. By doing so, there's always the chance that a burning ember left in the bore from the last shot, or from snapping caps on a percussion ignition system, could ignite the charge. If the charge ignites, a good scare, a few light burns, and maybe some singed hair will no doubt be the only result; but if some of the flame finds its way into a flask or horn, you could be holding a bomb in your hand.

Always heed the gun manufacturers' recommended maximum load warnings, which are established for good reasons. Load with the recommended granulation and type of powder. Most important, never load a muzzleloader with anything other than black powder, Pyrodex or some other black powder substitute recommended by the gun maker. While every container of Pyrodex is clearly marked "smokeless propellant," the powder has been formulated to produce black powder pressures in a muzzleloading gun. It also produces a cloud of smoke for those

muzzleloading purists who feel something's missing without it. Do not load a frontloading gun with any other smokeless propellant, however.

PROPER BULLET FIT

Safe loading practices dictate that a muzzle-loaded projectile must be seated solidly over a powder charge. If a projectile lies an inch or so over the powder, the only effect will most likely be inconsistent accuracy. But if a bullet is seated four, five, six or more inches over the powder charge and left there, or if the bullet works its way that far ahead of the powder charge, it could create erratic pressures that might cause the barrel to bulge or even burst. So the fit of a projectile within the bore is not only crucial to good muzzleloader accuracy, it's vital to muzzleloader safety. A projectile that fits too loose can work forward, creating a dangerous situation. It can be even more so when loading and shooting the bore-sized conical bullets than with other muzzleloader projectiles.

Conical bore-sized lead bullets for muzzle-loading rifles generally fall into one of two categories: "slip fit" or "interference fit." The best example of the former is the big hollow-based Civil War-era projectile known as the "Minie Bullet." This elongated projectile was cast slightly under-sized

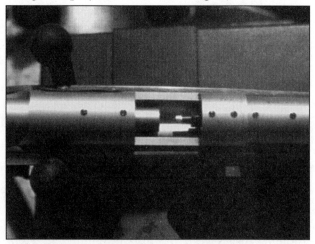

The ignition system of this in-line percussion rifle is protected somewhat but is still exposed.

Switching from a coarser grain powder like Pyrodex "RS" (left) to Pyrodex "P" (right) could create excessive pressures in some guns.

and Maxi-Hunter, Hornady Great Plains Bullet, and Buffalo Bullet Company's conical bullets. When these bullets are started into the bore, the rifling must engrave at least one oversized bearing surface. Once the rifling has cut the soft lead, the bullet can then be pushed easily down the bore with a ramrod. This may result in a more precise fit with the rifling, and it might indeed hold the bullet in the bore more securely. But lead has no memory. Once the rifling has cut into the soft lead, the bullet no longer offers much resistance to movements one way or the other, whether it's being pushed down the bore with a ramrod or jarred forward as the hunter leaps over some obstacle in the woods. Moreover, as the bullet is pushed down the barrel, this fit continues to loosen as minute amounts of soft lead are eroded by the lands. When loading, shooting and especially hunting with any bore-sized lead conical bullet, it must be seated solidly over the powder charge. And when hunting with bullets of either slip fit or interference fit design, the cap should be removed from a percussion ignition system and the ramrod pushed down the bore occasionally to prevent the bullet from slipping forward off the powder charge.

purposely so it could be loaded quickly and easily into the big .58 caliber rifled muskets during the heat of battle. The precise fit of a Minie relies on the thin skirt of a hollow base as it expands into the grooves by the burning powder charge. Little of any resistance is felt as one of these bullets is ramrodded down the bore. Should a gun be carried muzzle down, however, the bullet could easily slide off the powder charge. If it slides far enough forward, it could work the same as a barrel obstruction.

As for the "interference fit" design, classic examples include the Thompson/Center Maxi-Ball

Several years ago, an independent group of muzzleloading shooters held tests to determine how much pressure it took to pull a projectile off a

The hollow-based Minie bullets, fired from big Civil War rifle muskets like this Navy Arms Model 1863 Springfield, load easily and fit the bore so loosely that a projectile could slide forward with the muzzle carried down, creating a potentially dangerous situation.

powder charge. Bore-sized conical bullets, patched round balls and saboted bullets were fitted with tiny eyelets to which a string was attached. The different projectiles were then seated into the same .50 caliber bore, with the loose end of the string attached to a scale. The slip fit, bore-sized bullets took so little effort that the force didn't even register on the scale. Most of the interference fit bullets required less than four pounds of exertion to pull forward, while the old patched round ball registered an average of 20 pounds of force. The plastic saboted bullets offered the most resistance, requiring 40 pounds of exertion.

SAFETY ON THE RANGE

Perhaps it's the result of mandatory hunter safety education for beginning shooters and hunters, but today's shooters seem more safety-conscious than ever before. It could also be the fact that many shooters know someone with impaired hearing caused by over-exposure to the sounds of gunfire, or who has some degree of sight loss due to debris or powder fouling getting into an eye. Fortunately, new shooters tend to be more conscious about the need for hearing and eye protection. Because of the exposed ignition systems of most muzzleloaders, these needs have become even more evident.

Never forget that when loading a frontloader always keep face and hands clear of the bore.

Traditional side-hammer styled locks are not built with a safety (the half-cock notch of most such locks is not considered a safety).

Shooting at most public or private ranges generally means the participants are using primarily modern firearms, not muzzleloaders. Where adequate provisions exist, don't load and shoot from the same bench or table as other frontloaders. Most ranges don't provide a second facility for loading components, so muzzleloading shooters may have to improvise. If there's only one shooting position, at least the container of powder should be removed from the bench before shooting. Several years ago, I observed a shooter who wished he had done just that. He was shooting from an enclosed shack with two shooting positions, but with no other tables or benches for laying out loading components. Another shooter next to him was loading with pre-measured charges carried in small, sealed plastic tubes, while the man I observed was loading from a powder flask. After each shot, he carefully measured a charge of powder from his flask and discharged it into a separate measure. He then leveled off the powder charge and poured it into the muzzle of his rifle. Once the projectile was seated, he placed the rifle on the sandbags, sat down at the bench, capped the rifle, and fired. He repeated that process all morning, loading and firing in the neighborhood of 30 or more shots. What he didn't notice was that every time he leveled off a charge of powder, a few grains would fall onto the loading and shooting bench—exactly where he had put down the flask full of powder.

His last shot of the day was one he'll never forget. He sat down behind the modern in-line percussion hunting rifle, reached up with a capper and placed a cap on the nipple. He then sighted in on the target and squeezed off the shot. The explosion that followed sounded as if the shack had been hit by a mortar. Fire from the exploding cap had somehow reached the loose powder on the bench. Worse, some of the flash had found its way around the valve of the flask, igniting more than a quarter-pound of black powder inside the flask. Like a rocket, the heavy brass flask blew off the valve dispenser and headed toward the steel door, hitting it with enough force to punch a hole measuring two inches in diameter right through the metal. If that flask had been angled toward the shooter, or the second man at the adjacent bench, the results would have been disastrous.

When shooting at a range, never cap or prime a muzzleloader until you're sitting behind it at a bench, ready to fire. If shooting off-hand, wait until you are at the firing line, with the muzzle pointed down range. The other shooters at the range will greatly appreciate such safety precautions.

When loading and shooting repeatedly, take time to wipe the fouling from the bore. For best accuracy, do this between every shot; but for safety's sake, do it at least after every second or third shot. Nothing looks worse than a shooter who is literally wrestling with a ramrod, trying to force another projectile down a fouled bore. This can be dangerous, too, especially when loading with the kind of frail wooden ramrod that comes with most rifles. More than one black powder shooter has a nasty scar on his wrist or hand where a ramrod had snapped and left a nasty gouge.

A strong synthetic ramrod, similar to this polymer-coated fiberglass rod from Thompson/Center, could prevent a broken rod and a gouged hand during loading.

Good accuracy can never be maintained with a dirty bore. When fouling builds with each shot, the residue makes it difficult to seat the projectile at the same spot each time. And as the bore becomes even more fouled, it causes more drag or resistance for the projectile, hence higher pressures and poor accuracy. A fouled bore becomes really dangerous when it's so dirty the projectile ends up well off the powder charge.

Once a good load is established, take time to drop the ramrod into the bore over a fresh charge in a clean barrel, then mark it. That way it will take only a glance to indicate if the projectile has been seated all the way down. If the mark sits well above the muzzle, you'll know immediately if the projectile needs to be seated farther down, or the gun has been loaded with too much powder. If the rod drops past the mark, you'll know if the powder charge was too light (or maybe you forgot to pour in any powder at all!). With most percussion guns, removing a projectile that may have been loaded without powder behind it isn't the predicament it may seem. The nipple can be removed from most guns and a few grains of powder trickled in behind the projectile. The nipple can then be replaced, a cap placed on the nipple and the projectile fired out. Only a few grains can push many projectiles out of a barrel. If a ball or bullet moves forward only a few inches, repeat the process, tapping the barrel as the powder is trickled in. The idea is to get more powder behind the projectile.

Before capping and firing, first push the projectile down over the powder with a ramrod. The projectile should now shoot out from the muzzle. If the muzzleloader features a removable breech plug, the projectile can be pushed out either end of the barrel. If there's a hang fire, it's probably the result of not clearing the ignition system before loading. The burning powder charge more often than not burns away the moisture, cleaning solvent or oil, which may have prevented fire from reaching the powder charge. Succeeding shots will usually fire without any hesitation; but if there's a total misfire, the muzzleloader should be handled with great care. Stand at the bench with the rifle to your shoulder for a minute or so to make sure there's no pronounced delayed fire. Before moving the rifle, place another cap on the nipple, or prime the pan of a flintlock, then try to fire the gun again. If it still doesn't fire, repeat once more. After that, handle the rifle the same as if it were loaded without powder. As for a percussion gun, remove the nipple and trickle in a few grains of powder, replace the nipple and try shooting again. If it doesn't fire, you may have to pull the projectile and dump out the powder charge. If the front loader has a removable breech plug, break down the gun and push the load out with a ramrod; or use a compressed air discharger to shoot the load out. Once the barrel is clear, treat the gun as if it was being reloaded for the first time that day.

SAFETY IN THE FIELD

As with all hunting accidents, carelessness and poor judgment are the causes of most muzzleloader hunting accidents. Mistaking another hunter for game is easily the number one cause of serious injuries and fatalities; but according to a study of hunting accidents worldwide, accidental discharge of a muzzleloader is nearly as serious a problem. For example, the half-cock of a traditionally styled muzzleloader lock mechanism should never be considered a "safety." While in that half-cock position, the hammer of a percussion rifle sits close to, but not on, the percussion cap. This makes the ignition system less susceptible to being fired accidentally than when the hammer sits directly on the percussion cap. Accidental discharge would result from the rifle falling over and hitting the hammer, or when a rifle slips from a shooter's hands. On the other hand, the tip of the sear and the half-

This muzzleloading whitetail hunter is asking for an accident. He's not wearing a safety belt and his rifle could easily slip from its precarious position and discharge as it hits the ground.

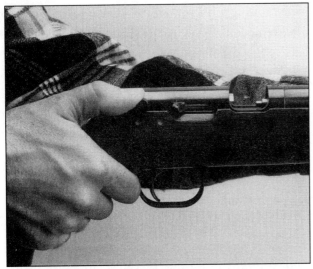

The sliding thumb-operated safety of this Thompson/Center Fire Hawk prevents the trigger from being pulled accidentally.

cock notch (in the tumbler) are both easily broken, and it doesn't take much of a blow for a hammer to fall and fire the rifle. More than one black powder hunter has been injured after slipping on a wet log, striking his hammer on the way down. Several companies now offer "cap covers," which slip directly over a capped nipple and absorb the fall of a hammer.

Modern in-line percussion rifles are built with modern safeties, much like those found on contemporary centerfire hunting rifles. Most are in the form of a trigger lock, which prevents the trigger from being pulled and disengaging the sear from the hammer. During a hard fall, the sear itself could still break, or the pin holding the sear in place could shear, allowing the rifle to fire. One of the safest muzzleloaders on the market today is the Knight in-line percussion rifle, which features a double safety system. The primary safety, which is thumb-operated, is the standard trigger lock safety just described. The secondary safety is in the form of a knurled collar positioned at the rear of the hammer. It fits on a threaded portion of the hammer shaft, and when the hammer is pulled to full cock (there is no half-cock) this safety turns

forward. Once it's in the forward position, an effective hammer block forms. Should the hammer fall, the safety, which is now in the forward position, will bottom out against the rear of the receiver before the nose of the hammer can strike the capped nipple.

With both primary and secondary safeties engaged on the Knight in-line rifles, the chances of both safeties failing should the rifle fall from, say, an elevated stand is unlikely. For the hunter who simply hates the idea of having to rely on two safeties, the rear secondary safety should be used when hunting from an elevated platform, and the side trigger lock safety employed when hunting on the ground. A great feature of the threaded secondary safety is that it's quiet. If suddenly a big whitetail buck should appear directly under a

Climbing into an elevated stand while carrying a loaded muzzleloader is a dangerous practice.

When hunting whitetails from an elevated tree stand, the hunters should always be aware that a dropped rifle can discharge accidentally with fatal consequences.

hunter's stand, he can slowly turn the safety to the rear without making a sound. Several other modern in-line rifles now feature double safeties as well. The traditional side-hammer rifle shooter can find additional comfort with one of the cap covers installed. It takes only a second to reach up and slip the cover off the capped nipple. Should the rifle slip from winter-chilled hands and fall to the frozen ground below, the cover will protect the cap from being struck by the hammer. Whether a shooter hunts with a modern in-line rifle with double safeties or a traditional side-hammer muzzleloader fitted with a safety cover, there's no use taking unnecessary chances. Never try to climb into a stand with a rifle slung over your shoulder. And

when raising a rifle into a tree stand with a lanyard, first remove the cap from the nipple. If it's a flint-lock rifle, simply dump out the priming powder before pulling it up.

Hunting with a muzzleloading side-by-side shotgun presents another safety concern. During a hunt, it's not uncommon to fire only one barrel. Before reloading the fired barrel, always take a second to remove the percussion cap from the barrel that's still loaded. After all, it's foolish to stand at the muzzle of a loaded and capped bore. Once the first barrel has been reloaded, recap both nipples and continue hunting. If you've fired the same barrel several times without shooting the other, you may also want to drop a ramrod down over the unfired load now and then to make sure recoil hasn't caused the shot load to move forward. This often happens when loading with a one-piece plastic wad unit rather than with a combination of card and cushion wads.

As for transporting muzzleloaders, most states insist that a percussion gun must first be uncapped and the priming powder removed from a flintlock. A few states even require a frontloader to be cased before it's transported. Several serious accidents have resulted from a shooter or hunter reaching into a vehicle and having the hammer catch on the edge of a seat or in a loose-fitting seat cover. As the rifle is pulled from the vehicle, muzzle first, the hammer falls and discharges the load, striking whoever happens to be standing at the muzzle. In at least several instances, shooters have claimed that static electricity caused a muzzleloader to fire. If you've ever slid out of a pickup with nylon seat covers and witnessed a blue arc jumping from your finger tips, you know this is possible.

With more and more hunters now relying on the excellent four-wheel ATVs to get in and out of the woods, an unfortunate number of accidents involving muzzleloaders have occurred. Most often

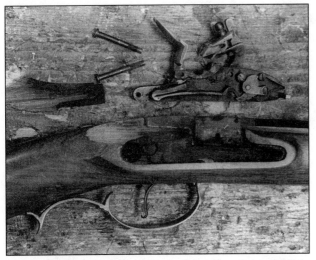

Poor loading practices resulted in the catastrophic failure of this flintlock.

these involve careless drivers who overturn their vehicles, causing a hammer to strike the ground or the vehicle itself. Most of these accidents can be avoided by removing the cap (or priming) from the gun and slipping it into a case, then strapping it to a carrier rack. The Gun Boot made by Kolpin Manufacturing is a good accessory for such ATV owners. The company makes attachments that allow this form-fitting hard case to be attached to the ATV directly, protecting the muzzleloader from rain, snow and mud—and man-made accidents.

When all is said and done, shooting and hunting with guns of frontloading design remains one of our safest pastimes. This safety record can in large part be credited to the "hands on" aspect of muzzleloading, which forces shooters to think about the next step when loading and shooting a frontloading long gun or handgun. Building and shooting one shot at a time leaves little doubt in a shooter's mind about the status of his or her rifle. No matter what type of muzzleloader you're shooting or hunting with, always fall back on common sense—especially when you're not sure about what you're doing. *The following precepts have been generally accepted as the "Ten Commandments" of muzzleloading. Be sure to live by them.*

THE TEN COMMANDMENTS OF MUZZLELOADING SAFETY

1. USE ONLY BLACK OR REPLICA BLACK POWDER. Pyrodex is the most commonly known replica black powder.

2. TREAT EVERY GUN AS IF IT WERE LOADED. Never point a gun at anything you don't intend to shoot. Keep the muzzle pointed in a safe direction at all times. Never lean over the muzzle. Make priming the pan or capping the nipple the last step in loading.

3. BE SURE OF YOUR TARGET BEFORE FIRING. Be aware of the location of other people around you. Know what is behind your target. Never fire into water or at flat, hard surfaces. Round balls are prone to glance or ricochet.

4. BE SURE YOUR GUN IS IN FIRING CONDITION BEFORE YOU PULL THE TRIGGER. Make sure the ball is firmly seated, the gun is not overcharged, and there is no obstruction in the barrel.

5. TREAT A MISFIRE OR FAILURE TO FIRE WITH EXTREME CARE. Keep the gun pointed in a safe direction down range, and wait at least one full minute before repriming.

6. MAKE SURE YOUR GUN IS UNLOADED BEFORE STORING IT. Store the gun, powder and caps separately.

7. PROTECT YOUR EYES AND EARS WHILE SHOOTING. Always wear shooting glasses and ear plugs to prevent possible damage.

8. NEVER SMOKE WHILE LOADING, SHOOTING OR HANDLING BLACKPOWDER PROPELLANTS.

9. NEVER DRINK ALCOHOLIC BEVERAGES BEFORE OR WHILE SHOOTING.

10. USE COMMON SENSE AT ALL TIMES

Courtesy of Dixie Gun Works

FORMULA FOR SUCCESS: ACCESSORIZE

The variety of muzzleloading accessories currently available is tremendous. Nearly every muzzleloading gun maker now offers a wide spectrum of helpful gadgets to give black powder shooters more choices than they probably will ever need. In fact, several major companies have been built around the need for quality muzzleloading accessories. Even in a book this size, it's impossible to cover each and every accessory available, but in this chapter we will concentrate on "must have" accessories for the proper loading, shooting and maintenance of a frontloading gun. Actually, there are several different approaches to accessorizing a muzzleloader. One is to get by with only the bare necessities—for loading and cleaning—that will make life simple, if not austere. And then, there's the overboard approach: buy every muzzleloading gadget currently on the market. The happy medium is to own what's needed to make the job as simple and enjoyable as possible. In covering the different types of muzzleloading accessories, five

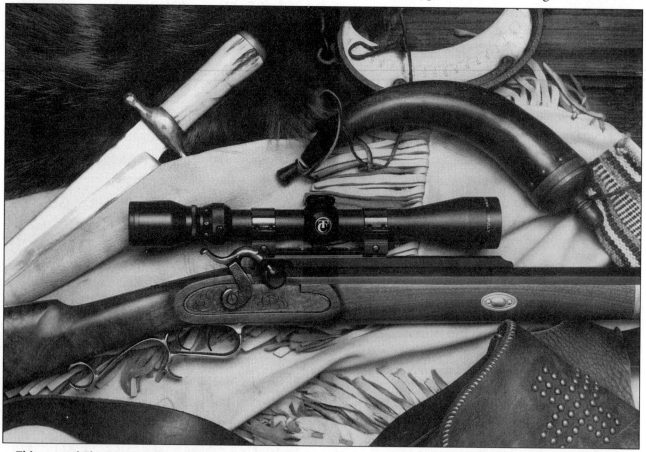

This scoped Thompson/Center Hawken is surrounded by nice but expendable accessories that are generally not used by today's black powder big game hunters.

Other than powder, projectile and fire for ignition, the only accessory needed is a ramrod for seating projectiles over the powder charge.

classifications are included: 1) General Loading and Shooting; 2) General Cleaning and Maintenance; 3) Range Accessories; 4) Authentic Accoutrements; and 5) Hunting Accessories.

I. GENERAL LOADING AND SHOOTING

It doesn't take much to load and shoot a muzzle-loading gun. The basic necessities are powder, projectile and fire for the ignition system. A ramrod is actually the only accessory required. However, without the use of other loading and shooting accessories, it would be impossible to ram two identical loads down a barrel and on their way to the target. Accuracy with a muzzleloading gun relies on a shooter's ability to load a rifle the same exact way for each and every shot. What follows is a round-up of accessories that will help achieve this consistency.

1. POWDER MEASURES

A reliable powder measure is easily the most important accessory a muzzleloading shooter can own. All the attention given to loading with the right type and granulation of powder, or loading with the proper type and diameter of projectile, is wasted unless the shooter loads each round with the exact same amount of powder. We've all seen the movie versions of "Davy Crockett" and "Daniel Boone" as they poured a charge of powder directly from their powder horns straight into the muzzle of "Ol Betsy" without taking time to measure. Perhaps in the heat of an Indian fight, Davy or Daniel might have trickled enough powder down the bore to fire a shot; but when the time came to place a shot on game for the table or during a shooting match, you can bet they used a powder measure.

Black powder shooters once relied on powder measures made from a wide range of materials, often nothing more than the tip of a deer antler or a piece of wood hollowed out to hold a powder charge. In much the same manner, a contemporary black powder shooter on a tight budget can easily fashion his own powder measure, such as an empty brass cartridge case or a piece of plastic tubing that's been

Powder charges that are carefully measured, with every grain accounted for, are vital for good accuracy.

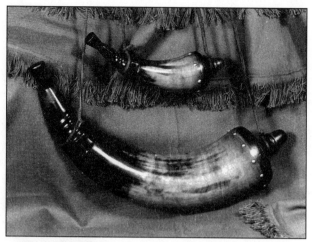

This matched set of powder and priming horns from Dixie Gun Works is ideal for complementing a nice flint rifle.

capped at one end. The goal is to measure out the same amount of black powder or Pyrodex each time, whether the powder charge requires the measure to be filled once, twice or even three times. If a load is to be used strictly for hunting big game, hunters need to know the velocities and energies involved in order to dole out the actual weight of the powder charge. One way to know how much powder a home-made measure holds is to weigh it on a balance beam scale, or borrow another shooter's adjustable measure. If a charge of Pyrodex needs to be weighed, keep in mind that its actually about 20 percent lighter than black powder by weight. It has also been formulated for loading on a volume-to-volume basis with black powder.

Most powder measures sold today are of the "adjustable" type, which allows shooters to increase or decrease the size of the powder cavity or chamber. Most are simple brass tube-type arrangements featuring an internal plunger that pulls down from the bottom of the measure to increase the volume of the powder charge, or slides back in to measure out a lighter charge. The amount of powder measured is commonly indicated by a scale located on a plunger protruding from the bottom of the measure. Most top quality measures feature a way to keep the

setting locked in place. A major benefit of owning an adjustable measure is that it can be used for loading different powder charges for different guns, as well as tailoring new loads for a favorite muzzleloader.

Dixie Gun Works, Thompson/Center Arms, Navy Arms, Traditions, Connecticut Valley Arms, Michaels of Oregon and a number of other accessory suppliers all offer adjustable measures of this design, any one of which should work fine. Most are adjustable from one to 120 grains, and some feature a funnel-like spout that swivels out of the way as the measure is filled, then swings back over the measure and levels the powder charge, making certain that every granule of powder goes into the muzzle and not on the ground. Some measures have a base that can be unthreaded from the bottom of a plunger, to which is attached a vent or nipple pick to clear the flash channel. The adjustable measures currently available range from a simple push-pull adjustment type to such added features as a funnel, vent pick, or

This heavy brass powder flask and adjustable measure from Modern Muzzleloading rank among the best.

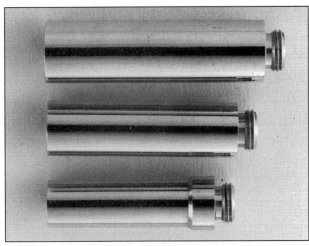

Interchangeable flask spouts encourage shooters to pour powder charges directly from the powder flash into the muzzle, creating a dangerous situation.

cap storage compartment. In any event, when buying a powder measure, don't lose sight of its real purpose: to measure out powder charges with consistency.

When replacing an older powder measure with a new one, make sure the new measure provides the same charges as the old one. Even though the new measure may be set for the same powder charge used previously, it could be measuring out slightly more or less powder. In fact, with all of the adjustable measures on the market, buyers will discover that, when set at the heavier settings, there could be as much as a 20 percent variation in the charges measured. For example, if all measures were set at 100 grains, they could actually measure anywhere from 90 to 110 grains by actual weight. An old measure, when checked by weighing a charge on a scale, might well reveal that you've actually been loading, shooting and hunting with a powder charge ten grains lighter or heavier than you'd assumed.

2. POWDER FLASKS AND HORNS

While not as important as a good powder measure, a container of sorts for carrying a supply of powder to the range or into the deer woods is preferable to slipping a one-pound can into a jacket pocket or shooting pouch, as more than one black

powder burner has done. Many others still use a small plastic bottle with a moisture-proof cap for carrying four or five ounces of black powder or Pyrodex when hunting, especially in wet weather. Like powder measures, the variety of powder flasks and powder horns seems almost limitless. Dixie Gun Works' huge 700-page catalog includes more than five full pages of different powder flasks and horns, including traditional styles from the past and modern flasks designed primarily for muzzleloading hunters in the 1990s. Whatever type is used, make sure it's reasonably weather or water resistant. Not many horns and flasks available can be classified as "waterproof," because of their spring-powered dispensers. The design of many authentically-styled horns allows moisture to seep in when submerged in water. On the other hand, not many shooters have a real need for a waterproof horn or flask. As long as the dispenser (or spout) can be closed to keep powder from spilling out, most any arrangement will work. Some just work a little better than others, such as the heavy brass cylindrical powder flask made by Modern Muzzleloading, Inc. Measuring about 1½ inches in diameter and five inches in

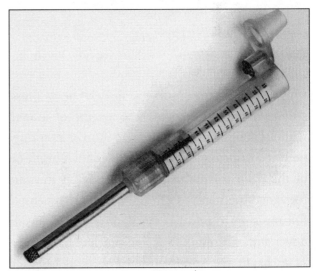

Both black powder and Pyrodex are loaded by volume measurement. An adjustable U-View measure made by Thompson/Center can be easily changed when working up loads.

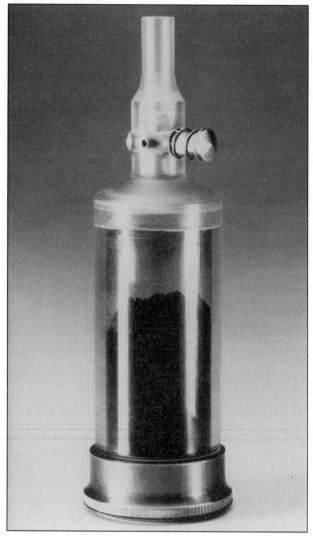

The transparent sides of Thompson/Center's U-View powder flask allow shooters to see how much powder remains inside.

It also helps settle the granules to ensure a consistent powder charge each time. This arrangement requires that the measure be pulled from the recess of the flask dispenser and the powder charge then poured into the barrel, keeping the flask away from the muzzle. Some flasks encourage shooters to thread in a spout to hold the desired powder charge. A finger is first placed over the open end and the spout filled by opening the dispenser valve, whereupon the charge is poured into the barrel (with the spout still attached to the flask). This is a dangerous practice that could well cost a shooter a hand, however. A spark or ember in the barrel could ignite the powder as it's poured into the bore, and it in turn could explode the quarter-pound or more of powder inside the flask. Always dispense powder into a separate measure, then pour it into the barrel—never directly from the flask or a spout attached to the flask.

The U-View Powder Flask from Thompson/Center allows shooters to fill a flask quickly without losing a grain of powder. The entire bottom of this flask unthreads from the body, which is then filled by pouring powder directly from the can. The see-through body of this flask also lets shooters know at a glance how much powder remains inside. The U-View flask is small enough to slip into a jacket pocket or a shooting pouch, yet large enough to hold powder for 10 to 12 shots. Many of the larger flasks, such as the heavy brass model from Modern Muzzleloading, hold upwards of a quarter to one-third of a pound of powder, or enough for 20 to 30 shots. Flasks that big are better suited for use at the range or when working up loads. Once filled with powder, these containers can weigh a pound or more, adding considerable weight to a shooting pouch and making them impractical for carrying in a jacket pocket.

Most black powder shooters and hunters now steer away from powder horns. A well-built, decorated horn can be a thing of beauty, though, and when time is taken to fit and seal the base plug

length, the body of this flask is made of heavy brass, strong enough to support the weight of a man without denting or collapsing. The top of its spring-powered dispenser has a recess that allows insertion of the open end of an adjustable powder measure (designed specifically to fit the flask). To dispense a full measure of powder, the flask is turned upside down and, with both flask and measure held in the same hand, the spring-powered valve is operated with the thumb. By tapping the side of the flask against the other hand, the powder will flow freely from the flask into the measure.

The tough Lexan plastic bullet starter from Connecticut Valley Arms is a simple arrangement that stands up to hard every-day use.

into a horn, the result is a moisture-tight fit. Trouble is, you won't get that kind of workmanship in a powder horn costing $30 to $40, but more likely twice that much for a top quality model. A sturdy, well-built and inexpensive powder flask is still hard to beat for everyday loading and shooting.

3. BALL OR BULLET STARTER

When buying a ball or bullet starter, simple is usually best. The goal is a tight-fitting patch and ball, an oversized conical bullet, or a snug-fitting sabot and bullet combination loaded through a muzzle and into the bore far enough so that a ramrod can seat a projectile over the powder charge. Most starters are simply a round, square or rectangular-shaped piece of wood with a four- or five-inch section of strong hardwood or nylon dowel rod protruding from one side. Most feature a second half-inch section of rod that also protrudes from a ball or wood block as well, usually located at a 90% angle from the rod itself. Its purpose is to push the projectile in flush with the muzzle. When loading a stubborn ball or bullet, most shooters grasp the long rod, centering the short section on the projectile, and then forcing it into the barrel with a hard slap on the back side of the ball with the palm of the other hand. When loading bore-sized conical bullets or saboted bullets with a delicate hollow-point, take care to prevent damage to

that fragile nose. Once the projectile is past the muzzle, push the ball or bullet on into the bore with the long rod another four or five inches. The ramrod is then slipped into the bore until the projectile is seated over the powder charge.

"Uncle Mike's" line of accessories (from Michaels of Oregon) includes several well-built ball or bullet starters. One is a hardwood ball with a brass-tipped, four-inch nylon rod, plus two shorter 3/8" brass starters, one for .44/.45 caliber guns and another for .50/.54 caliber muzzleloaders. The company also carries a more sophisticated ball and bullet starter featuring the same hardwood ball and a short brass starter, plus a longer brass-tipped stainless steel rod. It also features a tapered brass bore guard that keeps the stainless rod centered and away from the rifling. Shooters might also take a look at the almost identical "Hunter" bullet starter from Traditions or the "M-P" bullet starter from Modern Muzzleloading. In addition to their T-Handle-shaped starters, both double as ramrod extensions for turning most ramrods into more effective cleaning or range-loading rods. Once the tip of the heavy brass rod is unthreaded, a 10x32 threaded shank is exposed. It can then be screwed into one end of most ramrods, adding about five inches to their length. An

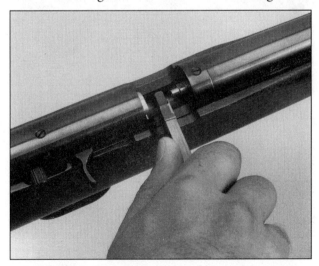

A straight in-line capper makes the capping proce-dure on this Thompson/Center Fire Hawk a breeze.

aluminum ramrod provided with all Knight in-line percussion rifles (and a growing number of others) is also threaded at the other end, allowing shooters to thread their cleaning jags into place as well. The longer rod is also used to swab the bore of an in-line rifle, one that features a removable breech plug all the way through from the receiver end, eliminating wear on the rifling at the muzzle. The starters carried by both Traditions and Modern Muzzleloading also feature recesses in their aluminum handles. The starters can then be slipped over the end of the ramrod when a really tight ball or bullet is being pushed down the bore. Many black powder shooters often drill a half-inch deep hole of 5/16" or 3/8" diameter into the wooden ball of their starters, turning them into comfortable palm savers or ramrod assist handles.

4. CAPPERS

It's possible for a shooter—be it with a percussion rifle, shotgun or pistol—to go through life without ever owning a capper; but once they've used one, it's a good bet they won't ever be without it again! To start with, many percussion muzzleloader shooters, when the time comes to cap the ignition system,

Modern Muzzleloading offers a complete line of accessories, including this multi-purpose bullet starter, capper, and de-capper (left to right).

Cappers come in all shapes and sizes. The molded plastic Thompson/Center Star-7 capper shown sells for a fraction of what metal cappers cost.

open a tin of percussion caps, pull one out with their fingers and place it on the nipple of the gun. Most of the time this practice works just fine—but not always. Capping a modern in-line percussion rifle by hand can actually be close to impossible. The nipple on many designs is so protected by the receiver that it's very difficult to reach in with one's fingers and slip a cap on the cone of a nipple. The same is true when trying to slip caps on the nipples of a percussion revolver. And when hunting in temperatures well below freezing, trying to do this with numbed fingertips becomes even more difficult. With a good capper, this task can actually become the easiest step in loading and firing a percussion muzzleloader

Today's cappers, whether metal or plastic, come in a wide range of sizes, shapes and designs. Costs can range from just a few dollars to as much as $30 or more, depending on the quality. The simplest cappers are injection-molded plastic with short fingers for holding a percussion cap securely in a tight-fitting recess. The shooter simply reaches in with the capper, slips the hollow cavity of the cap over the nipple and pulls the capper away, leaving the cap on the nipple. Some cappers won't work with many of the in-line guns, especially rifles that have been fitted with scopes. The fingers simply aren't long enough to reach the nipple. Remington and Modern Muzzleloading, however, do offer low cost "in-line" plastic cappers. These allow in-line rifle shooters to reach in and place a cap on the nipple.

In-line cappers have been around since before the Civil War, when they were used extensively with percussion revolvers such as the Colt 1851 Navy or Remington Model 1858 Army. Designs vary somewhat, but most range from two to four inches in length and feature an internal spring and plunger that feed percussion caps to an open end, where the cap is held securely by a flat spring. A shooter can now reach in, slip the cap on the nipple, then pull the capper away by moving it directly out to the side. The spring releases its grasp on the cap, which now remains in place on the nipple. Pushing an external plunger moves the next cap into the opening at the end, where the spring holds it until needed. Such cappers work well for capping revolvers, shotguns, traditional side-hammer rifles or modern in-line rifles.

During the heyday of percussion sporting guns, which ran from about 1840 into the early 1960s, a number of ingenious and well-built cappers were used by sportsmen and target shooters of the time. Outside configurations ranged from oval to teardrop in shape, but internally most operated in about the same manner. The caps were gravity-fed down to a spring-powered gate, which was manually operated

The oval brass capper from Cash Manufacturing is a handy large-capacity rifle capper.

The teardrop-shaped capper from Cash Manufacturing was originally designed for use with percussion revolvers, but it works well with many in-line rifles as well. The capper holds 100 No. 11 percussion caps.

by thumb pressure on an external button. This allowed a cap to slide down into an open recess, so when pressure was released on the external button, spring pressure held the cap in place until it was slipped onto the nipple.

Several companies now offer copies of these cappers, but none can equal the quality of those made by Tedd Cash (Cash Manufacturing, Waunakee, Wisconsin). He produces two different styles: an oval-shaped "rifle" capper holding about 75 No. 11 percussion caps, and a rear drop-shaped "revolver" capper that holds 100 percussion caps. The end of this rifle capper is too large to fit into the nipple recess at the rear of a percussion revolver cylinder, and many in-line percussion rifle shooters will discover that it won't work with their guns, either. The revolver capper made by Cash features a curved, tapered end that fits easily into the nipple recess of a revolver or the receiver of an in-line percussion rifle (with or without a scope). The curvature of this capper, however, is for right-handed shooters. The cut-out for capping a percussion revolver is located on the right side of the frame, which means the handgun must be capped right-handed. Some in-line percussion rifles feature a receiver that allows a nipple to be capped from either side. A left-handed shooter who tries capping from the left will soon discover that the cap is facing toward

"Uncle Mike's" mechanical priming powder dispensers make priming a flintlock pan a cinch, providing enough FFFFg for a whole day of shooting.

him and not the nipple. When an unscoped rifle is involved, the capper can be turned upside down and used; but when a scope sits directly above the receiver opening, the capper is unable to extend far enough to be placed on the nipple.

5. FLINTLOCK PRIMERS

Shooters who own a flintlock rifle, pistol, musket or fowler will need a small container for packing the super fine FFFFg priming powder. Those who load with FFFg black powder often prime with the same powder, but flintlock shooters who are successful at big game hunting or in target competition will quickly comment that ignition is greatly improved when priming with the finer powder. In the past, flintlock shooters relied on two powder horns. A larger type carried the FFg or FFFg powder used for the main charge in the barrel, while a much smaller second horn held the dust-like priming powder for the ignition system.

More and more, flintlock shooters have turned to handy mechanical pan primers, which quickly dispense the few grains of FFFFg needed for ignition with a flintlock frontloader. Rightnour Manufacturing Company (Mingoville Pennsylvania) offers several well-built brass pan primers. One style automatically drops in two to three grains of powder when the plunger dispenser is placed in the pan and the primer pushed downward. Small pistol pans may only require one charge, while the larger pan of a big flintlock musket, such as the .75 caliber Brown Bess, accommodates two or even three charges from a priming device. The company also offers its primer with a plunger dispenser, which allows powder to trickle out until the plunger is released. Either style will hold enough of fine priming powder for 25 or 30 shots, depending on how much priming powder is used for each shot.

Finally, many of the accessories discussed in this chapter also fit into the other categories established earlier. The powder measure, powder flask, ball/bullet starter, capper and pan primer are all accessories the shooter will need at the range, as well. And a stylish set of powder horns is definitely an authentic accoutrement for a custom flintlock rifle.

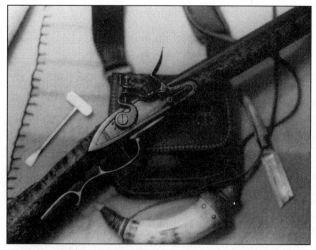

Shown with a custom flintlock rifle are a "possibles" bag, handcrafted powder horn, handmade patch knife and hammer-forged flinter's tool. All complement this beautiful custom flintlock rifle.

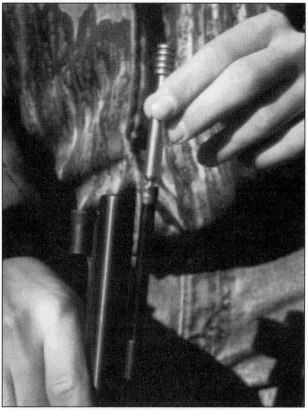

A cleaning jag, which is threaded into the end of most rifle ramrods, is used to wipe the bore between shots, or for cleaning the barrel at the end of the day.

The accessories discussed here represent just some of the basic accessories required for loading and shooting a muzzleloader.

II. GENERAL CLEANING AND MAINTENANCE

Once a muzzleloader is fired, whether once or twenty times, its owner is committed to cleaning the gun. The dirty and corrosive fouling left behind from burning charges of blackpowder or Pyrodex must be thoroughly scrubbed from the bore—and any other fouled surface—or the gun will be a total ruin in as little as one day. In the following chapter, we give an in-depth look at various cleaning methods and techniques. Here we'll discuss some of the accessories needed to ensure the job is done correctly.

First, a cleaning jag that fits properly is a "must have" accessory. Not only is it needed for a thorough cleaning of a dirty bore at the end of a day's shooting, it's also needed to wipe fouling from the bore. When buying a cleaning jag, make certain it's for the proper caliber. Often it's hard to distinguish a .45 caliber jag from a .50, or a .50 from a .54 caliber cleaning jag, just by looking at them. More than once, a .54 caliber jag has ended up in a .50 caliber jag package, and vice versa. If the cleaning jag turns out to be for a caliber larger than the rifle in question, chances are it won't even fit into the bore. But if the jag is of a smaller caliber, it will likely fit the bore so loosely that the serrated edges on the jag won't grip the patch tight enough to return it once the ramrod or cleaning rod is pulled upward. Occasionally, a jag meant for a .54 caliber will still slip into a .50 caliber bore, riding right on top of the rifling lands. It may still go into the smaller bore, but there's not enough room for the cleaning patch to fit between the jag and rifling.

The most common type of cleaning jag features a cylindrical head with a series of grooves encircling the circumference. When a tight-fitting cleaning patch is compressed into these grooves, the jag will grip it tight enough to pull the patch up and out of the bore. Most cleaning patches run $1\frac{1}{2}$ to two inches in diameter. To allow enough room for excess material, most jags feature a deep recess

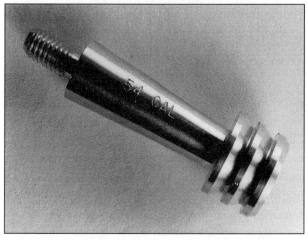

To clean a muzzleloader properly, a good cleaning jag is essential.

between the head and the point where the jag threads into the ramrod. Another kind of jag, designed for use with smaller diameter stainless steel auxiliary cleaning and loading rods, is nothing more than a cylindrical head. Excess material from a large patch simply folds in behind the jag and around the smaller diameter steel rod. Should one of these jags be threaded into a ramrod with a larger diameter, and then used to wipe the rifle bore, there's no recess to contain the excess cloth from the cleaning patch. The material and rod often won't fit through the bore; and even when they do fit there's a good chance the patch will get stuck in the barrel.

Most rifles available today come with a ramrod built for 10x32 thread cleaning jags and other accessories. Many older rifles, however, came with ramrods having smaller diameter 8x32 threads. When buying a jag, it's important to get a tip with the right threads. If there's a choice, buy a cleaning jag with steel threads, not brass ones. Steel is less likely to break, leaving a patch and jag in the bore. Shooters who do a lot of hunting may want to consider buying an auxiliary cleaning and loading rod made of much stronger materials than what goes into the ramrod of a rifle, such as polymer-coated

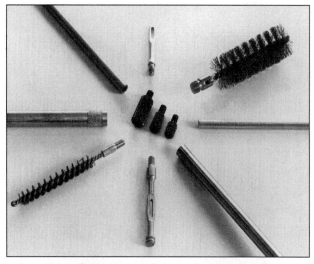

A variety of cleaning and ramrod accessory tips can make thorough cleaning of a muzzleloader faster and less tedious.

fiberglass or stainless steel. These rods are available in lengths longer than that of the rifle barrel, providing the extra length needed for easier cleaning and loading (they also reduce wear and tear on the ramrod).

A wide range of cleaning tips, which thread into the tip of the ramrod or into a cleaning/range rod, are also available. When wiping the bore for accuracy, some shooters rely on a bristled bore brush made of nylon to knock fouling out of the rifling grooves. Often the brush is run down the bore a time or two, then pulled out and wrapped with a damp cleaning patch, which is then run back down the bore to remove the loose fouling. Don't try this with a brass bore brush, though. Once the shooter pushes a brass brush to the bottom of the bore and tries to pull it back out, the stiff bristles can bite into the rifling and refuse to budge. The more flexible nylon bristles have enough give to bend or fold, allowing the brush to be pulled out of the bore with reasonable ease. Most shooter find that a cleaning jag does just as good a job with fewer problems.

Another cleaning and maintenance accessory is a "worm" for fishing loose patches from the bore. There's also a "ball puller," a screw-like arrangement that threads into the ramrod or auxiliary rod and is

Auxiliary loading and cleaning rods come with a variety of handle styles, all helping to save wear and tear on the ramrod. Note the nylon bore guides, which keep the steel rods from marring rifling at the muzzle.

Old oil and dust were wiped from the bore of a rifle that had been cleaned and stored several months earlier.

Knight rifle designer Tony Knight uses an auxiliary loading rod to push a tight-fitting sabot and bullet down on top of the powder charge.

used to pull a projectile, one that may have been loaded before powder was dropped in. Most in-line percussion rifles come with the take-down tools necessary to disassemble them for cleaning, but the traditional side-hammer percussion gun shooter will sooner or later find a need for the proper nipple wrench.

III. RANGE ACCESSORIES

The flimsy wooden rods that come with some of today's reproduction muzzleloading rifles are often barely suited for the job of loading the rifle, let alone the repeated use and abuse of cleaning or loading and wiping the bore when working up loads. Even when the ramrod is made of a tough synthetic material or a high tensile-strength aluminum, it's long enough to

fit the length of the bore and, without any extension, can make wiping the bore between shots tedious. Jack Garner (Tennessee Valley Manufacturing, Corinth, Mississippi) offers an excellent stainless steel rod that should last a black powder shooter a lifetime, even with heavy use. The rod itself is made of $1/4$" diameter stainless steel, and is available in 36" or 45" lengths. The rod is fitted with a comfortable $1^3/4$" hardwood ball that fits comfortably into the palm of the hand when seating a tight-fitting projectile. It comes threaded for 8x32 accessory tips. Tennessee Valley Manufacturing ships the rod with a cleaning jag, ranging from .32 caliber to 12 gauge. The rod is also fitted with a tapered nylon bore guard, which keeps the steel rod centered in the bore to prevent wear on the rifling at the muzzle.

Trade blankets at rendezvous and historical encampments offer specialized accessories and clothing from a certain period in American history.

Michaels of Oregon, Dixie Gun Works and a few others offer similar stainless steel range and cleaning rods. The handles may vary slightly on some of these, but the basic design is about the same. Mountain State Muzzleloading Supplies (Williamstown, West Virginia) markets a tough range rod made from a super-strong space age synthetic material that stays flexible in the cold. It also remains rigid enough in warm weather for sure loading, is not abrasive to the bore, and is guaranteed for life against breakage. Mountain

State's "Super Rod" features a grooved handle for a positive grip and comes with a cleaning jag installed in a choice of .32 through .58 caliber and 36- or 48-inch lengths.

Finally a good solid rest contributes greatly to tight down range groups. It's hard to beat plain old sandbags for a rock-solid rest, whether they're fashioned from sections of tire inner tubes, empty shot bags, or commercially available leather bags filled with sand. Shooters who like the "store bought" look have a variety of different shooting rests available. Only one's budget or ingenuity is the limiting factor.

IV. AUTHENTIC ACCOUTREMENTS

When attempting to recreate a past era, today's black powder shooter is often faced with the difficult task of putting together a complete set of clothing styled for that era, plus a very authentic compliment of loading and shooting accessories that also date from the same period. By shopping the catalogs of big black powder suppliers, such as Dixie Gun works or Mountain State Muzzleloading Supplies, and scrutinizing the many "trade blankets" at black-powder rendezvous and re-enactments, the nostalgia buff can outfit himself in short order for almost any era of American history.

Except for some of the leather goods produced for followers of the Civil War, most of these goods are the products of small craftsmen whose attention to detail is reflected in relatively high prices. To put together a complete outfit and a set of shooting accessories styled for the Revolutionary War or Civil War can cost more than a thousand dollars—and that's not including the cost of the muzzleloader itself.

V. HUNTING ACCESSORIES

Black powder hunters today are avoiding the use of pouches or bags with which to carry all of their loading accessories and components into the field. Instead, they're learning to get by with less, and

With three or four speed loaders, plus a capper, most hunters are set for the day. The Traditions speed load tube features a built-in short starter.

they're enjoying the hunt more. My first bag, like most, was made of heavy leather, and except for a couple of small inside pockets, it was basically one big compartment covered by a generous fold-over flap. Little things like a tin of percussion caps, maybe a nipple wrench, or even a spare flint for a flintlock, could be stored away inside the bag's small internal pockets. But that's where all resemblance of organization ended, because every other accessory I owned was simply tossed helter-skelter into the bag's main compartment. There you could eventually unearth a ball or bullet bag filled with projectiles, a flask filled with powder, an adjustable powder measure, a capper filled with No.11 percussion caps, often a spare tin of caps, a small container of bullet or patch lubricant, patches for round balls, a ball or bullet starter, often bulk patching and patch knife, a cleaning jag, cleaning patches, a small squirt bottle

of black powder cleaning solvent, a nipple wrench, a couple of spare nipples, a patch puller, a worm for removing a stuck ball, and generally a few take-down tools. That bag easily weighed ten pounds, and I often felt (and sounded like) a Yankee Panhandler as I headed for the deer woods with that heavy old bag tipping me over to one side. I now travel a lot lighter, though; in fact, everything I need for a full day of hunting weighs a pound or less and can fit into a jacket pocket.

Even for those who still rely on a pouch for carrying everything needed to load and fire, the pouches have become a lot smaller. Instead of a big leather pouch hanging from the shoulder, most are now small enough to carry around the waist, using either belt loops sewn right onto the backside of the pouch, or a nylon waist strap with a quick-detachable buckle. Inside, these nylon pouches hold

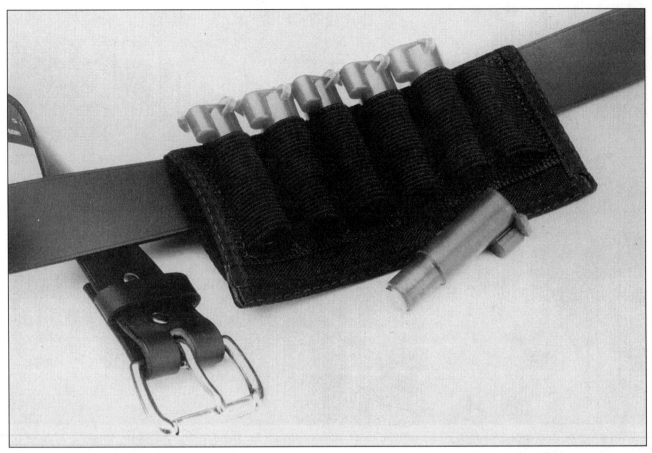

The Thompson/Center Quick Shot belt carrier holds six 4-N-1 loaders charged with pre-measured powder charges and projectiles.

enough to load five to ten rounds, plus a cleaning jag and enough patches to wipe the bore between shots. A growing number of black powder hunters now rely almost exclusively on "speed load" tubes or "speed loaders," which simplify loading even further. Most are simple plastic tubes with a moisture proof cap that snaps onto each end. Some feature a center partition that separates the powder and bullet. Others are hollow tubes about four inches long, with a cavity running from end to end. Either design enables muzzleloading hunters to carry a complete load in each tube.

Those speed load tubes featuring a partition seem to be the most popular with hunters, especially those who shoot more than one caliber rifle. The compartments on each end of the tube are large enough to hold powder charges of 110 or 120 grains, or a projectile for bores as large as .58 caliber. The shooter simply snaps open the end holding the pre-measured powder charge, pours the powder in the bore, then snaps open the projectile end, removing the ball or bullet and starting it into the bore. A tube with a built-in starter will speed up loading even more. Some are made of a special clear plastic, with grain increments marked on the outside to serve as a powder measure as well.

When buying a speed load tube with a single cavity running from end to end, shooters must buy tubes for a specific caliber. To load, a projectile is started into one end far enough for the cap to be snapped over the nose of a ball or bullet. A powder charge is then poured into the other end and the cap snapped in place. In actual use, the cap on the powder end must be removed and the powder poured in through the

These speed loaders from Traditions make it easier to keep loading components organized. Each loader contains the powder charge and projectile needed for a load.

muzzle. Next, the cap over the projectile is removed, the tube is placed over the muzzle, and the projectile is pushed through the tube and into the bore with a short starter. With no partition to keep powder and projectile separated, proper fit of the projectile in the tube is critical. If a .54 caliber tube were to be used with a .50 caliber rifle, the projectile would fit so loosely that some of the powder would find its way around the projectile, making it impossible to achieve an exact charge behind the projectile each time. The powder will also tend to cake up because of the lube used on most bore-sized conical bullets, making them difficult to load. When it comes time to reload a rifle in the field, speed load tubes really live up to their reputation. With a pre-measured powder charge, and with everything except the percussion cap held in one neat container, most

shooters can get a second load down the barrel in a matter of 20 seconds or so. Moreover, several mechanical loaders are now available that effectively shorten reloading time even more.

Thompson/Center's 4-N-1 Quick Shot is basically a two-compartment loader, with one end featuring a powder compartment with a moisture-proof snap-on cap. The other end has a recess for holding a pre-lubed Maxi-Ball or Maxi-Hunter bullet. To use, the powder cap is flipped open, the powder then poured into the bore, the base of the bullet inserted into the bore. When the shooter pushes down on the top of the loader, a built-in plunger rams the Maxi into the bore. This causes the rifling to engrave the over-sized front bearing band. The bullet is then seated over the powder charge with a ramrod. Remington's Cyclone Quick Starter and Big Bore

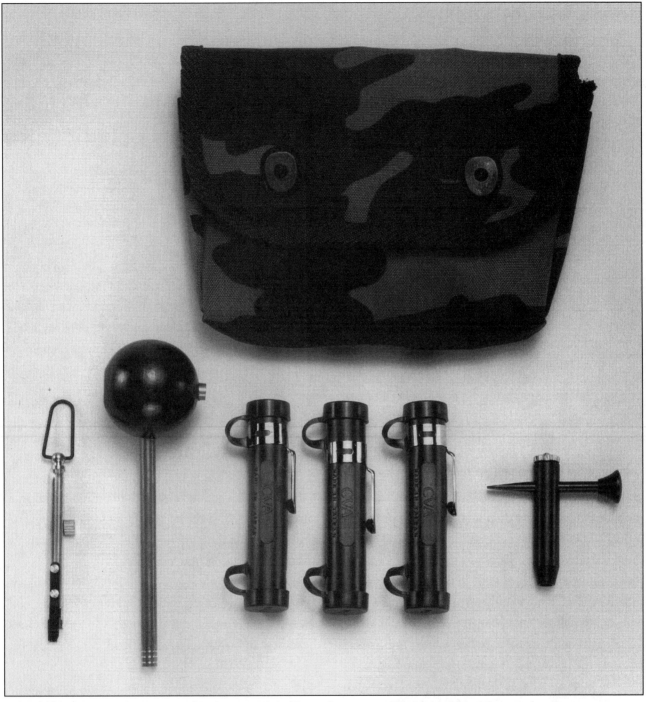

Everything needed for a day in the deer woods is pictured: a capper filled with percussion caps, a short starter, three speed load tubes with pre-measured powder charges and projectiles, and a nipple wrench with a compartment for a spare nipple.

Express Mag-Charger operate basically the same. A special pre-loaded tube is inserted into the loading device and the entire load, including powder and projectile, is rammed into the bore with a hard down-stroke on the starter. With a film of waxed paper or plastic food wrap sealing each end of the loading tube, the powder charge and projectile can be pushed easily through the moisture-proof seal and into the barrel.

Another handy mechanical starter is the EC-Loader from Traditions, which holds three complete loads ready to be rammed into the barrel with a built-in plunger starter. The EC-Loader features a revolving cylinder with three "chambers" for holding a premeasured powder charge and projectile. To use, the loader is placed over the muzzle and a plunger starter is pulled upward, allowing the cylinder to rotate. When one of the chambers aligns with the bore, the powder charge automatically drops through the muzzle and, with a hardy push on the starter, the projectile is started down the bore.

Because the success of a muzzleloading hunt often hinges on how quickly the black powder hunter can reload for a follow-up shot, these speed load tubes and loaders eliminate the need for carrying a powder flask or horn, a powder measure, or often a short starter. In fact, most hunters these days don't want, or need, to carry all the components for a dozen shots. Four- or five-speed loaders thrown into a pocket, along with a capper, is all that's needed for a day in the deer woods, chasing after elk or stalking a black bear. Shooters who have worked up a good, hard-hitting load and have properly sighted in their rifles will more than likely not need a follow-up or finishing shot. If they do, though, these loaders will put a rifle back in service in a matter of seconds. Indeed, the fully equipped black powder shooter can almost always find use for a well-designed accessory, especially when loading and shooting from the bench, or when giving a muzzleloader a thorough cleaning at the end of a day at the range or following a muzzleloading hunt. *Hunters are finding that times afield are usually more enjoyable and successful when loading essentials are kept to the bare necessities and are well-organized. Today's wide range of accessories allows muzzleloading hunters to pursue their sport with as few or as many gadgets as they desire.*

20

KEEP 'EM CLEAN!

Each year, thousands of deadly accurate, high quality muzzleloading rifles are lost because of simple neglect. Most were probably fired only a few times, then removed to some forgotten corner of the house without being properly cleaned. In only a matter of days, a fine frontloading rifle barrel that was once capable of delivering tight down-range groups is rendered into an unserviceable hunk of scrap metal. Once the bore has been lost to improper care, its only useful purpose is as a costly reminder of the dollars lost because a few minutes weren't spent cleaning the frontloader before it was put away.

Both black powder, the traditional muzzleloader propellant, and the modern substitute, Pyrodex, leave behind corrosive fouling or residue after a muzzleloading gun has been fired. It doesn't matter if it's been fired once during the course of a hunt, or dozens of times at the range or during competition.

In short, a gun that's been fired must be cleaned—ideally that same day. The fouling left behind by a single shot is enough to ruin a bore overnight. The shooter who packs along a box full of shooting components, accessories and cleaning supplies every time he or she spends time at the range has absolutely no excuse for not cleaning a black powder gun. Usually five or six cleaning patches soaked with a good black powder cleaning solvent or even plain water or saliva can knock most of the fouling from a bore. The hunter who suddenly finds success just as the sun begins to dip below the horizon can ill afford not to take a few minutes to wipe the fouling from the bore before field-dressing, tagging, dragging out, and otherwise attending to a downed animal. All that's needed are a cleaning jag for the rifle and a few cleaning patches, all of which can fit easily into a small zip-lock plastic sandwich bag.

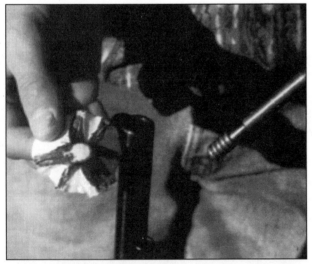

Only a single shot has left fouling in the bore. Unless time is taken to wipe the bore clean, the corrosive residue could ruin the barrel.

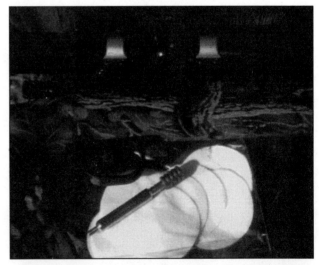

A zip-lock bag with cleaning patches and a cleaning jag are all that's needed to give a muzzleloader a quick field cleaning.

Unless it's cleaned almost immediately, the fouling left behind from one shot is enough to destroy the bore of this rifle.

Fouling left by burning charges of black powder or Pyrodex is totally water soluble, which means fouling can be thoroughly removed from the bore of a muzzleloader with nothing more than a little water or saliva. A number of excellent black powder cleaning solvents are on the market that can cut fouling much faster than plain water. However, to avoid nasty chemical odors, many hunters simply carry dry cleaning patches into the deer woods. When it's time to wipe the bore, they simply pop one in their mouth, dampen it with saliva, then swab the fouling from the bore of a fired front-loader. Those who shoot at the bench, and who have all of the cleaning supplies needed to give the muzzleloader a thorough cleaning, should scrub the bore and other fouled surfaces spotless as soon as they're finished for the day. If other commitments or projects sidetrack the shooter, he should at least take a few minutes to run a half-dozen cleaning patches through the bore to wipe away fouling. In the same light, by the time a black powder hunter gets a whitetail out of the woods and hangs it on a meat pole following a successful hunt, it could be well into the evening. Far too often, that dirty rifle will be left until the next day, or even longer, when only a few quick patches through the bore could have saved it from ruin.

Black powder and Pyrodex fouling is extremely hygroscopic; i.e., that thin film of residue left in a bore can literally pull moisture right out of the air. The heat from burning powder charges, moreover, burns away protective lubricants left in the bore from the last cleaning, and this only serves to compound the problem. During damp weather or in areas of high humidity, the corrosive fouling can pull moisture from the air and, within hours, begins to work on the unprotected metal surface of the bore. Even when time has been taken to wipe away most of the fouling from the bore—whether with solvent, water or saliva-dampened patches—owners

After the bore has had a quick field cleaning, it should be coated with a good lubricant, such as Break Free, to protect it until a more thorough cleaning job is done the next day.

of frontloaders should always follow up with several dry patches, especially if a thorough cleaning must be put off until the following day. The smallest amount of fouling left in the bore, remember, is enough to create a rough spot and destroy accuracy. Don't add to the problem by leaving the bore wet; and after wiping it dry, follow up with a liberal coat of lubricant. One of the water-displacing lubricants, such as WD-40, Remington Rem-Oil or Break Free, can create a barrier that prevents small pockets of residue from drawing moisture overnight. Tending to the bore in this manner will buy some time until the next day—but no longer.

With rifles equipped with a removable breech plug, it's a good idea to break it free before putting a rifle aside until the next morning. Fouling which builds at the face of the breech plug can dry and harden into a cinder-like crust making it impossible to break the plug loose. Even if the rifle has been fired several times, the fouling should stay soft for an hour or two following the last shot of the day. After that, it starts to set up like concrete. More than one high quality in-line rifle has ended up back at the factory because a shooter waited too long to remove the breech plug.

THE IMPORTANCE OF HOT SOAPY WATER

Strange as it may seem, the most widely used (and cheapest) "cleaning solvent" for muzzleloading guns is nothing more than hot water and a generous measure of liquid dishwashing detergent. Surprisingly, in most instances it will clean a muzzleloader barrel as spotlessly and quickly as many commercial black powder cleaning solvents on the market. As mentioned, black powder and Pyrodex fouling can be cleaned from the bore of a muzzleloader with nothing more than water; but the residue left behind by patch and bullet lubricants are usually more stubborn and require a detergent to clean metal surfaces completely. Such brand names as Dawn, Palmolive and Ivory break down these lubricants easily and allow them to be removed from the bore as quickly as the powder fouling. Many experienced black powder shooters feel that the hotter the water, the better. Actually, cold soapy water can and does thoroughly remove powder and lubricant residue from the bore. Hot soapy water does speed up the process, though, and really hot water does heat up the metal of the barrel and promotes the drying process. Once the bore has been scrubbed free of fouling, several dry patches should be run through the bore to remove moisture.

This line of cleaning patches for the black powder shooter— called Rusty Duck—is great to have for quick clean-up of a dirty rifle.

Non-petroleum greases, such as this special Polymer All- Purpose Grease from Rusty Duck, are used to lubricate the threads of a removable breech plug.

Then prop the barrel so that the muzzle is pointed straight down, allowing any remaining moisture to drain out. Once the bore has been thoroughly cleaned and dried, several passes with a lubricated patch will keep the bore bright and shiny until next time the rifle is loaded and fired.

BLACK POWDER CLEANING SOLVENTS

When it's impractical to fill a sink with hot soapy water and give a rifle a thorough scrubbing, there's a great selection of black powder cleaning solvents available that can thoroughly clean even the dirtiest barrel. Among these solvents is Rusty Duck "Black Off," an extremely powerful black powder cleaning product produced by Hydra-Tone Chemicals, Inc. (Fort Mitchell, Kentucky). This maximum-strength

cleaning solvent quickly breaks down black powder fouling; in fact, 90 percent of the fouling left in the bore of a muzzleloader after two or three shots can usually be removed with two or three patches soaked with this solvent. Four or five patches usually clean most bores spotless. Following up with a couple of dry patches, and another with protective lubricant, cleans the bore more than adequately. Black Off comes in several different-sized containers, from four ounce to a full gallon. Hydra-Tone Chemicals also offers cleaning patches that have been pre-soaked with the solvent, along with a number of other gun care products for muzzleloaders. Knight Solvent Concentrate from Modern Muzzleloading, Inc. (Centerville, Iowa) is another powerful black powder cleaning solvent. It eliminates fouling from the bore and any other metal surface almost immediately and is available in various sized containers (and pre-soaked patches as well). This same solvent also comes in an aerosol can, producing a foaming solvent that loosens tough fouling quickly. After sending a few squirts through the muzzle of a dirty barrel, set it aside for ten minutes or so. This procedure can cut cleaning time nearly in half. The aerosol is especially useful for cleaning hard-to-reach spots, such as inside the receiver of a modern in-line percussion rifle or the nipple recesses of a percussion revolver.

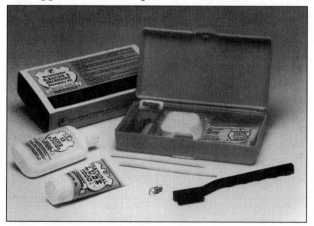

Thompson/Center's All Natural cleaning kit makes it easy for black powder shooters to give a muzzle-loader a thorough scrubbing.

Pyrodex "EZ Clean" is a cleaning solvent specially for-mulated to clean Pyrodex fouling from metal surfaces.

Hodgdon Powder Company (Shawnee Mission, Kansas) claims that its Pyrodex is not all that different from black powder. It burns cleaner, too, and has fewer fouling properties. Most available black powder solvents do a reasonably good job of cleaning Pyrodex fouling as well. Even so, Hodgdon has formulated a special solvent for cleaning residue left from Pyrodex loads known as Pyrodex EZ Clean. It comes in an eight-ounce spray bottle for easy application and makes cleaning a breeze. Best of all, this special Pyrodex solvent reduces the foul odor generated by damp Pyrodex or black powder fouling. Thompson/Center No. 13, Birchwood Casey No. 77, Hoppe's No. 9 Plus, and Dixie Gun Works Black Solve are all proven cleaning solvents as well. Some are exceptionally strong concentrates for use in full strength for tough cleaning jobs, or they can be diluted to last longer and still do a great job on fouling.

HOW TO CLEAN MUZZLELOADING LONG GUNS

Muzzleloading long guns feature either a "fixed breech," a "hooked breech" for removing the barrel, a modern in-line percussion ignition system with a removable breech plug, or one without a removable breech plug. How each of these muzzleloading long gun styles is cleaned varies from one design to another. Frontloading models with a fixed breech plug and non-removable barrel are probably the toughest to keep clean. Most guns of this design are usually long-barreled and full-stocked "Kentucky" rifles, featuring barrels that are "pinned" to the stock. As a result the barrel is held in place by round steel or brass pins that fit through a hole drilled through the long forestock and "tennons" attached to the bottom of the barrel. A few early flintlock muskets, such as the British Brown Bess, also featured pinned barrels. For purposes of repair or modification, these pins can be tapped out and the barrel removed. But if these pins are removed each time the barrel is cleaned, the pins holding the barrel in place would soon loosen and slide out in the field. Most muzzleloaders of this design are

Small amounts of residue can seep down between the pan and barrel of a custom flintlock. To clean the rifle properly, the lock must be removed and fouling wiped from internal lock surfaces.

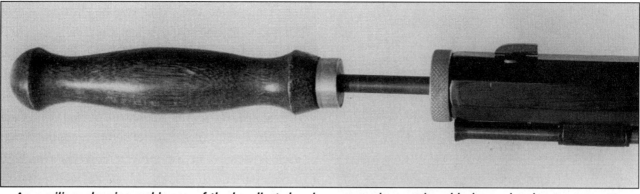

An auxiliary cleaning rod is one of the handiest cleaning accessories a serious black powder shooter can own, especially one that has a tapered muzzle guide.

cleaned with the barrel attached to the stock. To make the job a little easier, many traditional long rifle shooters remove the lock before starting the cleaning job. Often a small amount of flash from the pan of a flintlock can find its way down between the pan and the side of the barrel, leaving small amounts of fouling on the bottom of the barrel and the internal parts of the lock. Removing the lock will enable shooters to clean these areas thoroughly.

The bore of a pinned barrel is usually cleaned simply by using a cleaning jag on the ramrod. An auxiliary cleaning rod can also be used to run a series of solvent or water-soaked patches down the barrel until the last bit of fouling has been removed. The vent hole of a flintlock is easily cleaned with a small pick or pipe-cleaner, whereas the nipple of a percussion gun is removed with a wrench. The flash channel, leading from the base of the nipple into the barrel, can be wiped clean with a pipe cleaner or anything small enough to fit into the small diameter hole. An old tooth brush is a great cleaning accessory for scrubbing fouling from the pan and frizzen of a flintlock, around the drum and nipple of a percussion gun, or from any other outside surface.

One of the features that made the Thompson/Center Hawken an immediate success during the early 1970s was its hooked breech system, by which the barrel could be removed from

the stock assembly in a matter of minutes. One simply removes a flat wedge or key that passes through the fore-stock and a tennon attached to the bottom of the barrel. Once the key is removed, the muzzle of the barrel can be lifted upward, whereupon a hook located at the rear of the breech plug disengages a precision-cut recess in the face of the tang. The barrel can then be removed for cleaning.

Cleaning the barrel is accomplished in one of several different ways. One is to run a number of wet patches down the bore until all fouling is removed. Most hooked breech rifle shooters, however, prefer to place the breech end of the barrel into a container filled with soapy water. A

The "hooked breech" feature of Thompson/Center's Hawken makes it easier to remove the barrel from the stock assembly for cleaning.

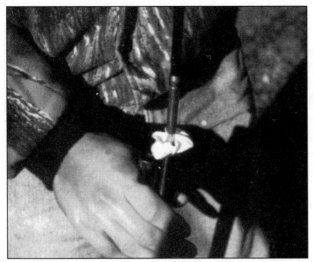

A cleaning jag enables a shooter to push a damp patch down the bore, then pull it back out.

damp patch is then pushed into the muzzle with a jag or cleaning rod, forcing air in the bore out through the nipple or vent hole as the rod works its way down the barrel. Finally, as the rod is retracted, the cleaning solution is pulled in through the nipple or vent hole, filling the barrel. When the patch appears at the muzzle, it's pushed back down the bore, forcing out the solution. This process is repeated until every bit of fouling has been removed from the bore with only one patch used.

Most modern in-line percussion rifles—which do not feature a removable breech plug—are cleaned in roughly the same manner. Before the

receiver end of the barrel can be dunked into a container of hot soapy water, though, the action must be removed, starting with the hammer and trigger. That leaves the shooter with only the barrel, receiver, breech plug and nipple, all of which can be submerged in a cleaning solution. With the receiver and breech end of the barrel submerged, the barrel itself is cleaned in the same manner as a hooked breech barrel.

The modern in-line percussion ignition systems featuring fully removable breech plugs are the most user-friendly among today's muzzleloading guns. These are shipped with all the tools needed to fully disassemble the gun. Once the nipple and breech plug are removed, the bore is ready to be cleaned, starting from the breech end, much like the barrel of a modern bolt-action centerfire rifle. The fastest and easiest way to clean a modern in-line with a removable breech plug, though, is to stick the muzzle down into a container of cleaning solution. Then, with a ramrod or cleaning rod (with jag attached), a damp patch is pushed in from the breech end and all the way to the muzzle, then pulled back to the receiver. After 20 or 30 strokes, all fouling should be thoroughly wiped and flushed from the bore.

The Hoppes Black Powder Cleaning Kit stores handily in its own box organizer.

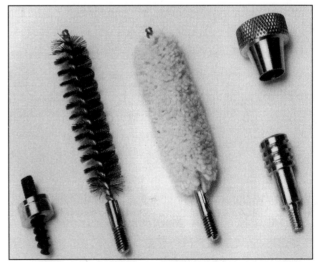

A variety of accessory tips for the ramrod or cleaning rod can make the cleaning job faster and easier.

One of the great advantages of owning and shooting a rifle with a removable breech plug is that it allows you to look through the bore and know that it's clean. Also, by cleaning from the breech end, the wear found on the rifling at the muzzle is greatly reduced. Other advantages of a removable breech plug include the ability to remove a projectile that started down the bore before a powder charge was poured in, and also to extract both the powder and bullet at the end of a rainy day in the woods (instead of shooting it out). It's a lot easier to wipe down and clean a rifle that hasn't been fired than one filled with burned powder fouling.

Depending on how a barrel is attached, and whether or not the gun in question has a removable breech plug, single-shot muzzleloading pistols are cleaned the same as a rifle similar in design. The same is true with muzzleloading shotguns. Most copies of the big .58 caliber Civil War rifled muskets feature a barrel held in place by a long tang screw and two or three barrel bands. These can all be easily removed so that the barrel can then be pulled from the stock for cleaning.

Flush tubes, or barrel flushers, allow barrels of some traditionally styled and in-line rifles to be cleaned without removing the barrel from the stock assembly. To do this, the nipple must be removed and replaced with a special adapter attached to a short section of rubber tubing. The loose end of this tube is then dropped into a container of cleaning solution, whereupon the barrel is cleaned much the same as a hooked breech barrel. Each time the ramrod, cleaning jag and patch are pulled toward the muzzle, the cleaning solution is pulled into the bore through the rubber tubing, then pushed out with a down stroke on the rod. It's a great way to clean a percussion gun without taking it down all the way.

Most manufacturers of modern-in-line percussion rifles that have a removable breech plug don't recommend the use of flush tubes. The

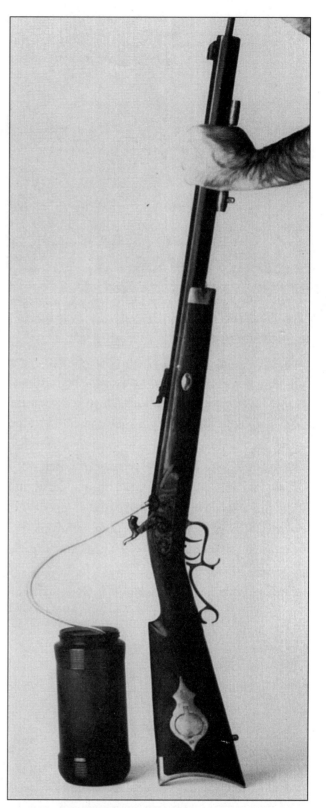

The Uncle Mike's Barrel Flusher, plus some hot soapy water, enables a black powder shooter to clean a fouled muzzleloader without making a mess.

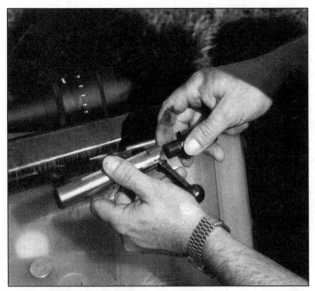

The bolt of a modern in-line rifle must be broken down before fouling can be removed from its internal surfaces.

breech plug on these must be removed each time the gun is cleaned. The threads *must* be scrubbed free of fouling, then lubed with a high temperature, non-petroleum based grease, such as white lithium grease. If the breech plug is not removed for just one cleaning, it's likely the average shooter won't be able to remove it for the next—at least, not with the take-down tools that were shipped with the rifle. To have the frozen plug removed, the gun must be taken to a gunsmith or shipped back to the factory. Either way, it can be an expensive lesson. So if your gun is equipped with

a removable breech plug, be sure to remove it every time the gun is cleaned.

HOW TO KEEP PERCUSSION REVOLVERS CLEAN

Most of the popular percussion revolvers fall into two basic categories: either the open-topped Colt design or the closed-frame Remington design. These two cap and ball revolvers may be loaded in basically the same manner, but how they are disassembled and cleaned varies as much as their appearances. The Colt-styled percussion revolvers are broken down easily into three major parts groups in a matter of minutes. Most feature a small wedge that runs through the rear of the barrel assembly and a milled slot in the cylinder pin. With the muzzle of the pistol pointing to the right, the wedge is tapped downward with a hammer made of plastic, wood or brass. Once the wedge has cleared the slot in the cylinder pin, the barrel can be removed. For a handgun that's extremely dirty, the hammer may have to be placed at half cock, and the cylinder rotated so the loading lever appears between two chambers. A little leverage may be required to break the barrel assembly free. With it removed, the cylinder can be slipped from the cylinder pin, leaving the three parts: barrel assembly, cylinder and frame or action.

Percussion revolvers are available in two basic designs: the open-framed Colt style (left) or the closed frame Remington style (right). Each breaks down differently for cleaning.

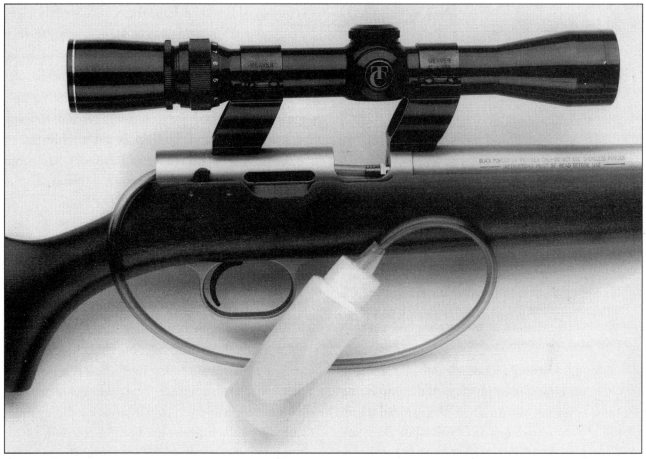

Thompson/Center's "Expediter Cleaning Kit" helps speed up the cleaning process without making a mess.

When disassembling a Remington-type revolver, the loading lever drops downward and the removable cylinder pin is pulled from the face of the frame. The cylinder then drops out, leaving the barrel attached to the frame and action. For cleaning purposes, that's as far as a Remington-style percussion revolver, or any modern variation of the same design (such as the Ruger "Old Army"), should be broken down. The removable barrel assembly of a Colt percussion revolver, on the other hand, makes it easier to clean. Some shooters remove the loading lever and submerge the barrel in hot soapy water for a few minutes, then run five or six patches through the barrel to knock out the fouling. The barrel is then dried and lubricated. The barrel can also be cleaned almost as fast by pushing damp patches through the bore. Either way, be sure

to scrub away the fouling that often accumulates at the rear of the barrel housing, on the plunger of the loading lever, and in the loading lever recess.

When fouling is removed from the bore of a Remington revolver design, make certain none of

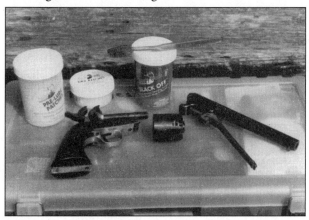

This Navy Arms Model 1851 Colt Navy has been disassembled for cleaning

The nipple and removable breech plug of a modern in-line rifle are considered "wear" parts and must be replaced from time to time.

the cleaning solution gets down into the working mechanism. Hold the handgun with the grip facing upward, or upside down. Then push several damp cleaning patches through the bore—but take care that none of the dirty solution trickles down into the action. Once the barrel is cleaned, wipe away any fouling left inside the frame, and be sure to wipe away fouling from the cylinder pin of either design. To clean the cylinder of a percussion wheel-gun takes the most time. There are, after all, five or six dirty chambers to scrub out. The easiest way is to soak the cylinder in a hot soapy water solution for several minutes. Then wrap a generous patch around a cleaning jag and insert it in each chamber. With the patch held stationary, rotate the cylinder six or seven times. With the cylinder submerged, move the cleaning patch back and forth lengthwise in the chamber a half-dozen times. It won't take much effort to remove fouling from the smooth walls of the chambers. Any cleaning patches that pull off can be easily retrieved with the tip of a screwdriver. Some percussion revolver shooters remove the nipples each time they clean the

cylinder, while others leave them in. When the right nipple wrench is used, it take mere seconds to turn out the five or six nipples, which makes cleaning easier and ensures that the threads of the nipples won't rust. Either way, the recess around each nipple must be scrubbed free of fouling—and nothing works better for this job than an old toothbrush.

Once the barrel, frame and cylinder have been cleaned, thoroughly dried and lubricated, the revolver is ready for reassembly. The cylinder pin of a Colt handgun contains a series of shallow grooves, which are given a light application of grease before the cylinder is slipped back onto the pin. The Remington pin doesn't have these grooves, so some shooters place a small dab of grease in the pin hole of the cylinder before sliding the pin back into place. Actually, a little lube on either design helps keep the cylinders rotating freely. Before reinstalling the cylinder on either type, always place the hammer at half-cock, which releases the cylinder stop. Once the cylinder has been installed on a Colt handgun, the barrel assembly can be slipped back into place and the wedge tapped back through the barrel housing. In the Remington design the cylinder pin is inserted back through the front of the frame and cylinder.

CARING FOR STOCK WOODS

When cared for in a proper manner, the metal parts of a muzzleloading rifle, pistol, shotgun, musket or percussion revolver will last indefinitely. Wood, on the other hand, can deteriorate rather quickly; if not cared for, the life span of a wood stock or handgun grip can be shortened considerably. Oil seepage from the barrel, trigger and other metal surfaces can cause discoloration of—and even serious damage to—stock woods. Spraying the metal surfaces of a muzzleloader liberally with an aerosol oil without first removing the stock could also do as much harm as good. Even

Shooters who burn a lot of powder should invest in a "cleaning box" and fill it with all of the accessories, cleaning solvents and lubricants one needs to keep black powder guns in near-perfect condition

When headed for a long range hunt, it's important to put together a travel repair kit.

though excess oil is wiped away with a soft cloth, some inevitably finds its way down between the wood and metal parts. The oil won't be absorbed by the steel, but some woods will suck up oil like a sponge. One solution is to use oil sparingly when the barrel or action has not been removed from the stock before lubrication. Another is to make sure all internal stock surfaces—barrel channel, lock mortise and trigger inlet—are also finished. Bare, unfinished wood absorbs excess oil immediately, while a tough finish forms an oil-resistant barrier. Some shooters, especially muzzleloading hunters who head out into bad weather, will take time to disassemble their rifles and coat all internal stock surfaces with a good finish.

Thompson/Center's "Natural Lube 1000+ Bore Butter," an all-natural biodegradable lubricant, has virtually no ill effects on stock woods. In fact, the lube makes an excellent wood conditioner. Wiping internal stock surfaces with a light coat of this lubricant each time the muzzleloader is cleaned creates a protective barrier that helps petroleum-based oils from seeping into the wood. Lightly wiping the outside surface of a stock with the lube each time the gun is cleaned will eventually give the stock a pleasing satin luster.

GENERAL MAINTENANCE

The current popularity of muzzleloading guns made of "stainless steel" has created a major misconception among black powder shooters, especially newcomers to the sport. Because these guns are made of stainless steel, many shooters think they can keep shooting until the cows come home, then simply toss the gun back into a corner until the next outing. Wrong! Stainless steel is just as susceptible to the corrosive effects of black powder or Pyrodex as is blued mild steel. Stainless steel barrels and actions may buy some more time during wet weather, but however many times they're shot these guns still must be cleaned like any other muzzleloader.

The care and maintenance of a muzzleloader, whether blued or stainless steel, encompasses more than simply cleaning the gun after each time it's shot. Some parts of a black powder gun are considered "wear" parts and must be replaced from time to time. The part that best fits this definition is the nipple. This hollow cone on which the percussion cap is placed takes a real beating each time the hammer falls. A powerful mainspring slams the hammer down with enough force to explode the priming charge inside the cap; and as the exploding force pushes the hammer upwards at the precise moment of ignition, some of that force is absorbed by the nipple. Most nipple designs feature a tapered flash channel to put a hotter flame into the ignition system. It also causes eventual erosion of the exit hole at the base of the nipple. As this hole grows larger, it can adversely affect the efficiency of the entire ignition system. It can also

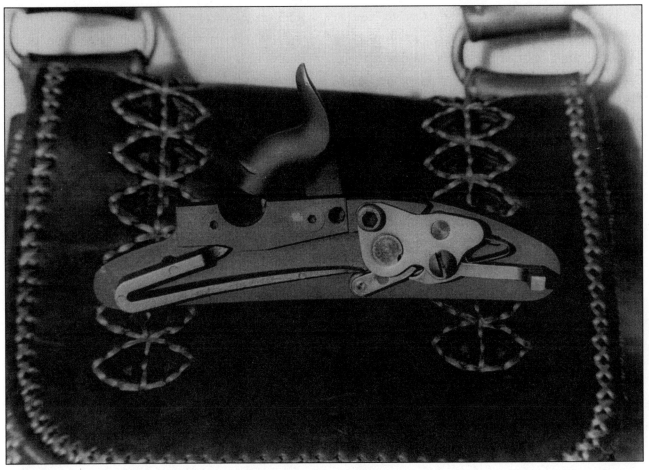

Muzzleloading hunters who travel long distances should always take along spare parts, like the main spring and sear spring of this traditional percussion lock.

allow more blow-back as the main powder charge ignites, throwing fouling back at the shooter. Therefore, when cleaning a percussion muzzleloader always check the condition of the nipple, replacing it as soon as the cone of the nipple appears battered, or the exit hole of the flash channel becomes eroded. To prevent ignition problems, experienced percussion shooters often replace a nipple after every 300 or 400 shots, whether or not it shows signs of damage or wear.

Likewise, the removable breech plug of some rifles should be replaced after every thousand rounds. If a rifle has been fired that many times, it's likely the breech plug has been removed at least a hundred times. The slightest damage to the threads of a breech plug can make it more difficult to remove for cleaning. Where most shooters experience problems, though, is with the shoulders or recess at the rear of the plug. If these begin to round or wallow out, a takedown tool won't fit properly. Eventually, it will be difficult to get a fit solid enough to break the plug loose.

Ramrods represent another wear item that needs replacing from time to time, especially wooden ramrods. With any ramrod, though, check the tips attached at one or both ends. Some can eventually begin to work loose, causing a tight-fitting jag and patch to be left in the bore. Quality-type rods feature a pin that runs crosswise through the tip and the rod itself. A rifle that isn't fitted with a ramrod made of some solid material, or with tips that are simply pinned in place, should be replaced.

There's nothing more frustrating than to have a muzzleloader out of service because a small screw is lost or a spring is broken. This can be costly when hundreds or even thousands of miles from home on a backcountry muzzleloading big game hunt; but even when close to home, getting replacement parts can take a month or more. One way to eliminate the headache is to determine which parts of your muzzleloader are essential. Most traditional side-hammer lock mechanisms are fairly simple. With a few replacement screws and springs, plus a screwdriver and a small set of Vise-Grips, anyone can learn to rebuild a lock.

Many muzzleloader manufacturers offer field repair kits containing all the parts needed to take care of lock problems. The repair kit I most often hunt with includes a complete plunger hammer assembly, a trigger assembly, a replacement breech plug, a spare nipple, and spare screws for attaching the trigger and stock to the barrel assembly. On several hunts in Alaska and the Northwest Territories, I even went to the trouble of sighting in a second scope, complete with quick-detachable rings, in case something happened to my primary scope. Remember, the farther you travel away from the source of replacement parts, the more you should be prepared for the unexpected—and that could include a back-up rifle.

To sum up, the main apprehension among new or would-be black powder shooters is cleaning. The thought of cleaning fouling from the bore and other surfaces of a black powder gun after each use has definitely kept many from coming into the sport—which is unfortunate and unnecessary. Cleaning a frontloader of any design can usually be done in 10 to 15 minutes. Amazingly, some shooters will put off this easy job for days, apparently willing to take a chance that the gun may be lost forever.

HISTORICAL REENACTMENTS

In the classic movie, "Jeremiah Johnson," Robert Redford and the rest of the cast did much to glamorize the life of that hardy breed of western adventurers who have come to be know as mountain men. The film depicted Redford as an individual driven to the mountains in search of solitude, and there he discovered a life filled with challenges that could only be appreciated by someone struck with wanderlust. What Clint Eastwood's movie hits of the 1970s did to popularize the big Smith & Wesson .44 magnum revolver, "Jeremiah Johnson" did for the revered Hawken rifle of the past, introducing more people to the name than anything before or since, indeed, it was probably no coincidence that the best-selling muzzleloader of the 1970s was the Thompson/Center "Hawken." While the modern film version of this frontloader displayed lines and features that were a far cry from those of an original Hawken, it was in fact a genuine "Hawken." It said so, right on the barrel!

Whether they are true copies of guns from the past or not, modern reproductions of guns like the Thompson/Center Hawken have allowed millions to enjoy a taste of the past. No shooter can pick up a frontloading rifle and fire it without wondering what it must have been like to shoot and hunt with a gun of similar design 150 or 200 years ago. And despite its fading importance, nostalgia continues to offer many black powder shooters a portal through which they can step back into time.

From the previous chapters in this book, it's appparent that muzzleloading has indeed become a hunting oriented sport, and that the guns which now dominate the market were designed and built primarily for the hunter. On the other hand, there exist literally hundreds of authentic reproductions, many of which are almost exact duplications of the originals they copy. So if your goal is to relive history, the muzzleloader you own and shoot can become a direct link to the past.

Since the early 1970s, interest has been growing in reliving history, either through authentic reenactments of battles, encampments, or some colorful era of American history. Participants spend

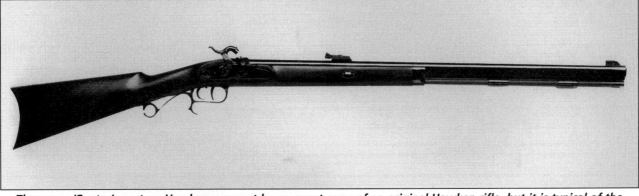

Thompson/Center's custom Hawken may not be an exact copy of an original Hawken rifle, but it is typical of the half-stock rifles carried by the mountain man during the fur trade period.

For hundreds of thousands of black powder shooters, muzzleloading provides an important link to the past.

thousands of hours (and dollars) to purchase or craft authentic clothing, camp gear, shooting and loading accessories. Serious re-enactors or rendezvous goers are spending more time studying the period so that they might own everything that belongs properly to a given period. Attend one of these get-togethers with a gun that's totally wrong for the era or event, and you're sure to be the target of disapproving stares. If a piece of wardrobe isn't exactly correct, most of the other participants are likely to share advice. But show up with a muzzle-loader that dates from a later time period and you'll probably be asked to leave or put the gun away. One thing is for certain—you'll not be invited to compete in any of the shooting competitions.

Following is a brief look at the guns generally accepted at various reenactments of popular historical periods in the U.S.

COLONIAL AND PRE-REVOLUTIONARY WAR

• Modern copies–custom or reproduction– of early flintlock English, French or German smoothbore muskets, fowlers or long guns.

• Reproductions of the English "Brown Bess" and French "Charleville" flintlock muskets available from some companies copy guns dating from the 1760s.

• Custom-built flintlock rifles of early English or German design, especially the European jaeger or early American-built flintlock rifles of similar design.

REVOLUTIONARY WAR

• Reproductions of the British "Brown Bess" flintlock musket or French "Charleville" flintlock musket.

A visit to an historical rendezvous encampment is like walking—or riding—back into history.

• Shooters depicting American patriots are appropriately armed with a stylish Pennsylvania flintlock long rifle of 1770 to 1780 design.

WESTWARD EXPANSION

• Members of the Lewis & Clark Expedition were armed with early flintlock smoothbored muskets, plus the 1803 Harpers Ferry flintlock rifle (reproductions are available from Dixie Gun Works, Navy Arms Company, and a few others).

• Flintlock rifles of pre-1800 styling.

FUR TRADE ERA
(CIRCA 1825 TO 1850)

• The guns of the "mountain men" include almost all of the earlier flintlock guns used in this country.

• Flintlock smoothbores, known as the Indian trade gun.

• Early percussion rifles with a "drum and nipple," depicting the early transition from flintlock ignition.

• Rocky Mountain fur trappers continued to rely on flintlock guns until the end of the period.

• Reproductions of flint or percussion Hawken, Leman or Henry-styled rifles are popular with the modern-day "Jeremiah Johnson" crowd.

CIVIL WAR

• Reproduction rifled muskets from Dixie Gun Works, Navy Arms Company, Traditions and a few others offering modern copies of the colorful .58 caliber Remington "Zouave," Springfield Model 1861 and Springfield Model 1863 rifled muskets.

• Gibbs Rifle Company (Martinsburg, West Virginia) offers a line-up of Parker-Hale .577 caliber British Enfields based on original patterns (other companies offer modern copies of the Enfield rifled muskets).

A muzzleloader of proper design is usually the first step in reliving a given period of the past.

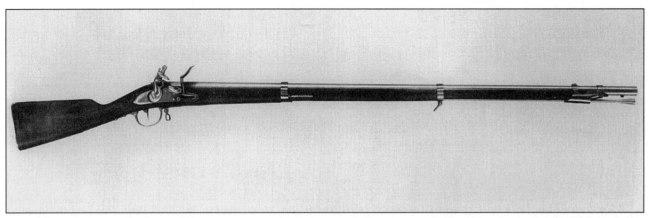

The Dixie Gun Works reproduction of the French Charleville flintlock musket is ideal for Revolutionary War era events.

• Dixie Gun Works catalogs a percussion Sharps rifle and carbine, plus a modern copy of the Confederate C.S. Richmond rifled musket.

• Navy Arms Company markets a faithful reproduction of the Smith carbine.

The following section lists several organizations that can help source the prized possessions of muzzleloading shooters.

NATIONAL MUZZLE LOADING RIFLE ASSOCIATION
P.O. BOX 67
FRIENDSHIP, INDIANA 47021

• Established in 1933, it has done more to promote the muzzleloader shooting sports than any other organization. Through state chapters, the N.M.L.R.A. is also deeply involved with a number of rendezvous reenactments in the U.S. Its monthly publication, *Muzzle Blasts*, informs readers what's happening where. Most rendezvous from the fur trade era and Revolutionary War reenactments are promoted in this publication. The magazine also presents excellent feature articles on guns and accessories from different periods, and it is a tremendous source of information for researchers of a given period. The N.M.L.R.A. can also put members in touch with smaller regional organizations and associations specializing in this subject. The N.M.L.R.A. also conducts a number of sanctioned muzzleloading matches around the country, including the National Championships held on its home range in Indiana.

NORTH-SOUTH SKIRMISH ASSOCIATION, INC.
507 N. BRIGHTON COURT
STERLING, VIRGINIA 20164

• Each year, Union and Confederate forces meet each other near Winchester, Virginia, to "battle it

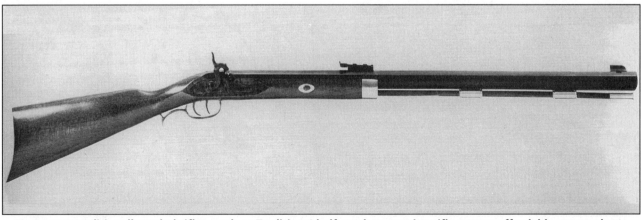

Numerous traditionally styled rifles, such as Traditions' half-stock percussion rifle, are an affordable approach to an authentically styled hunting rifle.

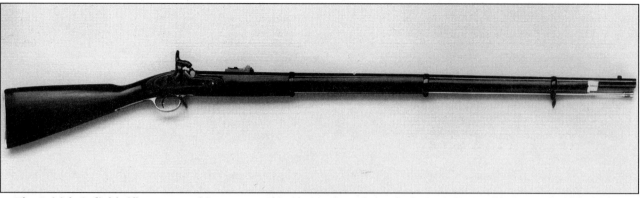

The British Enfield rifle was used by troops of both North and South during the Civil War. The Parker-Hale three-band Enfield from Gibbs Rifle Company is an excellent recreation of the colorful rifle musket.

out." Established in 1950, the N-SSA oversees numerous skirmishes and battle reenactments across the country. One of the most colorful muzzle-loading shooting events of the year takes place on the N-SSA's range in Virginia. Tens of thousands of Civil War buffs in full North and South regalia meet to compete with both original and reproduction .58 caliber rifled muskets, plus a wide range of other long guns and sidearms dating from the 1860s.

THE LONGHUNTER
P.O. BOX 67
FRIENDSHIP, INDIANA 47021

• This arm of the National Muzzle Loading Rifle Association is responsible for keeping all big game records. The organization publishes periodically a new records book for big game trophies harvested by muzzleloaders and that meet minimum qualifying scores. All scoring is recorded by recognized official scorers using the Boone & Crockett scoring system. The Longhunter organization also publishes a bi-monthly magazine known as *The Longhunter Journal.*

INTERNATIONAL BLACKPOWDER
HUNTING ASSOCIATION
P.O. BOX 1180
GLENROCK, WYOMING 82637

• The first organization to address the wants and needs of today's black powder hunter, the I.B.H.A. lobbies for better muzzleloader seasons and represents black powder hunters at meetings where state muzzleloading regulations and changes are scheduled for review. *Blackpowder Hunting,* a quarterly magazine published by I.B.H.A., reports on muzzleloading hunting opportunities across the U.S. and worldwide. Membership includes both traditional and modern in-line percussion rifle shooters.

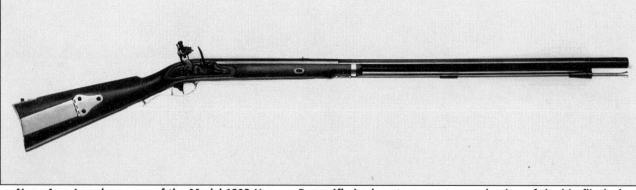

Navy Arms' modern copy of the Model 1803 Harpers Ferry rifle is almost an exact reproduction of the big flintlock rifle carried by the Lewis & Clark Expedition.